W9-BLB-367

THE BIBLE

Larry Richards

NELSON BOOKS
A Division of Thomas Nelson Publishers
Since 1798

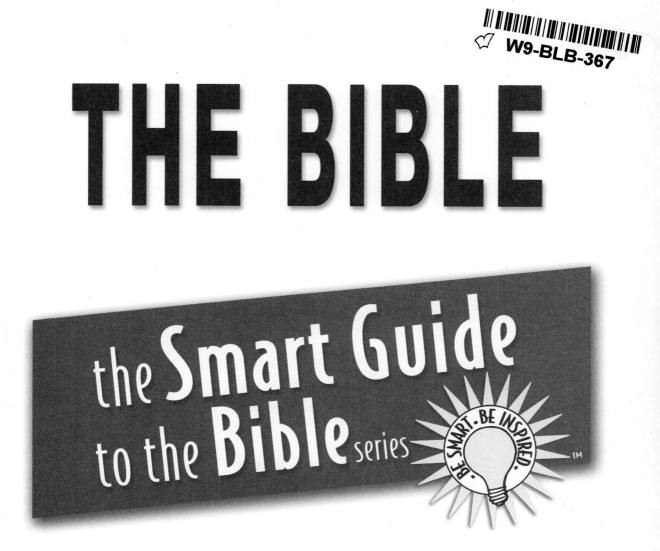

www.thomasnelson.com

The Bible
The Smart Guide to the Bible™ series
Copyright © 2006 by GRQ, Inc.

All rights reserved. No portion of this book may be reproduced, stored in a retrieval system, or transmitted in any form or by any means—electronic, mechanical, photocopy, recording, or any other—except for brief quotation in printed reviews, without the prior permission of the publisher.

Published by Nelson Reference, a Division of Thomas Nelson, Inc., P.O. Box 141000, Nashville, Tennessee 37214.

Originally published by Starburst Publishers under the title *The Bible: God's Word for the Biblically-Inept*. Now revised and updated.

Scripture quotations are taken from The New King James Version® (NKJV), copyright © 1979, 1980, 1982, 1992, Thomas Nelson, Inc., Publishers.

Managing Editor: Lila Empson
Associate Editor: W. Mark Whitlock
Scripture Editor: Deborah Wiseman
Assistant Editor: Amy Clark
Design: Diane Whisner

ISBN 1-4185-0988-4

Printed in the United States of America
07 08 09 9 8 7 6 5 4 3 2

Introduction

What's Unique About the Bible?

It's a collection of sixty-six individual books written by many different persons over a span of nearly 1,500 years. Yet it is one book, sharing one life-changing message. The Bible claims that its message is from God himself. More than 2,600 times the writers of the Bible claim to speak or write God's words—not their own.

How Did We Get the Bible?

Books of the Bible were written by different individuals and reflect their individual styles and circumstances. Yet the words they penned accurately convey the message God intended to communicate.

The first thirty-nine books of the Bible are called the Old Testament. They were mostly written in Hebrew, although parts of Daniel and Ezra were written in Aramaic, a related language. The Jewish people regarded these books as sacred, and they meticulously copied them word for word, with every care taken to avoid transcription errors. About a hundred years before Christ, the Old Testament was translated into Greek.

The twenty-seven books of the New Testament were written in Greek between about AD 40 and AD 95, and they were quickly recognized by believers as sacred. A number of individuals authored these books. Chapter and verse divisions were added much later to make it easier to find and remember the location of specific teachings. Most modern English translations of the Bible take great care to accurately express in our language the meaning of the Hebrew and Greek so we too can understand God's message.

But Can We Really Trust the Bible?

The answer to that question is yes. No other source claiming to provide knowledge about God was written by so many different authors over so many centuries—and yet conveys a totally consistent message. No other religious or secular source contains the hundreds of predictions about the future provided in the Bible. And in no other source has prediction after prediction been exactly fulfilled, often hundreds of years after they were made. The only way this is possible is that God, who alone can declare "the end from the beginning" (Isaiah 46:10 NKJV), revealed the future.

Yet perhaps the most compelling reason to trust the Bible is that through this unique book millions have established a personal relationship with God and find strength, joy, and peace in him. As we establish and live in a trust relationship with the God of the Bible, we learn by experience that we can rely on this book, which truly is God's Word.

A Word About Dates

Experts differ about dates in the Bible. But archaeologists keep making new discoveries so that many dates can now be fixed with confidence. Where significant disagreements exist, the most commonly recognized date is generally given. However, note that in the Time Lines "c" indicates *circa*, meaning "around that date."

Why This Book About the Bible?

Reading the Bible can change your life. That's something no book about the Bible can promise. But just opening the Bible and starting to read can be confusing. While the Bible tells a single story, it's a story that has many parts. To understand the nature and contribution of each part, we need to know how that part fits into the big picture. This book will help you see that big picture, so that the Bible will make sense to you whenever and wherever you open it.

About the Author

Dr. Larry Richards is a native of Michigan who now lives in Raleigh, North Carolina. He was converted while in the Navy in the 1950s. Larry has taught and written Sunday school curriculum for every age group, from nursery through adult. He has published more than two hundred books that have been translated into twenty-six languages. His wife, Sue, is also an author. They both enjoy teaching Bible studies as well as fishing and playing golf.

One Final Tip

God, who gave us the Bible, is present whenever we read it. So it helps to read the Bible prayerfully. People who open their hearts to God and ask him to speak to them tell us that he really does. So open your heart, ask God to speak to you as you read, and you'll be surprised how wonderfully the Bible will enrich your life!

If you feel awkward or strange when you pray, or don't know what to say, try the written prayer below. There is no "magic" in the words. It is only a guide.

Understanding the Bible Is Easy with These Tools

To understand God's Word you need easy-to-use study tools right where you need them—at your fingertips. The Smart Guide to the Bible™ series puts valuable resources adjacent to the text to save you both time and effort.

Every page features handy sidebars filled with icons and helpful information: cross references for additional insights, definitions of key words and concepts, brief commentaries from experts on the topic, points to ponder, evidence of God at work, the big picture of how passages fit into the context of the entire Bible, practical tips for applying biblical truths to every area of your life, and plenty of maps, charts, and illustrations. A wrap-up of each passage, combined with study questions, concludes each chapter.

These helpful tools show you what to watch for. Look them over to become familiar with them, and then turn to Chapter 1 with complete confidence: You are about to increase your knowledge of God's Word!

Study Helps

The thought-bubble icon alerts you to commentary you might find particularly thought-provoking, challenging, or encouraging. You'll want to take a moment to reflect on it and consider the implications for your life.

Don't miss this point! The exclamation-point icon draws your attention to a key point in the text and emphasizes important biblical truths and facts.

death on the cross
Colossians 1:21–22

Many see Boaz as a type of Jesus Christ. To win back what we human beings lost through sin and spiritual death, Jesus had to become human (i.e., he had to become a true kinsman), and he had to be willing to pay the penalty for our sins. With his death on the cross, Jesus paid the penalty and won freedom and eternal life for us.

The additional Bible verses add scriptural support for the passage you just read and help you better understand the underlined text. (Think of it as an instant reference resource!)

How does what you just read apply to your life? The heart icon indicates that you're about to find out! These practical tips speak to your mind, heart, body, and soul, and offer clear guidelines for living a righteous and joy-filled life, establishing priorities, maintaining healthy relationships, persevering through challenges, and more.

This icon reveals how God is truly all-knowing and all-powerful. The hourglass icon points to a specific example of the prediction of an event or the fulfillment of a prediction. See how some of what God has said would come to pass already has!

What are some of the great things God has done? The traffic-sign icon shows you how God has used miracles, special acts, promises, and covenants throughout history to draw people to him.

Does the story or event you just read about appear elsewhere in the Gospels? The cross icon points you to those instances where the same story appears in other Gospel locations—further proof of the accuracy and truth of Jesus' life, death, and resurrection.

Since God created marriage, there's no better person to turn to for advice. The double-ring icon points out biblical insights and tips for strengthening your marriage.

The Bible is filled with wisdom about raising a godly family and enjoying your spiritual family in Christ. The family icon gives you ideas for building up your home and helping your family grow close and strong.

Isle of Patmos
a small island in the Mediterranean Sea

something significant had occurred, he wrote down the substance of what he saw. This is the practice John followed when he recorded Revelation on the **Isle of Patmos.**

What does that word really mean, especially as it relates to this passage? Important, misunderstood, or infrequently used words are set in **bold type** in your text so you can immediately glance at the margin for definitions. This valuable feature lets you better understand the meaning of the entire passage without having to stop to check other references.

the big picture

Joshua

Led by Joshua, the Israelites crossed the Jordan River and invaded Canaan (see Illustration #8). In a series of military campaigns the Israelites defeated several coalition armies raised by the inhabitants of Canaan. With organized resistance put down, Joshua divided the land among the twelve Israelite

How does what you read fit in with the greater biblical story? The highlighted big picture summarizes the passage under discussion.

what others say

David Breese

Nothing is clearer in the Word of God than the fact that God wants us to understand himself and his working in the lives of men.[5]

It can be helpful to know what others say on the topic, and the highlighted quotation introduces another voice in the discussion. This resource enables you to read other opinions and perspectives.

Maps, charts, and illustrations pictorially represent ancient artifacts and show where and how stories and events took place. They enable you to better understand important empires, learn your way around villages and temples, see where major battles occurred, and follow the journeys of God's people. You'll find these graphics let you do more than study God's Word—they let you *experience* it.

Chapters at a Glance

BE SMART. BE INSPIRED.

BE SMART. BE INSPIRED.

PART II: The New Testament

The Old Testament • Part One

What Is the Old Testament?

The Old **Testament** is a collection of thirty-nine books that were written between 1450 **BC** and 400 BC. They tell the story of God's special relationship with one human family, the family of Abraham, Isaac, and Jacob, which became the Jewish people. Through this people God revealed himself to all mankind. And through this people God set in motion a plan to save all who would believe in him from the terrible consequences of **sin**.

testament
covenant

BC
before Christ, as opposed to AD, which means "in the year of our Lord"

sin
"any" violation of God's will

Why Is It Called the "Old" Testament?

This collection of thirty-nine books is called the Old Testament in contrast to the New Testament. The New Testament is a collection of twenty-seven books, all of which were written in the first century. The New Testament continues and completes the story begun in the Old Testament.

Find Out About God—by Reading the Old Testament!

People have different ideas about what God is like. Anyone who wants to find out can begin by reading the Old Testament. What's in the Old Testament?

The books of the Old Testament are divided into five different kinds of writings. Fascinating questions are raised and answered with these Old Testament writings.

Questions the Bible Raises and Answers

Pentateuch
the first five books of the Old Testament; a five-scrolled book

The Pentateuch

Genesis, Exodus, Leviticus, Numbers, Deuteronomy	Where did the universe come from? What makes human beings special? Why do people do wrong and evil things? Does God care what happens to us? How can I know what God expects of us?

History

Joshua, Judges, Ruth, 1 and 2 Samuel, 1 and 2 Kings, 1 and 2 Chronicles, Ezra, Nehemiah, Esther	What is God's plan for the world? Does God control what happens in history? Does it pay a nation to honor God?

Poetry

Job, Psalms, Proverbs, Ecclesiastes, Song of Solomon	Can I find meaning in life apart from God? How do I communicate with God? How can we survive suffering? What guidelines help me make wise choices?

Major Prophets

Isaiah, Jeremiah, Lamentations, Ezekiel, Daniel	Does God ever reveal the future? What prophecies have already come true? What sins is God sure to judge? How will the world end?

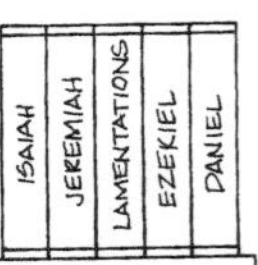

Minor Prophets

Hosea, Joel, Amos, Obadiah, Jonah, Micah, Nahum, Habakkuk, Zephaniah, Haggai, Zechariah, Malachi	How much does God love us? Do people really "get away with" being wicked? What kind of society will God bless? What kind of society is he sure to punish? Is our country in danger today?

Genesis 1–11

Let's Get Started

Genesis 1

No one was present at the creation of the **universe**, so where did Moses, who wrote the first five books of the Old Testament, get his information? From the only person who was present when the world began: God. The Bible is a book of revealed truth, or **revelation**. These early chapters of **Genesis** don't argue that God exists. They assume that God exists, and they describe a beginning about which only God could know.

created
Isaiah 40:18–31; Genesis 1:1–2:3

universe
stars, space, and all that exists

revelation
what God has communicated to us

Genesis
the name means "beginnings"

God created
God made the universe from nothing

Genesis

. . . the book of beginnings

Who	Moses
What	wrote Genesis
Where	traveling in the wilderness
When	about 1400 BC
Why	to reveal the truth about God and his relationship to human beings

What's Special About Genesis 1?

the big picture

Genesis 1:1–2:3

The Bible begins, "In the beginning **God created** the heavens and the earth" (Genesis 1:1 NKJV). The rest of the passage tells how God shaped our universe, paying special attention to shaping the earth as a home for humanity.

1. **The Genesis story of Creation was a truly NEW and DIFFERENT account of origins.** Moses didn't get his ideas of Creation from earlier peoples. It was revealed to him by God.

Adam
Genesis 2:8–23

image and likeness
like God, people have intellect, emotions, will, etc.

dominion
responsibility to care for

deity
a god

2. **God is the focus of Genesis 1**. ("God" appears 32 times.) God designs and creates a stable, dependable universe that he says is "good," and he clearly cares about what he has created.

3. **Human beings are special, since only they were created in the image and likeness of God**. God gave human beings **dominion** over his creation, and from the very beginning they have been special to God.

Ancient Ideas About Origins

	Mesopotamian	Egyptian	Greek	Genesis
View of the Gods	Many competing gods/ goddesses	Many related gods/ goddesses	Many warring gods/ goddesses	One God
Nature of the Gods	Good and evil, petty, warring	Nature deities, manipulative	Adulterous, petty, limited	Good, all-powerful
Relation to Man	Mankind sprang from the blood of slain **deity**	No moral or personal relationship	Both subject to fate; no real interest in humanity	Humans created in God's image; loved by God
Material Universe	Corpse of the goddess Tiamat	Five myths give five explanations	The universe existed before the gods	One God is the Creator and Designer of all

What Difference Does It Make?

Some believe that the universe is impersonal and "just happened." If this is true, one day our sun will burn out and the earth will become a dead, icy speck spinning through endless space. Long before that we will all die and be forgotten. But what if our universe is personal, created by a God who cares for human beings? Then we have hope. God may have a plan for our universe, and death may not be the end for those he loves! Whether or not God created makes all the difference in the world!

Then He Made Man and Woman

the big picture

Genesis 2:4–25

This chapter gives details about the creation of human beings. God first created Adam and placed him in a beautiful garden, the Garden of Eden (see Illustration #1). Adam explored the garden and named the animals. When Adam realized something was missing, God formed Eve from Adam's rib. Adam realized that Eve was a person like himself, a partner he could love.

go to

Eve
Genesis 2:8–23

Satan
Isaiah 14:12–14; Revelation 12:9

What's Special About Genesis 2?

1. **Genesis 1 tells us how Creation happened.** God said . . . and it was so (Genesis 1:3, 6, 9, 14, 24). "God formed man of the dust of the ground" and breathed into his nostrils the breath of life (Genesis 2:7 NKJV). The careful and unusual attention God gave to forming man reminds us that we are special, different from the animals.

what others say

Ronald F. Youngblood

"Create" is a special verb in the Old Testament. It always has God as its subject; it is never used of human activity. You and I may make or form or fashion, but only God creates.[1]

2. **The breath of life.** The life God breathed into Adam was different from the life given to animals. An animal ceases to exist when it dies. When we die, our bodies return to dust, but we continue to exist as conscious, self-aware people forever.

3. **Woman created.** Woman was created as a helper suitable to Adam. The Hebrew phrase means a "comparable companion"—a person who was Adam's equal, not his servant. God intended man and woman to be partners in their life on earth.

Satan Made Me Do It

the big picture

Genesis 3

Satan, in the form of a serpent, tricked Eve into disobeying God. Then Adam also disobeyed God. This sin had terrible consequences for the whole human race.

SATAN: Also called the evil one, the devil, and the great serpent. Satan was once an angel named Lucifer and led other angels in a rebellion against God. Satan and his angels hate God and are intent on thwarting God's plans. Ultimately God will triumph and send Satan and his followers to what we call **hell**.

hell
Matthew 25:41

Tigris and Euphrates
Genesis 2:14

The Fall is the disobedience of Adam and Eve, and explains how two people created by a good God could produce a race marred by crime, injustice, hatred, and war. When Adam and Eve sinned, their very natures were warped and twisted. They passed on this twisted nature to all their offspring.

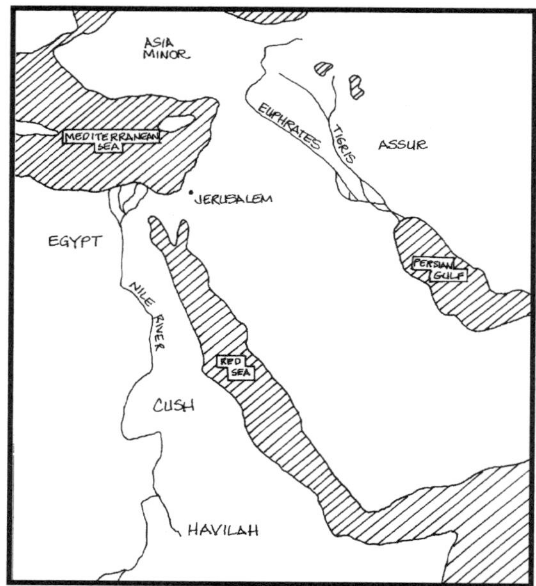

Illustration #1
Map of Eden—The first human civilizations developed in the Mesopotamian valley (modern Irac [Iraq] and Iran). Genesis places Eden in this area, listing four streams as Eden's boundaries. The only two known today are the Tigris and the Euphrates.

Why Did God Let It Happen?

Why put the **Tree of the Knowledge of Good and Evil** in Eden? God created human beings in his image. Since God distinguishes between right and wrong and makes **moral** choices, Adam and Eve too had to be given the opportunity to make a true moral choice.

hell
a place of fire and unending punishment for Satan and his followers

Tree of the Knowledge of Good and Evil
signifies the ability to know good and evil by personal experience

moral
doing as well as knowing what is right

temptation
an inward pull to doing wrong

What's Special in Genesis 3?

1. **Eve was vulnerable to temptation.** Because (1) She didn't know what God had said (compare Genesis 3:4 with Genesis 2:16–17), (2) She began to doubt God's motives (Genesis 3:4–5), and (3) She relied on her own senses and judgment rather than on God's Word to determine what was truly "good" for her (Genesis 3:6). The result was disaster!

Some have argued that Adam and Eve's decision to disobey God was freeing. They assume that to be "free" is to be able to do whatever we want, whenever we want to. But true freedom is found in choosing what is right and good, and for that we need God's guidance.

2. **The Tree of the Knowledge of Good and Evil**. God had said, "In the day that you eat of it you shall surely die" (Genesis 2:17 NKJV). The day Adam and Eve ate, the processes leading to **physical death** were initiated. That day they also died spiritually and morally, and were alienated from God. People who remain alienated from God will be separated from God forever. The Bible calls this a "**second death**."

3. **The Fall dramatically affected Adam and Eve**: (1) They felt shame and tried to cover themselves (Genesis 3:7), (2) They became afraid of the God who loved them, and tried to hide from him (Genesis 3:8, 10), and (3) They felt guilty and began to blame God and each other (Genesis 3:12).

4. **Additional consequences of the Fall** (Genesis 3:16). Women are driven to look to men for approval, and men try to rule over and subordinate women.

5. **God didn't turn against Adam and Eve**. He sought them out and then covered them with animal skins. This symbolic act was history's first **sacrifice for sins**.

died spiritually
Ephesians 2:1–3

second death
Revelation 20:12–14

sacrifice
Leviticus 17:11

sins
Ephesians 2:1–4

only evil all the time
Genesis 6:5

physical death
the body dies spiritual death: loss of relationship with God

second death
separation from God forever

sacrifice for sins
death of a substitute as a covering for sins

sin nature
the desire and tendency to choose to disobey God

genealogy
a list of family ancestors

What's Special in Genesis 4 and 5?

the big picture

Genesis 4–5

These chapters show that Adam and Eve's offspring really did inherit their parents' **sin nature**. Their son Cain murdered his brother Abel. A few generations later Lamech broke the pattern of one husband/one wife by taking two wives, and justified murdering a man who wounded him. A lengthy **genealogy** brings us to the days of Noah, a time of wickedness when mankind's thoughts were only evil all the time.

1. **Genesis 3 relates Adam and Eve's fall.** Genesis 4 shows that their sin nature was transmitted to their offspring. People are not sinners because they do wrong, but choose wrong because they are sinners.

all around him were wicked men
Genesis 6:5

Noah's faith
Hebrews 11:7

2. **Genesis 5 lists men who were supposed to have lived hundreds of years.** Is this credible? Medical science has now linked most diseases that shorten human life, and aging itself, to gradual damage to our genes and chromosomes. People who lived shortly after God created Adam and Eve would have suffered very little genetic damage. We should expect them to have lived substantially longer than we do.

3. **People speculate about the age of the universe and when human beings first appeared.** Genesis gives no hint of when the events it describes took place. The purpose of these early chapters of Genesis is to tell where the universe and human beings came from, not when God's creative work was done.

Lots and Lots of Water

the big picture

Genesis 6–9

These chapters tell the story of a great Flood by which God wiped out most life on earth. The family of one man, Noah, survived the Flood. He obeyed God's command to build an ark in which to preserve pairs of land animals that would then replenish the earth.

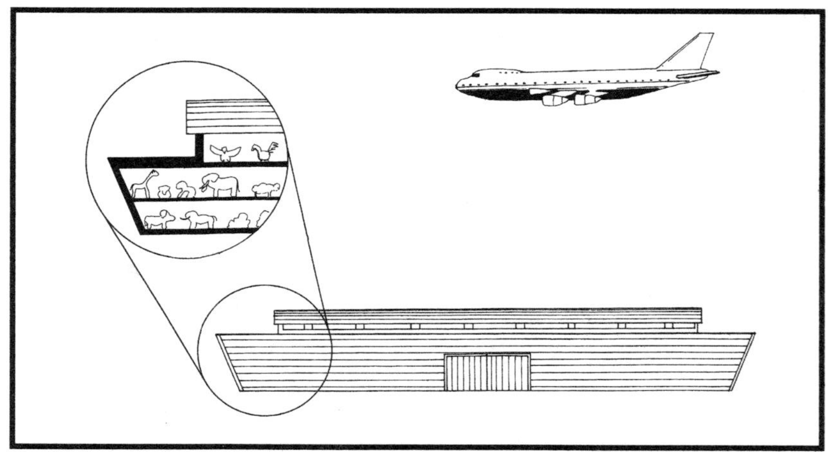

Illustration #2
The Ark—Noah's ark was an unpowered wooden boat that was 450 feet long, 75 feet wide, and 45 feet high. It took Noah and his sons 120 years to build, but when finished, the ark was roomy enough for Noah's family, all the animals, and food for everyone. This floating zoo would be home to Noah's family for over a year.

NOAH: Noah was a man who walked with God even though men all around him were wicked men. God told Noah he was about to wipe out the wicked with a great Flood. When he was told to build an ark (see Illustration #2), Noah trusted God and did as God said. Noah's faith is praised in the New Testament.

What's Special in Genesis 6–9?

1. **The cause of the Flood was human sin.** The New Testament points to the Flood as evidence that God is a **Moral Judge** who will punish the guilty. The story of the Flood is a warning.

2. **God's promise.** After the Flood God promised never again to destroy all life on earth by water. The rainbow that appears after storms is a visible reminder of that promise.

3. **Government's task.** After the Flood God told Noah that from then on, "whoever sheds man's blood, by man his blood shall be shed" (Genesis 9:6 NKJV). This is viewed as the institution of human government.

Moral Judge
God, in his commitment to punish sin

ziggurat
a tower with stairstep sides

Was There Really a Great, Worldwide Flood?

The Flood was an act of God that revealed God as mankind's judge. It is a warning that there will come a time in the life of every person and every nation when God will no longer overlook wrongdoing.

Peoples around the world, from the Middle East to China to the jungles of South America, tell tales of a flood that wiped out most human life. The best explanation is a tradition that goes back to a "real" event!

One Tall Tower

the big picture

Genesis 10–11 Around the World

Genesis 10 contains a table of nations that accurately identifies regions in which ancient ethnic groups lived. Genesis 11 relates that God caused ancient peoples to speak different languages when Noah's descendants failed to spread out and populate the earth as God intended. The last verses of Genesis 11 set the scene for the introduction of Abram, a key figure in the Bible.

The Tower of Babel was a **ziggurat** (see Illustration #3), a pyramid-like construction common in the ancient Middle East and in South America. The ancients built temples on the tops of these tow-

Babylon
Isaiah 13:1–11; Revelation 18:1–24

ers. They were inventing their own religion, trying to reach God by their own efforts.

The Bible and other writings from the ancient Near East view Babel as the first city-based civilization. Its evil aspects are reflected in Scripture's portrayal of Babylon, which was founded on the site of ancient Babel.

Beginnings in Genesis

Universe (1:1)	Promise (3:15)
Light (1:3)	Sacrifice (3:21)
Life (1:20)	Procreation (4:1)
Human Beings (1:27; 2:7)	Judgment (6:7)
Marriage (2:24)	Government (9:5–6)
Sin (3:6)	"Religion" (9:8–17)
Consequences (3:14–19)	Language (11:1–9)

Illustration #3
Ziggurat—Towers like this were constructed by the people of Mesopotamia over 5,000 years ago, and by the people of Central America 2,000 years ago.

Chapter Wrap-Up

- Genesis gives a unique account of the origin of the universe that has no parallels in the ancient world (Genesis 1).
- God created human beings in his own image and likeness, making human beings special (Genesis 1:27; 2).
- When Adam and Eve disobeyed God they died spiritually, and transmitted their sin nature to all their offspring (Genesis 3).
- The truth of the Bible's account of the Fall is seen in the big and little evils that mar society and each person's experience.
- The Genesis Flood revealed God as a Moral Judge who must and will punish sin (Genesis 6).

Study Questions

1. What difference does it make whether or not God "created"?
2. What makes human beings special?
3. How does the Bible explain the evils around us and our own tendency to do what we know is wrong?
4. What was the Fall and what were its consequences?
5. What does the Flood tell us about God?

Genesis 12 – 50

Let's Get Started

The first eleven chapters of Genesis relate the early history of the human race. Beginning with Genesis 12, the Bible sets a very different course by reporting God's choice of one man. The man was Abraham, and his descendants were the Jewish people. The rest of the 905 chapters that make up the Old Testament trace the history of this one family, and what God has done through them. Through Abraham's descendants God has revealed himself, dealt with sin, and reopened the way for a personal relationship with him.

Abraham
"father of a multitude"

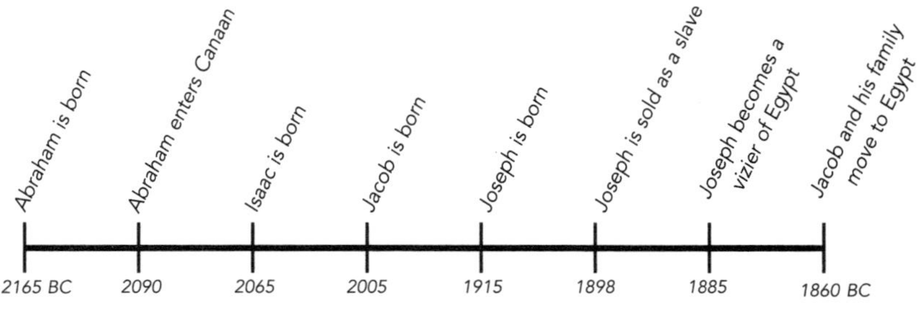

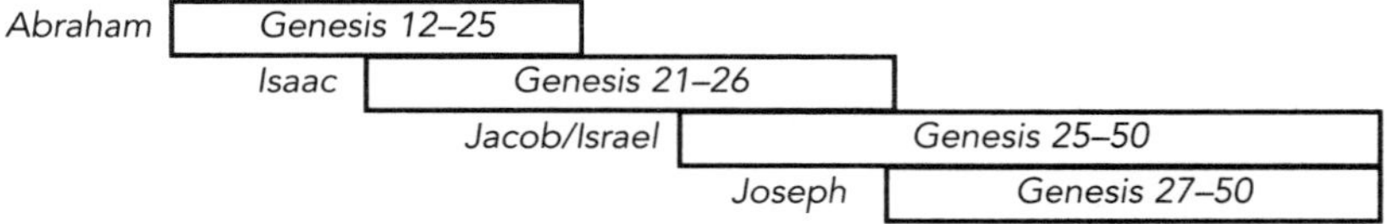

Time Line #1
Important Persons and Events in Genesis 12—50

I Choose You!

ABRAHAM: When God spoke to Abram he lived in the wealthy but idolatrous city of Ur (see Illustration #4). Abram chose to follow the Lord. Later his name was changed to **Abraham**.

Illustration #4
The Fertile Crescent—The outlined area was called "the Fertile Crescent." Broad river valleys supported agriculture and served as trade routes in Abraham's time.

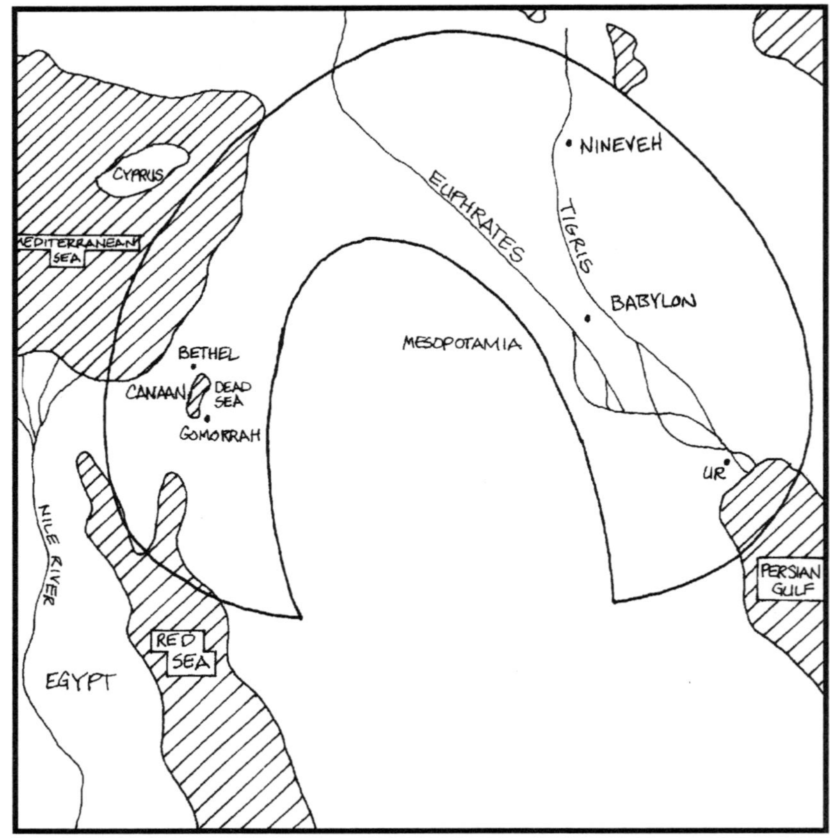

Abrahamic covenant
Genesis 12:1–3, 7

Abrahamic covenant
specific promises God made to Abraham

covenant
contract, oath, promise, or binding agreement

salvation
deliverance from sin

Abraham's Relationship with God Sets the Course of the Bible in Two Vital Ways

> **the big picture**
>
> **Genesis 12**
>
> God appeared to Abram and made a number of promises. These promises are known as the **Abrahamic covenant.** Abraham responded by leaving his homeland as God commanded, and by going to a land that God showed him.

1. God made **covenant** promises to Abraham. These outline God's plan for **salvation**, which becomes more and more clear as the Old Testament unfolds.

2. Abraham's **faith** in God is shown to be the key to a personal relationship with the **Lord**. Stories about Abraham in Genesis 12–25 portray a man who was flawed, as we are, but who trusted God.

righteousness
Genesis 15:6;
Romans 3:10, 21–22

The Abrahamic Covenant

The covenant promises God made are commitments to Abraham. A special covenant-making ceremony was performed, which was done in ancient times to make agreements legally binding.

Some of God's covenant promises have already been fulfilled. Others have been partially fulfilled and will be completely fulfilled at history's end.

faith
not belief "about" God, but trust "in" him

Lord
in the Old Testament, *Lord* usually indicates Yahweh; his power over his people, over the entire earth, and over all gods

righteousness
sinless in God's eyes

The Covenant Promises God Made to Abraham

Genesis	God's promises . . .	. . . the promise kept
Genesis 12:2	I will make you into a great nation.	From Abraham sprang both the Jewish and Arab peoples.
Genesis 12:2	I will bless you.	God protected and enriched Abraham during his lifetime.
Genesis 12:2	I will make your name great and you will be a blessing.	Jews, Muslims, and Christians honor Abraham as founder of their faith.
Genesis 12:3	I will bless those who bless you, and whoever curses you I will curse.	Throughout history, peoples who have persecuted the Jews have experienced national disaster.
Genesis 12:3	All peoples on earth will be blessed through you.	Abraham's descendants gave the world the Bible and Jesus, the Savior.
Genesis 12:7	To your offspring I will give this land.	Israel remains the Promised Land of the Jewish people, to be occupied at history's end.

Abraham's Faith

Bible stories about Abraham do not hide his weaknesses or sins. Yet Abraham had great faith in God. When Abraham was one hundred years old and his wife, Sarah, was ninety, God promised them a son. Abraham believed God, and God counted Abraham's faith as **righteousness**. The New Testament says,

glory
praise and honor

ROMANS 4:19–24 ***And not being weak in faith, he did not consider his own body, already dead (since he was about a hundred years old), and the deadness of Sarah's womb. He did not waver at the promise of God through unbelief, but was strengthened in faith, giving glory to God, and being fully convinced that what He had promised He was also able to perform. And therefore "it was accounted to him for righteousness." Now it was not written for his sake alone that it was imputed to him, but also for us. It shall be imputed to us who believe in Him who raised up Jesus our Lord from the dead.*** (NKJV)

what others say

Max Lucado

You do not impress the officials of NASA with a paper airplane. You don't claim equality with Einstein because you can write H_2O. And you don't boast about your goodness in the presence of the Perfect [God].[1]

Both Old and New Testaments teach that only those who trust God and his promises have a personal relationship with him.

Getting to Know Abraham

Some Bible stories about Abraham display his human weaknesses. Some reveal his trust in God. Reading one or two of the following stories from each of the two categories will provide an understanding of both the weaknesses and the faith of Abraham.

Abraham's weaknesses revealed	Abraham's growing trust displayed
Genesis 12:10–20	Genesis 12:4–9
Genesis 16:1–16	Genesis 13:1–18
Genesis 20:1–17	Genesis 14:1–24
	Genesis 15:1–20
	Genesis 19:1–29
	Genesis 22:1–19

God does not expect people to be "good" before he accepts them. God accepts people who trust him, and then he helps them become better.

what others say

Robert C. Girard

An amazing revelation! Since becoming a follower of Jesus Christ there is a part of me that wants what God wants. Through the Spirit's operation a new creation, totally tuned to God and in full accord with his will, is rising from the rubble of the old life.[2]

archaeology
the study of remains of ancient civilizations

Archaeology and Abraham

Some think that the stories about Abraham were made up. But **archaeology** makes it clear these stories contain authentic details. For instance, the raiding route that kings are said to have followed in Genesis 14 really was used two thousand years before Christ. Laws and marriage contracts dating from Abraham's time indicate Sarah's offer of her slave Hagar to Abraham, so that Abraham could have a son, was a common practice at that time. A person making up these stories hundreds of years later would not have been able to include so many authentic details.

Four hundred years before Abraham lived, in . . .

England	Stonehenge was erected as a ritual center.
Egypt	Pyramids were constructed as tombs for kings.
America	Pottery was invented in what is now Georgia.
Babylon	Astronomers used a highly developed geometry system.
Asia	Bronze ornaments and tools were in use in Thailand.

And All Those After You

the big picture

Genesis 21–27

These chapters tell the story of Isaac, Abraham's son by his wife, Sarah. Isaac is important because he inherited the covenant that God made with Abraham, and passed it on to his son, Jacob.

ISAAC: The son of Abraham and Sarah, Isaac, inherited the covenant promises God gave to Abraham. Isaac married Rebekah, and their son, Jacob, also inherited God's promises.

What About Women?

patriarchal
ruled by males

birthright
the oldest son's right to inherit

blessing
here, an oral last will and testament

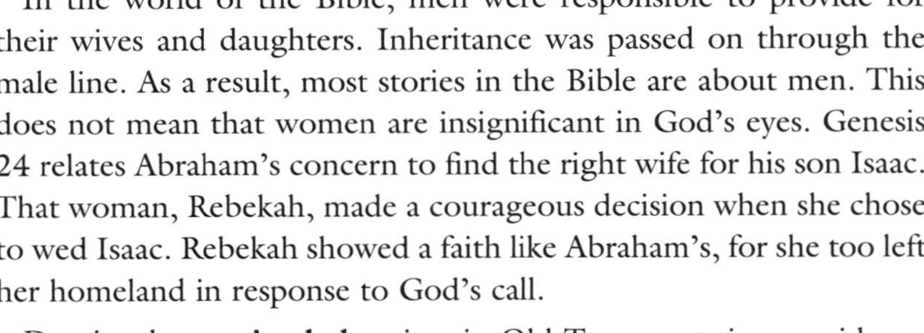

In the world of the Bible, men were responsible to provide for their wives and daughters. Inheritance was passed on through the male line. As a result, most stories in the Bible are about men. This does not mean that women are insignificant in God's eyes. Genesis 24 relates Abraham's concern to find the right wife for his son Isaac. That woman, Rebekah, made a courageous decision when she chose to wed Isaac. Rebekah showed a faith like Abraham's, for she too left her homeland in response to God's call.

Despite the **patriarchal** society in Old Testament times, evidence shines through that women also displayed faith in God.

the big picture

Genesis 25–50

These chapters tell the story of Jacob, who was next to inherit the covenant promises. Jacob's older twin, Esau, normally would have been his father's heir. But the materialistic Esau cared nothing for God or his promises, and traded his **birthright** to Jacob for a bowl of stew. Later, Jacob tricked his father into giving him Esau's **blessing**. When Esau threatened to kill Jacob, the latter fled to Haran. There Jacob married and had many children. Later, Jacob and his family moved to Egypt to escape a famine. The Israelites remained there four hundred years.

Getting to Know Jacob

JACOB: Jacob was the son of Isaac and Rebekah; he was the next to inherit God's covenant promises. God spoke to Jacob several times during his life. On one of these occasions God changed Jacob's name to Israel. The old name meant "deceiver," while Israel means "God perseveres." The people who descended from Jacob/Israel, and the nation they established, are also called Israel (Israelites) in the Bible.

Reading any two of the following stories will provide an introduction to the character of Jacob.

Jacob "steals" Esau's birthright.	Genesis 25:19–34
Jacob deceives his father.	Genesis 27:1–35
Jacob flees to his uncle Laban.	Genesis 27:41–46
God speaks to Jacob for the first time.	Genesis 28:10–22
Jacob marries two sisters.	Genesis 29:15–28
Jacob's wives compete.	Genesis 30:1–22
Jacob plans to return to Canaan.	Genesis 31:18–21
Jacob prays for protection.	Genesis 32:1–12
Jacob meets Esau again.	Genesis 33:11–20

concubines
secondary wives

polygamy
having several wives at the same time

narrative
storytelling

Jacob's Four Wives

The Bible reports that Jacob had two wives and two **concubines**, who all together bore him twelve sons. Muslims deduce from this that a man is allowed four wives. Christians teach that marriage is a relationship between one man and one woman. "A man shall leave his father and mother and be joined to his wife, and they shall become one flesh" (Genesis 2:24 NKJV).

The jealousy and unhappiness depicted in Genesis 29:31 to 30:24 show that **polygamy** is not a healthy state.

By the time of Isaac and Jacob, in . . .

Europe	The first trumpets were played in Denmark.
America	American Indians worked large open-pit copper mines in Wisconsin.
China	Astronomers kept careful records of eclipses.
Europe	Horses began to be used as mounts.
Egypt	Wine jars identifying vintages and orchards were placed in tombs of the wealthy.

When reading the Bible it's important to remember that **narrative** passages describe what did happen, not what should happen.

A Coat of Many Colors

vizier
chief official

the big picture

Genesis 36–50

Joseph was the favorite son of Jacob, but his jealous brothers sold him into Egyptian slavery. After many trials Jacob became **vizier** of Egypt, and God led Joseph to prepare Egypt to survive a great famine. Joseph was able to save the lives of his father and brothers during the famine by moving them from Canaan to Egypt, where their descendants lived for the next four hundred years.

JOSEPH: The story of Joseph is one of the most encouraging stories in the Bible. Joseph held on to his faith despite suffering and unfair treatment. His words to the brothers who had betrayed him sum up the lesson we can learn from his life: "You meant evil against me; but God meant it for good, in order to bring it about as it is this day, to save many people alive" (Genesis 50:20 NKJV). The story of Joseph reads like an exciting novel. Don't miss any of it.

what others say

Mother Teresa

Make sure that you let God's grace work in your souls by accepting whatever he gives you, and giving him whatever he takes from you. True holiness consists in doing God's will with a smile.[3]

Chapter Wrap-Up

- God gave Abraham covenant promises for himself and his physical descendants (Genesis 12:1–3, 7).
- The covenant promises outlined what God intended to do in the future.
- Abraham believed God's promise, and God credited Abraham's faith to him as righteousness (Genesis 15:6).
- All who trust God as Abraham did are the spiritual descendants of Abraham (Romans 4).
- The covenant promises given to Abraham were passed on to Isaac, Jacob, and to their descendants, the Jewish people.
- The rest of the Old Testament is the story of the Jewish people and how God worked out his covenant promises through history.

Study Questions

1. What is special about Abraham?
2. What is a covenant?
3. Why is it important to understand the Abrahamic covenant?
4. Who inherited the covenant promises after Abraham died?
5. Why is faith important for a person seeking a personal relationship with God?

Exodus

Let's Get Started

As Exodus begins, the **Israelites** are slaves in Egypt. Then God calls a man named Moses to free his people. Exodus is the story of how God acted to break the power of Egypt and free the Israelites. God then led the freed slaves to Mount Sinai (see Illustration #5), where he gave them the Ten Commandments.

Israelites
God's covenant people; descendants of Abraham, Isaac, and Jacob

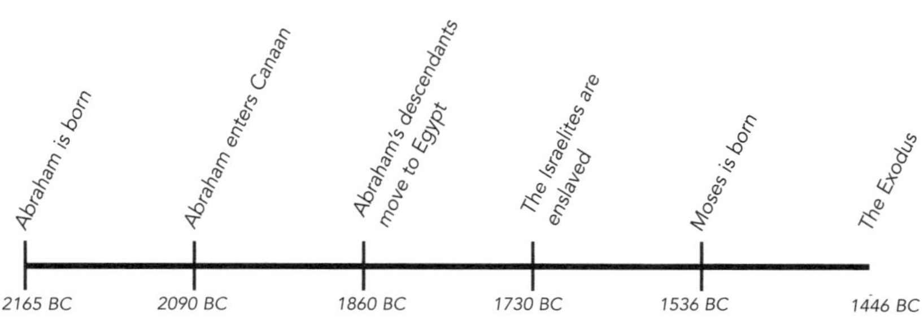

Time Line #2
Important Persons and Events in Exodus

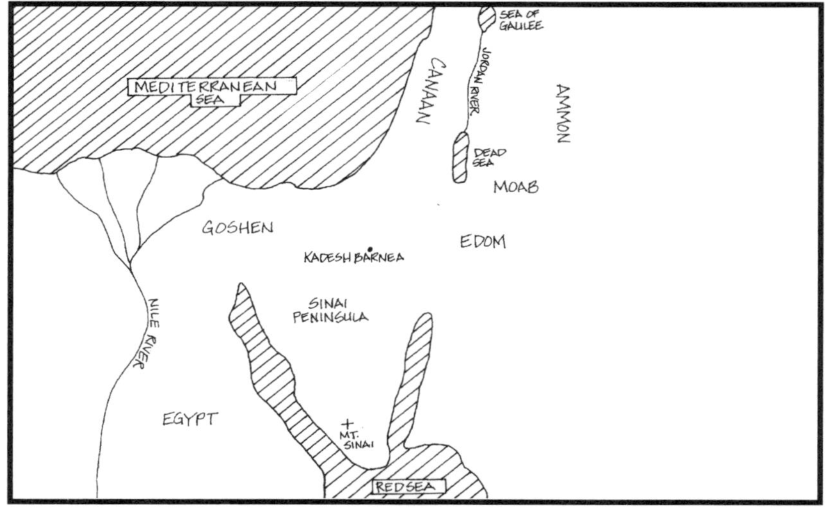

Illustration #5
Exodus Map—Use this map to locate where events in Exodus took place.

pharaoh
a title, king of Egypt

prophet
a person through whom God speaks and guides choices

Exodus

. . . exit to freedom

Who	Moses wrote
What	the story of the Israelites' deliverance from slavery
Where	in Egypt
When	around 1440 BC
Why	to provide a record of God's power and his commitment to Abraham's descendants

While the Israelites were in Egypt, in . . .

Africa	Horse-drawn chariots were added to the Egyptian army.
America	Sunflowers began to be cultivated and their seeds stored for winter food.
China	Human sacrifices were placed in the foundations of public buildings.
Syria	Glass began to be molded to form vessels and replace semiprecious stones.

Not Me, Lord

MOSES: Moses was an Israelite adopted into Egypt's royal family as an infant. When Moses was eighty years old, God called him to confront **Pharaoh** and free his people. God struck Egypt with ten plagues to win Israel's freedom, and Moses led the two million freed slaves to Mount Sinai. There God gave the Ten Commandments and a code of law for the Israelites to follow. Moses led the Israelites for forty years and died at age 120.

What's Special About Moses?

1. Moses was God's choice to deliver the Israelites from slavery.
2. Moses was God's choice to give us the Ten Commandments.
3. Moses was God's choice to give Israel his Law and is honored in Judaism as the Lawgiver.
4. Moses was God's choice to write the first five books of the Old Testament—Genesis, Exodus, Leviticus, Numbers, and Deuteronomy—and he was the first **prophet**.

A High Priest

AARON: Aaron was Moses' brother and his companion during the Exodus period; he became the Israelites' first high **priest**.

priest
middleman between God and the Israelites

What's Special in Exodus 1–6?

the big picture

Exodus 1–6

Although adopted into Egypt's royal family, Moses hoped to free the Israelites. Upon killing an Egyptian slave driver, Moses fled to the Sinai desert. Forty years later God told Moses to return to Egypt and free his people. Moses, having been humbled, told God how inadequate he felt for the task. God promised to be with Moses, and God also promised that Moses would be successful.

1. **The conditions under which the Israelites lived were truly brutal.** The plagues with which God later struck Egypt were a just punishment.
2. **God's words to Moses, when he announced that he was about to free Israel, help us to see what kind of person God is**. Here we see him as a God who keeps his promises, who hears the prayers of his people and responds to their suffering. He is a God who will act to deliver his people, and who has planned a wonderful future for them.

3. **Moses made excuse after excuse to explain why he was unable to accept God's commission.** God replied by telling Moses God's personal name. In Hebrew that name is YHWH, which means "the one who is always present." Moses would succeed because God was present with him, not because of his own ability. Here YHWH is translated "I AM." In English versions of the Bible, every time the word LORD appears with ORD in small capital letters, it means that the original Hebrew uses this special "I AM" name for God.

metaphysical
abstract, philosophical

judgments
acts of God intended to punish

miracles
direct, unmistakable, supernatural acts performed by God

supernatural
a direct exercise of God's power

what others say

William Sanford LaSor

[God's] existence is not a matter of being in the **metaphysical** sense—as if a philosophical statement— but rather in the relative or efficacious sense: "I am he who is there (for you)—really and truly present, ready to help and to act."[1]

The Bible is first of all a book about God and his faithful love for us.

Miracles!

the big picture

Exodus 7–19

When Pharaoh refused to free his Israelite slaves, Moses announced a series of plagues. Ten terrible **judgments** devastated the land of Egypt, and Pharaoh was forced to let the Israelites go. When Pharaoh changed his mind and pursued God's people, the Lord opened a path through the sea for the Israelites. But then the pathway closed, and the entire Egyptian army drowned. God's people were free to travel to Mount Sinai!

The Ten Plagues

What marks the ten plagues that struck Egypt as acts of God or **miracles**? Most involved natural phenomena and ordinary things like frogs, locusts, and hail. But:

1. These plagues were intense, far out of the ordinary.
2. They were announced ahead of time by Moses.
3. They began when Moses said they would begin.
4. They stopped when Moses asked God to stop them.
5. Many of them were selective, striking only the Egyptians and not the Israelites.
6. Both the Israelites and the Egyptians knew something **supernatural** was happening.

harden
Exodus 7:3–5; 7:13; 8:15

what others say

C. S. Lewis

A miracle is emphatically not an event without cause or without results. Its cause is the activity of God; its results follow according to natural law.[2]

Ten Miraculous Plagues

The Nile River is turned to blood	Exodus 7:19–25
Frogs cover the land	Exodus 8:1–15
Lice infest all of Egypt	Exodus 8:16–19
Flies swarm the Egyptians	Exodus 8:20–32
Egyptian herds die of disease	Exodus 9:1–7
Boils break out on the Egyptians	Exodus 9:8–12
Hail devastates Egyptian crops	Exodus 9:13–35
Locusts strip Egypt of vegetation	Exodus 10:1–20
Darkness blinds the Egyptians	Exodus 10:21–29
The firstborn sons of Egypt die, including Pharaoh's son	Exodus 11:1–10

Not only did God perform miracles to free Israel from Egypt, he performed miracles so that they could make it to Mount Sinai. After striking Egypt with the plagues, here's what else God did for the Israelites:

More Miracles

God shielded the Israelites	Exodus 14:5–20
God made a path through the sea	Exodus 14:21–25
God drowned an Egyptian army	Exodus 14:26–31
God purified undrinkable water	Exodus 15:22–27
God provided manna for food	Exodus 16:1–5, 13–35
God brought water from a rock	Exodus 17:1–7
God assured a military victory	Exodus 17:8–16
God displayed his power at Mount Sinai	Exodus 19:16–22

What's Special in Exodus 7–15?

1. **God told Moses he would harden Pharaoh's heart and that Pharaoh would refuse to let the Israelites go.** Some ask, "Was it fair to punish Pharaoh if he couldn't help resisting God?" But all God did to harden Pharaoh's heart was to progressively reveal more and more of his power. As the same sun that melts wax will harden clay, so God's revelation of himself softens the hearts of some and hardens the hearts of others.

lamb
Exodus 12:1–14, 21–28; John 1:29–34

Ten Commandments
Exodus 20:1–17

Passover
a yearly celebration reliving the night God won Israel's freedom from Egypt

2. **On the first Passover, a lamb was killed and its blood was sprinkled on the doorways of Israelite homes**. When the angel who struck the firstborn sons of Egypt saw the blood, it "passed over" those homes. The New Testament recalls this event in Jesus' title the "Lamb of God." It teaches that Jesus shed his blood in payment for our sins, that we might be saved from punishment for our sins.

3. **God told the Israelites to remember what he had done to free them by eating a Passover meal every year.** They were to serve the same food the people ate in Egypt on the night that God struck the firstborn sons of the Egyptians but spared his own people. Jewish families still celebrate Passover each spring.

4. **The miracles God performed in freeing the Israelites and bringing them to Mount Sinai are defining acts.** God is known throughout the Bible as the Creator who made the world, and the Redeemer whose mighty acts in history won the freedom of his people.

God's revelation of himself softens the hearts of some and hardens the hearts of others.

what others say

Norman L. Geisler

If God exists, then miracles are possible.[3]

Written in Stone

the big picture

Exodus 20–24

Moses led the Israelites into the wilderness to Mount Sinai. Clouds and lightning shrouded the mountain as God spoke to his people. God called Moses up to the mountaintop and gave him the Ten Commandments. God also gave Moses additional laws for the Israelites to follow.

What Are the Ten Commandments?

God gave Moses the Ten Commandments. The Ten Commandments teach basic morality. The first four reveal what it takes to have a good relationship with God. The next six show how to have good relationships with other people.

	The Commandments	How to Keep Them
A good relationship with God		
1.	Exodus 20:3—Do not put any other gods before me	Put God first in everything
2.	Exodus 20:4–6—Do not worship idols	Reject ideas about God that he himself has not revealed
3.	Exodus 20:7—Do not take my name in vain	Never speak or act as if God is not real and present
4.	Exodus 20:8–11—Keep the Sabbath holy	Set aside a day to rest and remember God
A good relationship with others		
5.	Exodus 20:12—Honor your mother and father	Show respect for your parents
6.	Exodus 20:13—Do not murder	Do nothing with an intent to harm another
7.	Exodus 20:14—Do not commit adultery	Be faithful in your commitment to your spouse
8.	Exodus 20:15—Do not steal	Respect the rights of others
9.	Exodus 20:16—Do not testify falsely	Respect others' reputations as well as their lives and property
10.	Exodus 20:17—Do not covet	Care about others, not about their possessions

Only a God who is himself loving, faithful, and good would command his people to live this kind of life.

what others say

Robert Schuller

God gave us these ten laws to protect us from an alluring, tempting path which would ultimately lead only to sickness, sin, and sorrow. Following the Ten Commandments will result in spiritual health, mental health, and physical health. Killing, lying, stealing, and adultery are bad for the health![4]

What's Special in Exodus 20–24?

1. **God gave these commandments to his own people.** God did not give the commandments to strangers and say, "Keep them and you will become my people." A people who have been saved by God will want to live the kind of life the commandments describe.

promises
Galatians 3:17–22

Law
the law of Moses; the Ten Commandments and other Old Testament laws God gave the Israelites

apodictic
laws that say "do," or "do not"

casuistic
rules about what to do in case this or that happens

2. God did not force the Israelites to accept his laws. He first explained what he expected of them. He warned of punishment for disobedience, and promised blessings if the Israelites obeyed. The people promised, "All the words which the LORD has said we will do" (Exodus 24:3 NKJV).

3. The agreement God and Israel made at Mount Sinai is called the Law covenant. In ancient times a covenant might be an oath, a contract, a treaty, or even a national constitution. The Law covenant is different from the covenant God made with Abraham. What are the differences?

In the Bible, only the Law covenant is a contract between God and the Israelites. The Abrahamic and other covenants of the Bible are oaths or pledges, promises stating what God says he will do.

Biblical Covenants

Question	Abrahamic Covenant	Law Covenant
Who made the commitments?	God only	God and the Israelites
Who must keep commitments?	God	God and the Israelites
What does the blessing depend on?	God's faithfulness	The Israelites' obedience
What happens if people sin?	God fulfills the covenant	God punishes the sinners
What happens if people obey?	God fulfills the covenant	God blesses the obedient
What kind of covenant is this?	Promise	Contract

4. Two kinds of laws are given in these chapters, apodictic and casuistic. Apodictic laws are universal and apply to all. The Ten Commandments are apodictic laws. Casuistic laws tell what a person should do in a specific situation. They apply only to people in the situation described. Exodus 22:5–6 and 23:4–5 are examples of casuistic or "case" law.

5. After the Israelites had been given God's Law, they knew:

- what they were to do,
- that in their life on earth God would bless them if they obeyed, and
- that God would punish them if they disobeyed.

But the Law did not change the Abrahamic covenant, nor the fact that God gives righteousness to those who have faith.

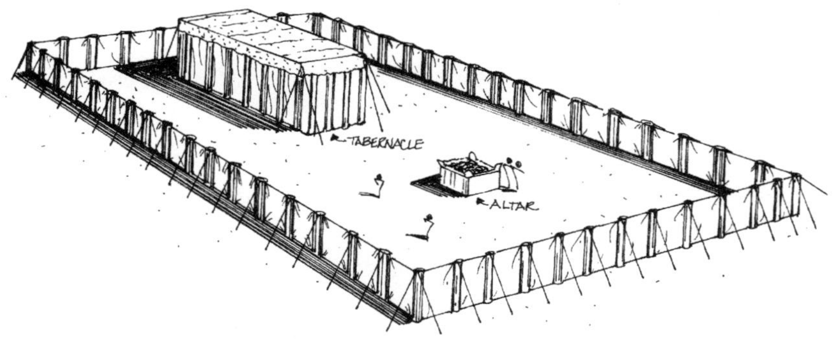

Illustration #6
The Wilderness Tabernacle—God designed each feature of the portable tent church that the Israelites carried with them.

We'll Take It with Us

the big picture

Exodus 25–40

With the Law God gave Moses the blueprint for a **worship** center. What to do was explained in minute detail. Moses and the Israelites followed God's instructions, and completed the worship center, which was called the **tabernacle.** (see Illustration #6). When all was ready, Moses and the people assembled to **dedicate** the Tabernacle to the Lord.

calf
Exodus 32:1–35

worship
honoring God with our praise

tabernacle
a tent, here the "tent of meeting" where God met with his people

dedicate
to set apart for the service of God

glory
in this case, a visible sign of God's presence

What's Special About Exodus 25–40?

1. **The tabernacle blueprint.** Why were God's directions so specific? Because each detail of the tabernacle taught a spiritual truth. For instance, God instructed there was to be only one door leading into the worship center to show that there is only one way to approach God—his way!

2. **The golden calf**. While Moses was on Mount Sinai, the Israelites urged Aaron to make an idol in the form of a calf. Many broke the first commandment and worshiped the idol, giving it credit for freeing God's people from Egypt. God punished those who were guilty, as the Law covenant specified that he should.

In spite of the fact that God's people broke his Law, God remained faithful to his promise to Abraham. When the tabernacle was completed, God filled it with his **glory** to show he truly was present with his people.

Chapter Wrap-Up

- Exodus tells the story of the Israelites' deliverance from slavery in Egypt.
- Moses was God's choice to confront Egypt's pharaoh and to announce the miraculous judgments that forced the Egyptians to free their slaves.
- After God freed the slaves, he gave them the Ten Commandments to teach his people how to maintain a healthy relationship with him and with one another.
- God promised to bless his people while they lived on earth, if they kept his commandments.
- God also gave Moses plans for a portable worship center, the tabernacle, where they could worship and offer sacrifices.

Study Questions

1. What makes Moses an important figure in the Old Testament?
2. What is a miracle?
3. What miracles did God perform to free the Israelite slaves?
4. What is the difference between a promise covenant and a contract covenant? Which kind is the Law covenant?
5. What can we learn from the Ten Commandments?

Leviticus • Numbers • Deuteronomy

Let's Get Started

At the beginning of Leviticus, the Israelites have been delivered from slavery in Egypt and brought to Mount Sinai. Moses had given them God's Ten Commandments, various other laws, and the blueprint for a portable worship center, the Tabernacle.

While at Mount Sinai, God will also reveal laws for **holy living**. Then the Israelites will set out for the land God promised to give Abraham's descendants. But a tragic rebellion will lead to thirty-eight years of wandering in the desert (see Illustration #7). Only after a new generation has replaced the men and women who left Egypt will the Israelites reach the borders of Canaan. There, just beyond the Jordan River, Moses will review the Law Covenant for the new generation.

holy living
a lifestyle fitting for people who are special to God

Where the Action Is

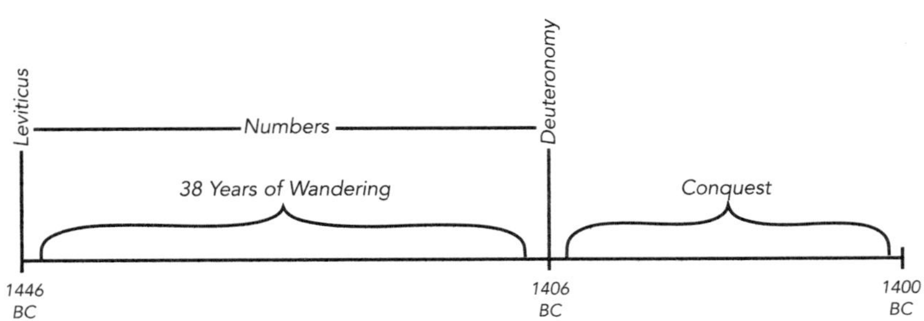

Time Line #3
Where the Action Is

Leviticus

. . . laws for holy living

Who	Moses wrote this
What	book of laws
Where	at Mount Sinai
When	around 1446 BC
Why	to remind the Israelites they were God's special people

Illustration #7
Map of Wilderness Wanderings—When the Israelites left Mount Sinai they traveled to Kadish Barnea, where they rebelled against God. After wandering in the desert for thirty-eight years, they traveled north to the plains of Moab. There, just across the Jordan River from the Promised Land, Moses reviewed God's Law.

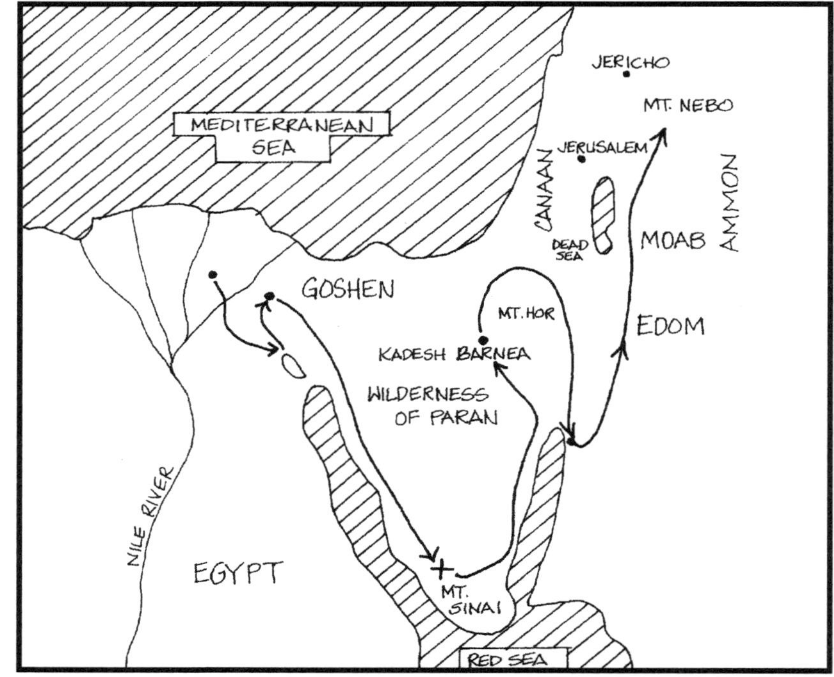

Laws, Laws, Laws

the big picture

Leviticus

This word means "about the Levites." One topic in Leviticus is that of rules for the Levites, who were the priests and worship leaders. Leviticus contains many rules that apply to all Israelites. These laws are intended to remind God's people that they belong to him. The major subjects in Leviticus are

- Offerings and sacrifices (Leviticus 1–7)
- Priests (Leviticus 8–10)
- Ritual law (Leviticus 11–15)
- The Day of Atonement (Leviticus 16)
- Practical holiness (Leviticus 17–22)
- Worshiping God (Leviticus 23–25)
- Conditions for blessing (Leviticus 26–27)

What's Special in Leviticus?

1. **Offerings and sacrifices** (Leviticus 1–7). When an Israelite wanted to approach God he or she brought an offering or a sacrifice. Sometimes a person wanted to approach God simply to

express thanks. Sometimes a person needed to approach God because he or she had sinned. These chapters describe the offerings and sacrifices an Israelite would bring to a priest, who would then burn them, symbolically presenting the offering or sacrifice to the Lord. The offerings and sacrifices described in these chapters are explained in the following chart.

atones
reconcile with God

uncleanness
contamination by contact, which temporarily limits participation in community worship

Sacrifices and Offerings

Offering	Passages	Content	Significance
Burnt	Leviticus 1; 6:8–12	Animal or bird	Symbolizes complete commitment to God
Grain (meal)	Leviticus 2; 6:14–23	Grain or bread with olive oil	Symbolizes devotion to God
Fellowship Peace	Leviticus 3; 7:11–36	Unblemished herd or flock animal	Symbolizes thanksgiving
Sin or Purification	Leviticus 4:1–5, 13; 6:24–30; 12:6–8; 14:12–14	The animal depends on what the offerer is able to provide	**Atones** for sin or **uncleanness**
Guilt	Leviticus 5:14—6:7; 7:1–6; 14:12–18	Valuable lamb or ram	Atones for sins violating others' rights or uncleanness

Many important Bible terms are associated with sacrifices and offerings. It is important to know the meanings of these terms. As we will see, a misunderstanding of them can even lead to confusion about why Jesus Christ was born, and about the meaning of his death on the cross. Below is a list of terms and their definitions. After reading them, it would be a good idea to turn your Bible to Leviticus 5:1–10 and underline each term.

Words Associated with Sacrifices and Offerings

Word	Meaning
Sin	Any violation of God's will
Guilt	Not guilt feelings, but a consequence of sin that makes a sinner subject to punishment by God
Confess	To acknowledge personal responsibility for a sin
Blood	Representation of life (see Leviticus 17:11)—making an animal sacrifice acknowledged the fact that death is the appropriate penalty for sin against God
Atonement	When an Israelite offered the blood of an animal and acknowledged his or her sin, the blood covered that sin and restored the Israelite's relationship with God
Forgiven	A forgiven person no longer has to fear divine punishment

sacrifice
Romans 3:21–26

ritual
having to do with worship practices

The New Testament teaches that Jesus Christ, God's Son, gave his life on the cross as a sacrifice to pay the penalty for our sins. When we acknowledge our guilt and trust Jesus as Savior, God forgives our sins freely and completely. The repeated Old Testament sacrifices were object lessons, teaching this special language of sacrifice and salvation.

2. **Priesthood** (Leviticus 8–10). Aaron and his sons were set apart as priests in a solemn ceremony, and the newly finished tabernacle was dedicated. Only Aaron's descendants were allowed to present an Israelite's offerings or sacrifices to the Lord.

3. **Different kinds of laws** (Leviticus 11–15). There are two basic kinds of law in the Old Testament. One kind is moral law. Moral law is about what is right and wrong and about the way we treat God and other people. The other kind of law is **ritual** law, often called ceremonial law. Ritual laws were rules the Israelites were to live by simply because they were God's people, rather than because they represented what was right or wrong in and of themselves. Ritual laws were about worship, because a person who violated a ritual law became unclean and could not join others in worshiping God.

what others say

Joni Eareckson Tada

God is telling his people what he expects of them in their worship. God wants his people to understand that all of life is spiritual; all of life's activities come under his domain. How we plow our fields or how we shop at the market. How we mate our animals or even how we talk to a gas station attendant. Everything we do can be a way of worshiping him.[1]

Which of the five rules below do you think are examples of ritual law? Remember, ritual laws have nothing to do with moral right and wrong. (See Appendix B for answers.)

1. Don't eat shrimp.
2. Offer a sacrifice after giving birth.
3. Don't commit adultery.
4. Help your enemy if his cattle get loose.
5. Wash your clothes after touching a dead body.

Terms of Ritual Law

Uncleanness: A person who broke a ritual law became ritually unclean. That person could not take part in worship or eat sacrificed meat. In some cases the unclean person had to be isolated from others. This is an important concept in the Old Testament, where the Hebrew word for "unclean" occurs 279 times!

unclean
Leviticus 13:45–46; 16:14–16, 29–34

blood sacrifice
Leviticus 17:11

Cleansing: An Israelite who had broken a ritual law and become unclean could be made clean again. Usually this called for a period of waiting and then either a washing with water or a ritual of **purification**, which involved offering a blood sacrifice. After this the Israelite could rejoin others for worship.

purification
to make ritually clean

worship
praising God for who he is and what he has done

4. **Ritual laws** (Leviticus 11–15). The ritual laws in this section of Leviticus cover what the Israelites could and could not eat, what to do when a person was born, when a person contracted an infectious skin disease, had a bodily discharge, died, etc. Ritual laws reminded the Israelites that God was concerned with every aspect of their daily lives.

5. **The Day of Atonement** (Leviticus 16). The sacrifices for sin described in Leviticus 1–7 could only atone for unintentional sins. What about the sins an Israelite committed knowingly, fully aware that he or she was doing wrong? Once a year on the Day of Atonement the high priest took a blood sacrifice into the inner room of the tabernacle, the Holy of Holies, to make an atonement for all the sins of the Israelites.

6. **Laws of practical holiness** (Leviticus 17–22). These chapters contain a variety of laws that the Israelites were to follow. Many of the laws were moral laws about relationships between people. Other laws were designed to strengthen the family, while still others were symbolic reminders that as God's people the Israelites were to be different from the peoples around them. "I the LORD am holy, and have separated you from the peoples, that you should be Mine" (Leviticus 20:26 NKJV).

7. **Worshiping God** (Leviticus 23–25). These chapters describe special festivals during which the Israelites gathered to **worship** God. Some of these same festivals are celebrated as religious holidays by Jews today.

Significance of Jewish Festivals

Jewish Festival	Date	Significance
Passover	14 Nisan (March/April)	Families share a meal and remember how God delivered the Israelites from slavery in Egypt
Unleavened Bread	15–21 Nisan (March/April)	Families offer sacrifices and eat bread without leaven as a reminder of the hurried departure from Egypt
Firstfruits	6 Nisan (March/April)	A harvesttime, thanksgiving celebration
Pentecost (Weeks)	5 Silvan (May/June	A thanksgiving celebration when newly ripened grain is offered and sacrifices are made
Trumpets	1 Tishri (September/October)	This is a day of rest—the first day of Israel's civil year
Rosh Hashanah		The religious year begins with Passover
Day of Atonement	10 Tishri (September/October)	The high priest enters the tabernacle and makes the yearly sacrifice for all the sins of the Israelites. The people fast on this solemn day
Tabernacles	15–21 Tishri (September/October)	For a week the Israelites live in outdoor shelters, reliving the travels of the Exodus generation to the Promised Land

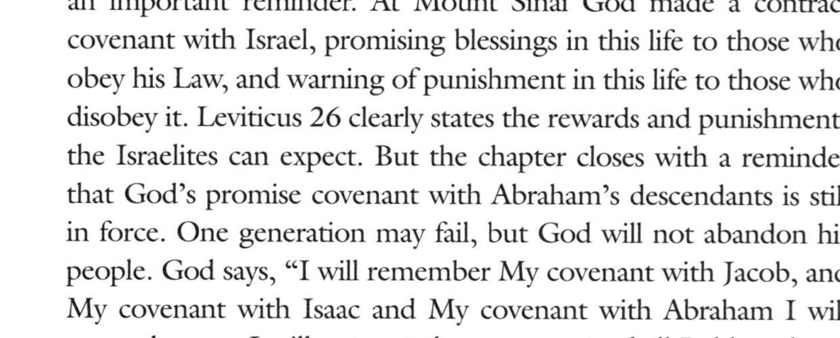

8. Conditions for blessing (Leviticus 26–27). Leviticus closes with an important reminder. At Mount Sinai God made a contract covenant with Israel, promising blessings in this life to those who obey his Law, and warning of punishment in this life to those who disobey it. Leviticus 26 clearly states the rewards and punishments the Israelites can expect. But the chapter closes with a reminder that God's promise covenant with Abraham's descendants is still in force. One generation may fail, but God will not abandon his people. God says, "I will remember My covenant with Jacob, and My covenant with Isaac and My covenant with Abraham I will remember . . . I will not cast them away, nor shall I abhor them, to utterly destroy them and break My covenant with them" (Leviticus 26:42, 44 NKJV).

Numbers

. . . the long journey

Who	Moses wrote this
What	narrative history
Where	after reaching the borders of Canaan
When	around 1406 BC
Why	to remind the Israelites of the consequences of rebelling against God.

Promised Land
the land God promised Abraham's descendants, modern Israel (Palestine)

We Won't Be There Tomorrow

the big picture

Numbers

The name is taken from two numberings of the Israelites, recorded in chapters 1 and 26. After having camped for a year at Mount Sinai, the Israelites, led by Moses, set out for Canaan. Upon arriving, the Israelites refused to trust God and rebelled. For the next thirty-eight years the Israelites wandered in the desert (see Time Line #3). During this time God provided for all their needs. When all the adults who had been freed from Egypt had died, Moses led a new generation that did trust him back to Canaan. Numbers has three main sections:

- Preparation for the journey (Numbers 1–10)
- Journeying toward Canaan (Numbers 11–21)
- Waiting on the plains of Moab (Numbers 22–36)

What's Special in Numbers?

1. **Preparation for the journey** (Numbers 1–10). There were many things to do during the year that the Israelites camped at Mount Sinai. A census was taken and listed 603,550 men. With women and children, the people numbered over two million! The tabernacle and its furnishings were constructed and dedicated (see Illustration #6). The descendants of Levi were set apart by God to care for the tabernacle, and jobs were assigned to various Levite families. When all these tasks were completed, the Israelites were ready to leave for the **Promised Land**.

refused to obey
Hebrews 3:7–19

Balaam
2 Peter 2:15–16

2. **Journeying toward Canaan** (Numbers 11–21). God was clearly present with the Israelites. His pillar of cloud and fire led them. His manna fed them daily. But instead of being grateful, the Israelites grumbled and complained. When they reached the borders of Canaan, Moses sent out men to explore the land. The men reported that Canaan was fertile but that Canaan's inhabitants were powerful and their fortified cities frightening. Terrified by the report, the Israelites refused to obey God's command to attack and take the Promised Land. Under the Law covenant, direct disobedience called for punishment. Moses prayed for the people, and the Lord pardoned their sin. But the Israelites could not avoid the consequences of their unwillingness to obey the Lord. Until the entire generation of those who were unwilling to obey God died out, the Israelites were forced to wander in the wilderness—waiting.

God's faithfulness underlined (Numbers 15–21). The first words of Numbers 15 remind us of God's faithfulness. The Israelites had rebelled. But God immediately told Moses, "Speak to the children of Israel, and say to them: 'When you have come into the land you are to inhabit, which I am giving to you . . .'" (Numbers 15:2 NKJV). Despite the repeated failures to trust and obey God reported in these chapters, God intended to keep his promises and give the Israelites the Promised Land.

While the Israelites wandered in the wilderness, in . . .

Mesopotamia	The city of Nineveh, capital of Assyria, was founded.
America	Indians in Nevada used duck decoys in hunting.
America	Indians living near the Great Lakes wore shells from the Gulf of Mexico as ornaments.
China	An alphabet of two thousand characters was in use.

3. **Waiting on the plains of Moab** (Numbers 22–36). As the years of wandering drew toward an end, the Israelites followed a major trade route east of Mount Sinai. They avoided some of their enemies but fought others. The ruler of Moab was frightened, and sent for a man named Balaam. Balaam was reputed to have influence with supernatural powers. The ruler of Moab hoped Balaam would be able to curse the Israelites and so weaken them. Balaam

tried to curse the Israelites, but God intervened and Balaam was forced to bless them instead.

Balaam was forced to confess, "There is no sorcery against Jacob, nor any divination against Israel" (Numbers 23:23 NKJV). God protects his people from evil spiritual powers.

Balaam's advice. Balaam wanted to earn the money the Moabites offered him, but Israel could not be cursed. So he suggested the Moabites try to turn God against his people! Following Balaam's advice, the Midianite ruler sent young women to seduce Israelite men and invite them to sacrifice to idols. Balaam reasoned God would punish the Israelites himself, and they would be defeated by his Moabite clients.

God did punish, but only the guilty. God remained faithful to his promises to the people as a whole.

The second census. At this point in Numbers the adults who left Egypt have died and have been replaced by their grown children. A second census showed that despite these deaths, the Israelites were as numerous as before, with over 600,000 men. The new generation learned from their parents' failure. This generation obeyed the Lord their God.

The Moabites are defeated. Various laws are reviewed in chapters 27–30. Chapters 31–33 relate the defeat of the Moabites and the request of several of Israel's tribes to be given the land the Moabites had lived on. These tribes agree to go with their brothers to help fight for Canaan.

Moses defines the boundaries of Canaan and makes plans. Moses explained to the Israelites how territory will be distributed to each tribe. With God on Israel's side, the question is not if his people will take Canaan, but what is to happen when victory is achieved!

Deuteronomy

. . . the law reviewed

Who	Moses preached
What	sermons reviewing God's Law
Where	on the plains of Moab
When	about 1406 BC
Why	to remind the new generations of Israelites what God expects

I'll Say It Again

the big picture

Deuteronomy

Deuteronomy means "second law." The new generation of Israelites was about to enter the Promised Land when Moses reminded them of all that God had done for them. He summarized the way God's people were to live in order to enjoy his blessing. The book ends with an account of Moses' farewell blessing and his death. Major sections of Deuteronomy are

- Remembering the journey (Deuteronomy 1:1–4:43)
- Reviewing God's Law (Deuteronomy 4:44–11)
- Rules to remember (Deuteronomy 12–26)
- Consequences to consider (Deuteronomy 27, 28)
- Covenant commitment (Deuteronomy 29, 30)
- Moses' farewell and death (Deuteronomy 31–34)

What's Special in Deuteronomy?

1. **Remembering the journey** (Deuteronomy 1:1–4:43). Moses retraced the thirty-eight-year journey from Mount Sinai to the border of the Promised Land. He urged the new generation to learn from history, and especially to develop a sense of wonder at the special relationship they had with the God of the universe.
2. **Reviewing God's Law** (Deuteronomy 4:44–11:32). Moses restated a number of laws given at Mount Sinai, including the Ten Commandments. Several themes in these chapters may raise questions.

Q: What does it mean to "fear the Lord"?

A: It doesn't mean "be afraid of." The phrase means "show" respect for" by seeking to please him.

Q: What does "love" have to do with Law?

A: Love moved God to give Israel the Law, and love moves people to keep it. The Law showed how to express love.

Q: Why did God tell the Israelites to totally destroy the Canaanites?

A: God was punishing the immorality and idolatry of the Canaanites. If allowed to remain, their practices would have corrupted God's people.

Read the following passages and indicate which question each helps to answer. In the spaces provided, write F for fear, L for love, or D for drive out (destroy). (See Appendix B for answers.)

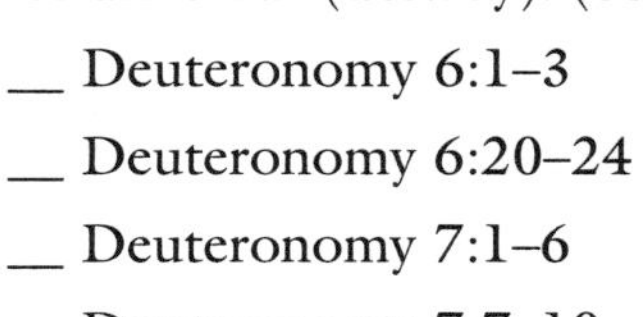

- __ Deuteronomy 6:1–3
- __ Deuteronomy 6:20–24
- __ Deuteronomy 7:1–6
- __ Deuteronomy 7:7–10
- __ Deuteronomy 10:12–22
- __ Deuteronomy 11:16–17

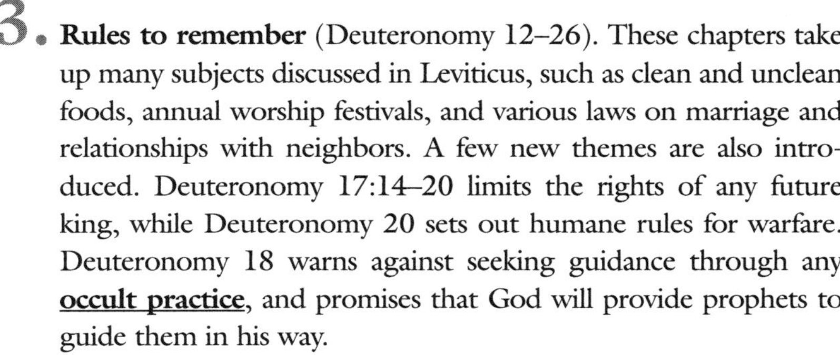

3. Rules to remember (Deuteronomy 12–26). These chapters take up many subjects discussed in Leviticus, such as clean and unclean foods, annual worship festivals, and various laws on marriage and relationships with neighbors. A few new themes are also introduced. Deuteronomy 17:14–20 limits the rights of any future king, while Deuteronomy 20 sets out humane rules for warfare. Deuteronomy 18 warns against seeking guidance through any <u>**occult practice**</u>, and promises that God will provide prophets to guide them in his way.

occult practice
Deuteronomy 18:9–22

occult practice
any practice used to make choices with non-Christian, supernatural guidance

legalistic
relying on good works rather than God

remnant
the few within Israel who continued to trust God

> **what others say**
>
> **Lewis Goldberg**
>
> Deuteronomy describes how God blessed and showered his love on them because of his grace and mercy. What the Lord expected from Israel in return was an outpouring of love. While some people misappropriated God's intentions and developed a **legalistic** substitute, a **remnant** in every generation always deeply loved, honored, and served the Lord their God.[2]

A Little Guidance

Old Testament Law gave rules to follow in daily life, but some situations simply were not covered in the Law. How could the Israelites know and follow God's will in such cases?

The Canaanites and other pagan peoples looked to the occult for guidance. They checked horoscopes, went to mediums or spiritists, practiced divination, and even engaged in witchcraft. God called these practices "abominations" and forbade them.

false prophet
a person God did not send who claims to have a message from God

brethren
fellow Jews

epitaph
eulogy; praise for the dead

God then promised to send prophets to his people, like Moses, by whom God would give them special guidance when it was needed. Deuteronomy 18 gives three tests for distinguising a true prophet from a **false prophet**. The true prophet will

1. be "from among their **brethren**,"
2. speak in God's name, and
3. predict the future accurately.

As we go on in the Bible we will meet many prophets God sent to his people. We will also read many of their amazing predictions about the future!

4. **Consequences to consider** (Deuteronomy 27, 28). The Law covenant is a contract covenant. When the Israelites kept the Law, God blessed them. When they disobeyed, God disciplined them. These chapters spell out both blessings for obedience and punishments for disobedience.
5. **Covenant commitment** (Deuteronomy 29, 30). Moses called on the Israelites to make a choice and to keep the covenant they had made with the Lord their God.
6. **Moses' farewell and death** (Deuteronomy 31–34). God chose a successor for Moses to lead the Israelites. Moses blessed the people whom he had led for forty years. Then Moses went to the top of Mount Nebo and looked over the Jordan River, where he was able to see the Promised Land. Moses died there, and God himself buried his faithful servant. The following, written some time after Moses' death, is a fitting **epitaph**.

Deuteronomy 34:10–12 ***But since then there has not arisen in Israel a prophet like Moses, whom the Lord knew face to face, in all the signs and wonders which the Lord sent him to do in the land of Egypt, before Pharaoh, before all his servants, and in all his land, and by all that mighty power and all the great terror which Moses performed in the sight of all Israel. (NKJV)***

Chapter Wrap-Up

- At Mount Sinai God gave the Israelites laws for holy living, which are found in Leviticus.
- The offerings and sacrifices specified in Leviticus remind us that everyone sins and that the penalty of sin is death.
- The offerings and sacrifices specified in Leviticus teach us that blood atonement is required if we are to be forgiven.
- Moral laws were about right and wrong actions, while ritual laws governed actions that made an Israelite ritually unclean and temporarily disqualified to participate in worship.
- Numbers reports the rebellion of the Israelites. As a result, God required them to wander in the desert for thirty-eight years, and then an obedient generation replaced the rebellious one.
- Deuteronomy records Moses' last words to the Israelites as they were poised to enter the Promised Land.
- Deuteronomy makes it very clear that those who know God are to have nothing to do with occult practices.
- Deuteronomy emphasizes the fact that God was motivated by love to give the Israelites his Law, and that only love for God can motivate a believer to obey the Lord.

Study Questions

1. What is the theme of Leviticus?
2. What Bible terms are linked with Leviticus's teaching on sacrifice? Why is it so important for us to understand these terms?
3. What is the difference between ritual law and moral law?
4. What made an Israelite unclean, and what could he or she do about it?
5. Why did the Israelites have to wander in the wilderness for thirty-eight years after leaving Mount Sinai?
6. What roles does love play in the Law God gave to Israel?
7. What is a prophet, and how could the Israelites tell a true prophet from a false prophet?

Joshua • Judges • Ruth

Let's Get Started

God delivered the Israelites from slavery in Egypt and gave them his Law at Mount Sinai. A new generation of Israelites was ready to take the land God promised to Abraham hundreds of years before. The conquest to come would be successful, because this generation was willing to trust and obey the Lord. But the bright days of the conquest would soon fade, and idolatry and unbelief would doom the Israelites to centuries of oppression by foreign enemies.

Canaan
the land God promised Abraham, from now on known as "Israel"

Joshua

. . . the conquest of Canaan

Who	An unnamed author wrote
What	this history of
Where	the occupation of **Canaan**
When	around 1400 BC
Why	to emphasize the importance of obedience to the Lord

We're Finally There

JOSHUA: Joshua succeeded Moses as the leader of the Israelites. He was a man of faith who had been Moses' right-hand man and military commander during the years of wandering in the wilderness. (Some believe that Joshua was once an officer in the Egyptian army.) He was a spiritual as well as military leader, and during his lifetime the Israelites were faithful to the Lord.

the big picture

Joshua

Led by Joshua, the Israelites crossed the Jordan River and invaded Canaan (see Illustration #8). In a series of military campaigns the Israelites defeated several coalition armies raised by the inhabitants of Canaan. With organized resistance put down,

Joshua divided the land among the twelve Israelite tribes. The book of Joshua covers:

- Preparation for the invasion (Joshua 1–5)
- The conquest (Joshua 6–12)
- Division of the land (Joshua 13–21)
- Joshua's farewell challenge (Joshua 22–24)

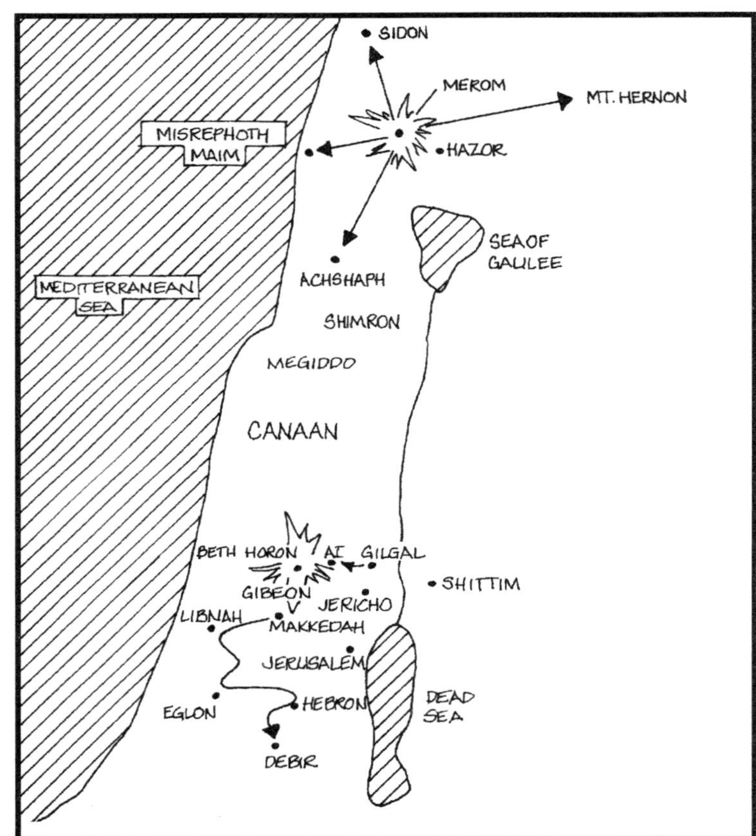

Illustration #8
Map of Conquest—Canaan was not a united nation when the Israelites invaded. It had been settled by a number of ethnic groups, each of which lived in a small fortified city-state. When the Israelites arrived, the kings of these city-states united against them. Joshua's first thrust into Canaan cut the country in two, and the Israelites defeated first the southern and then the northern coalitions. The campaign against the Canaanites is still studied in U.S. and Israeli war colleges.

What's Special in Joshua?

1. **Preparation for victory** (Joshua 1–5). The Israelites were about to attack a heavily populated land. These chapters of Joshua tell how God prepared them to meet the challenge. Four kinds of preparation are emphasized:

   A. *Spiritual preparation of Joshua*. Like Joshua, anyone who wants to be a spiritual leader must be ready to submit to God and to claim God's promises.

B. *Secret preparation of the way by God.* Israelite spies, sent to the walled city of Jericho, discovered that the population was aware of God and his power. They were terrified. When God asks anyone to take a risk for him, he will prepare the way.

C. *Sensitive preparation of the Israelites.* God opened a path through the Jordan River to show that he was with Joshua as he had been with Moses. God was sensitive to the Israelites' need for evidence of his presence with Joshua.

D. *Heart preparation by the people.* The men of Israel were **circumcised**, and the whole community celebrated Passover. These acts expressed commitment to the Lord.What's Special in Joshua?

circumcised
removed the foreskin of the male genitalia; signified faith in God's covenant promises

RAHAB: A woman who lived in Jericho and hid Israelite spies. Like others in the city she had heard that God performed miracles for his people. She shared their conviction that "the LORD . . . is God in heaven above and on earth beneath" (Joshua 2:11 NKJV). Rahab hid the spies, and when Jericho fell, only she and her family survived.

All the people of Jericho had the same information about God that Rahab did. But only Rahab chose to trust God rather than resist him. Faith is not just knowing the truth about God. Faith is responding to the truth we know.

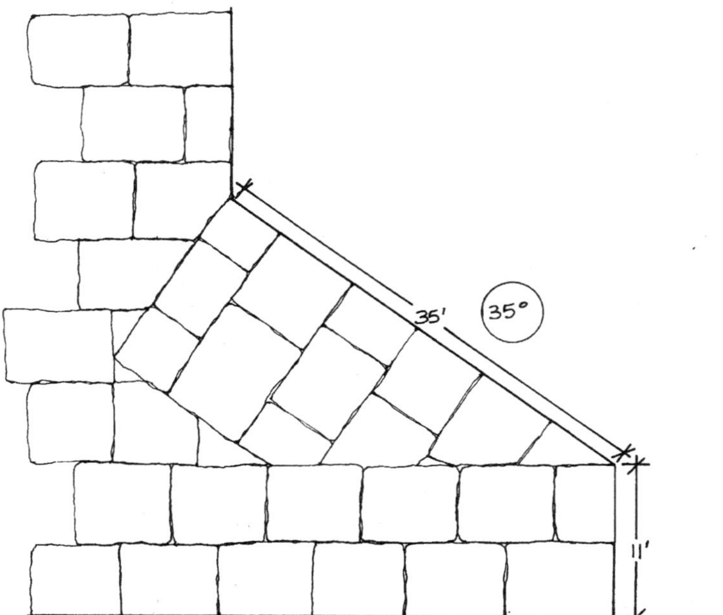

Illustration #9
The Walls of Jericho—Above an 11-foot base wall, smooth stones sloped 35 feet at a 35-degree angle to join massive main walls. The city of Jericho was impregnable to direct assault by an army without siege engines.

2. The conquest of Canaan (Joshua 6–12).

Jericho. Joshua 6–8 is devoted to the fall of Jericho, followed by a defeat at Ai. Jericho was a walled city (see Illustration #9) that blocked access to the only pass which led into the heart of Canaan. God instructed Joshua to have the Israelites march in silence around the city for six days. On the seventh day they circled the city seven times—shouted—and the walls fell down! Obedience to a seemingly foolish command of God led to a stunning victory.

lots
Proverbs 16:33; John 19:24

Ai. At Jericho an Israelite named Achan disobeyed God's command not to take any **booty**. When a force of Israelites was sent to attack Ai, a small nearby city, the Israelites were defeated and thirty-eight were killed. The two events placed side by side taught an important lesson. Obedience to God guaranteed victory. Disobedience guaranteed defeat. (Joshua 7–8)

Gibeon. The news of the victory at Jericho further terrified the Canaanites. One group, the Gibeonites, pretended to live outside Canaan and tricked the Israelites into making a treaty with them. When the deceit was discovered, Joshua insisted the treaty be honored because the Israelites had sworn in the name of the Lord their God. (Joshua 9)

booty
spoils taken in battle

clans
groups of closely related families

lots
like dice

Other victories. The southern and northern campaigns, which took several years, are briefly summarized in chapters 10–12.

The major lessons taught in the book of Joshua are summarized in the first stages of the battle for Canaan. Below is a list of places and respective lessons.

Battle for Canaan

Place	Lesson
Jericho	Obedience to God's will brings victory.
Ai	Disobedience to God's will brings defeat.
Gibeon	When uncertain about God's will, ask him for guidance.

3. Division of the land (Joshua 13–21).

Land for all (Joshua 12–19). The Old Testament presents Canaan as God's special possession, on which he settled the descendants of Abraham. Each tribe's holdings were given to it. Then the tribal territory was subdivided and distributed to **clans** and families by **lots**. Because God controlled the fall of the lots, each Israelite felt that God personally provided his or her home. Homesteads assigned at the conquest were to remain within the family, be passed from father to son, and never be sold.

premeditated planned and intended

Cities of refuge (Joshua 20). In Old Testament times the Israelites had no national or local police force. Violations of the Law were dealt with in the community. In the case of murder, a close relative of the victim was responsible for bringing the killer to justice. But the Law made a distinction between **premeditated** and accidental murder. Cities of refuge were established within one day's journey of any Israelite. A person who killed another could flee there and be safe until community elders determined whether the death was intentional or by accident. While murderers were put to death, those who killed accidentally were protected.

Cities for the Levites (Joshua 21). The tribe of Levi provided Israel's priests and worship leaders. The Levites were also to teach God's Law. Rather than being given a district of their own, the Levites were assigned towns and fields within the territory of the other tribes. Everyone needed access to those charged with communicating God's Word.

4. **Joshua's farewell** (Joshua 22–24). Many years after the victory over the Canaanites, Joshua summoned the Israelites and reminded them of all God had done. He challenged them to "fear the LORD, [and] serve Him in sincerity and in truth" (Joshua 24:14 NKJV). Joshua's final exhortation is as relevant today as it was thirty-four hundred years ago: "Choose for yourselves this day whom you will serve. . . . But as for me and my house, we will serve the LORD" (Joshua 24:15 NKJV).

Judges

. . . the long decline

Who	An unnamed author wrote
What	this brief history of events
Where	in Canaan
When	from about 1375 BC to 1050 BC
Why	to underline the importance of national commitment to the Lord

pagan
peoples who worshiped false gods

judges
Israelite leaders; spiritual, political, and military leaders

dispossess
put them out; cut off or separate from

the big picture

Judges

After Joshua died, the Israelites again and again turned from God to the idolatry of **pagan** neighbors. This led to oppression by foreign enemies, until God's people returned to him and prayed for deliverance. God then provided leaders called **judges** who threw out the oppressors. During the judges' rule, the Israelites were at peace and remained faithful to God, but they quickly went astray again after the judges died. The book of Judges has three main sections:

- Causes of the decline (Judges 1:1–3:5)
- Stories of the judges (Judges 3:6–16:31)
- Consequences of straying (Judges 17–21)

What's Important in Judges?

1. **Causes of the decline** (Judges 1:1–3:5). Not all the Canaanites were driven out during the conquest. Each Israelite tribe was told to **dispossess** those who remained, in order to protect God's people from spiritual and moral corruption. Some tribes failed to do so because of their lack of faith. Others directly disobeyed and when Israel became strong, they pressed the Canaanites into forced labor (see Judges 1:28). Again and again their turning to worship the idols of Canaan's pagan peoples would bring disaster.

what others say

Howard Hendricks

Homes should be training grounds to develop habit patterns that serve Jesus Christ. And then we'll avoid the tragedy described in Judges 2:10—another generation grew up, who knew neither the Lord nor what he had done.[1]

2. **Stories of the judges** (Judges 3:6–16:31). What was a judge? A judge was an individual whom God raised up to lead one or more Israelite tribes. The term "judge" may give the wrong impression. These gifted individuals exercised all governmental powers during their time in office—executive, legislative, and judicial. Most were also military leaders. The office of judge was not hereditary. God called individuals from different walks of life and empowered them to serve as judges.

JUDGES: Who were the judges? Twelve judges are named, and the chart below indicates the verses devoted to each judge. The stories given the most space have lessons to teach believers today.

The Twelve Judges

Judge	Number of Verses	Years of Peace Won
Othniel	4	40
Ehud	18	80
Shamgar	1	—
Deborah	53	40
Gideon	100	40
Tola	2	23
Jair	3	—
Jephthah	58	6
Izban	3	—
Elan	2	—
Adbon	3	—
Samson	97	20

DEBORAH: All ancient societies were patriarchal. Israel was no exception. Priests, town elders, political and military leaders, like the heads of households, were men. But at one time Deborah, a woman and a prophetess, emerged as the acknowledged leader, the judge, of several of the northern Israelite tribes. What counted were the obvious gifts and the calling by God of this exceptional woman, not her gender. What still counts today is not how society limits us, but how God enables us. (Judges 4:1–16)

GIDEON: The story of Gideon's victory with just three hundred men against a much larger army is a favorite in every Sunday school curriculum. What's more fascinating is that even though Gideon was deeply aware of his weakness and sought constant reassurance, he obeyed God before he was reassured. A weak person willing to obey God will be the strongest in the end. (Judges 6–7)

Martin Luther

When God contemplates some great work, he begins it by the hand of some poor, weak human creature, to whom he afterward gives aid, so that the enemies who seek to obstruct it are overcome.[2]

Philistines
warlike people from Crete who controlled coastal Canaan

moorings
a common commitment to shared values

JEPHTHAH: Jephthah (pronounced Jeff-thah) was the son of a prostitute. His father acknowledged Jephthah and brought him up as one of his own. When the father died, however, Jephthah was thrown out of the family, clan, and tribe. When war came, the tribal elders called Jephthah back to lead them. His letters to the invading Amorites show that Jephthah knew well the history of his nation's relationship with God. Early disadvantages need not limit the future of those who know God. (Judges 10:4–40)

Jephthah's Daughter: Read Judges 11:29–40. Then vote. Did Jephthah kill his only daughter as a sacrifice to the Lord?

YES___ NO___ (See Appendix B for the answer.)

SAMSON: Sunday school stories emphasize Samson's physical strength. The Bible emphasizes his moral and spiritual weaknesses. Although he was a judge, Samson never delivered his people from oppression by the **Philistines**. Finally Samson's passion for a prostitute led him to betray the secret of his strength, which eventually brought about his death. No matter how great our natural gifts, only complete commitment to God will enable us to live up to our potential. (Judges 16)

3. Consequences of straying (Judges 17–21). Judges closes with a description of three incidents that reveal what happens when a society loses its **moorings** by turning away from God's Word and his ways.

Straying from God Affects Us in Three Ways

	1. Spiritually	2. Morally	3. Socially
	Judges 17–18	Judges 19	Judges 20–21
The Act	Micah makes an idol and gets a Levite to serve as his priest.	A traveler threatened with homosexual rape turns his concubine over to the the rapists.	Civil war breaks out when the tribes attempt to punish the mob
The Result	Knowledge of God is lost or distorted.	Moral standards are abandoned and corrupted.	Social remedies break down.

Ruth

. . . simple faith

Who	An unnamed author wrote
What	this beautiful story of
Where	a young woman who honored God
When	during the days of the judges
Why	to show that even when a society abandons God, individual commitment is honored

kinsman
a close relative

redeem
to buy back

A Pillar of Faith

the big picture

Ruth

This book of the Bible takes its name from the Moabitess daughter-in-law of Naomi. Naomi left Israel during a famine and returned years later after her husband and sons died. Ruth committed herself to Naomi and to Israel's God. Although in poverty, Ruth's virtue and character won the admiration of a relative of Naomi's husband, who married her. The union led to the birth of Obed, the grandfather of Israel's greatest king, David.

NAOMI: After her husband and sons died in Moab, Naomi, which means "pleasant," changed her name to Mara, which means "bitter." Yet through the loving support of her daughter-in-law Ruth, Naomi found comfort and a future.

RUTH: Ruth's famous words to Naomi express her commitment. "Wherever you go, I will go; and wherever you lodge, I will lodge; your people shall be my people, and your God, my God" (Ruth 1:16 NKJV). Ruth's modesty and obvious commitment to her mother-in-law won the admiration of the community and the love of Boaz, whom she married.

BOAZ: An older man, Boaz was attracted to Ruth's character as well as her beauty. The story hinges on how Boaz played the role of the **kinsman redeemer**, and how, by marrying Ruth, he gained back Naomi's lost lands for their child, Obed.

What's Special About Ruth?

become human
Hebrews 2:14–18

death on the cross
Colossians 1:21–22

type
a person or thing which is like another in an important respect

1. **This gentle story, set during the days of the judges, is in sharp contrast to the stories told in Judges 17–21.** It reminds us that even when a society breaks down, people of faith can live fulfilling and beautiful lives.
2. **For thousands of years the relationship of Ruth and Naomi has served as a clear example of the costs and rewards of commitment.** It is no wonder that Ruth's words to Naomi (Ruth 1:16) have been woven into many marriage ceremonies.
3. **Boaz is a model of the Old Testament's kinsman redeemer.** When a man died childless, a near kinsman could marry the widow. Any son of the resulting union would gain the first husband's inheritance. But to rescue the lost estate, the redeemer had to be a near kinsman, and he had to be willing to accept the responsibility.

Many see Boaz as a **type** of Jesus Christ. To win back what we human beings lost through sin and spiritual death, Jesus had to become human (i.e., he had to become a true kinsman), and he had to be willing to pay the penalty for our sins. With his death on the cross, Jesus paid the penalty and won freedom and eternal life for us.

Chapter Wrap-Up

- The book of Joshua tells the story of the Israelites' conquest of Canaan.
- The miracle at Jericho taught the Israelites that obedience to God's commands assures victory, and their failure at Ai taught Israel that disobeying God leads to defeat.
- Judges relates incidents that happened during a long period of time in which the Israelites often strayed from God.
- The judges were political, military, and religious leaders that God provided when the Israelites looked to him for help.
- The Israelites suffered material, moral, and social decline during this era because of their failure to remain faithful to God.
- The book of Ruth reminds us that individuals can find blessing by trusting God even during times when their nations have turned away from him.

Study Questions

1. What time period do the books of Joshua, Judges, and Ruth cover?
2. What is the main message of the book of Joshua?
3. What is the main message of Judges?
4. What was a judge, and what did the judges do for the Israelites?
5. Name three of the four persons who are emphasized in Judges.
6. What is the main message of the book of Ruth?

1 Samuel • 2 Samuel • 1 Chronicles

Let's Get Started

During the age of the judges, Israel was a loose association of weak tribes, barely surviving in the Promised Land. In 1050 BC the last judge, Samuel, **anointed** Saul, Israel's first king. The flawed King Saul was succeeded by David, who became Israel's greatest king. David united the Israelites into a single nation, defeated every foreign enemy, and established Jerusalem as Israel's political and religious capital. When David died in 970 BC, the Israelites occupied ten times as much territory as when he became king.

anointed
set apart for a task by pouring oil on a person's head

Stories Told and Retold

This pivotal period of Old Testament history is so important that its stories are told and retold in the Bible. The chart below shows how the Bible books that feature Samuel, Saul, and David overlap.

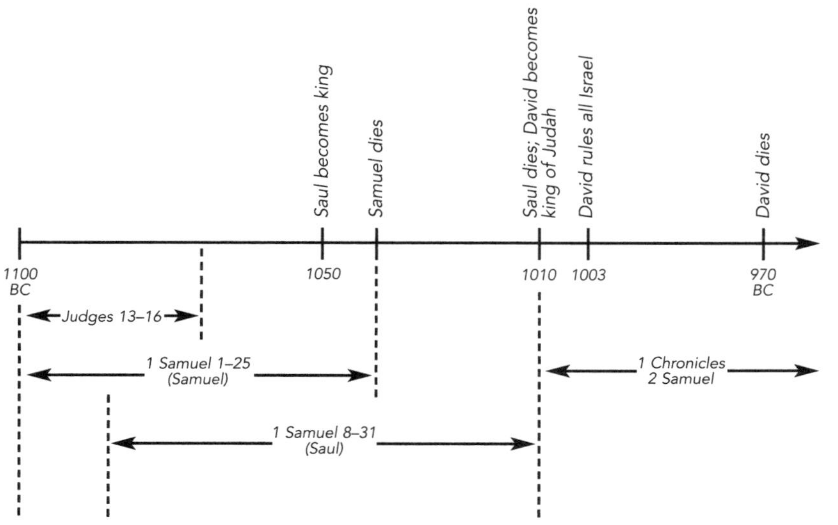

Time Line #4
Accounts of the New Beginning

1 Samuel

. . . origin of the monarchy

Who	An unnamed author wrote
What	this history of events
Where	in Canaan
When	from 1050 BC to 1010 BC
Why	to record how Israel became a united nation ruled by kings

Dedicated to the Lord

the big picture

1 Samuel

The book begins with the birth of Samuel and his dedication to the Lord. Early chapters highlight incidents from the ministry of Samuel, who was God's prophet and Israel's last judge. Pressured by the people in his old age, Samuel anoints Saul as Israel's first king. The focus of 1 Samuel then shifts to Saul, whose flaws lead to God's rejection of him as king. Most of the book traces the relationship between Saul and a newcomer to his court, David, who will become king when Saul dies. First Samuel may be outlined as follows:

- Samuel (chapters 1–7)
- Saul (chapters 8–15)
- Saul and David (chapters 16–31)

SAMUEL: As a child of three years, Samuel was dedicated by his mother to serve God at the tabernacle. He later became Israel's last judge and drove the Philistines from Israel's territory. When Samuel was old the Israelites demanded a king. On God's instructions Samuel anointed Saul, and later David, to become rulers of Israel.

What's Special in 1 Samuel 1–7?

1. **Hannah's prayer** (1 Samuel 1–2). Hannah prayed desperately for a son and promised to dedicate him to the Lord. Her prayer answered, Hannah brought three-year-old Samuel to the tabernacle, where he served God as priest, prophet, and Israel's last judge. Hannah's prayer of praise expressed her joy, which came as a result of returning to God what he had given her.

2. **Israel's defeat** (1 Samuel 4–6). When a Philistine army invaded, two Israeli priests brought the **ark of the covenant** to the battlefield at Aphek, counting on its magic powers to help them. The Philistines defeated Israel and captured the ark. But the trophy, which symbolized God's presence, caused such terrible plagues that the Philistines quickly returned it to Israel. Though the movie *Raiders of the Lost Ark* is fiction, the ark of the covenant did exist, and the God of the ark was and is real!

3. **Victory at Mizpah** (1 Samuel 7). Twenty years after the defeat at Aphek, Samuel purged idolatry from Israel and led the people back to God. When attacked by the Philistines again, Samuel prayed, and Israel won a great victory at Mizpah. It was such a decisive victory that it ended any immediate threat from the Philistines throughout Samuel's judgeship.

laws
Deuteronomy 17:14–20

ark of the covenant
Israel's holiest object; the gold-covered box contained the Ten Commandments, and symbolized God's presence on earth

What, No Backbone?

SAUL: Saul, Israel's first king, was a tall young man whose early successes won him the allegiance of his people. Despite his impressive physique, Saul was morally weak. Under pressure, Saul failed to trust God and was unwilling to obey him. The result was that God eventually rejected his kingship.

What's Special in 1 Samuel 8–15?

1. **A matter of motive** (1 Samuel 8). Moses laid down laws under which Israel's kings were to rule. But when the Israelites demanded a king centuries later, it was because they wanted to be like all the nations. Before, Israel had been different—responsible to and dependent on God rather than a human ruler. The demand for a king was an overt rejection of God's direct rule.

2. **Saul's flaws revealed** (1 Samuel 13; 15:1–26). Israel's kings were spiritual as well as political leaders. A king's commitment to God set the tone for the nation. Two incidents reveal why Saul was unfit to rule God's people.

The first incident. A massive Philistine army assembled to attack Israel. Samuel told Saul to wait, and that within seven days he would come and intercede with God. Saul waited, but more and more of

feared
Matthew 6:25–34; 10:16–31

trust
Psalm 23

foolishly
not stupid but morally wrong

his army left. Finally Saul offered a sacrifice himself. Samuel rebuked Saul by saying, "You have done **foolishly.** You have not kept the commandment of the LORD your God, which He commanded you" (1 Samuel 13:13 NKJV). Saul not only disobeyed God's prophet, he disobeyed God's Law. Only a descendant of Aaron was qualified to offer a sacrifice.

The second incident. God commissioned Saul to utterly destroy the Amalekites. When Saul failed, he made excuses: "I feared the people [his own army] and obeyed their voice" (1 Samuel 15:24 NKJV). This rejection of God's eternal authority resulted in God's rejection of Saul's earthly authority. All too often we hesitate to do what we know is right, out of concern for what others might think or say.

No End to Jealousy

DAVID: A towering Old Testament figure. As the youngest son in a large family, David guarded the family sheep. Living outdoors David developed a great awe of God the Creator, and while protecting his sheep from wild animals, David learned to trust God's living presence and power. David came to Saul's attention when as a teenager he faced and killed the giant Philistine warrior, Goliath. Enlisted in Saul's army as a junior commander, David's exploits thrilled the nation but aroused Saul's jealousy. David married one of Saul's daughters, but eventually the paranoid and hostile Saul determined to kill his son-in-law, whom he saw as a rival. Chapters 16–31 feature many stories about David's adventures during the years that he first served, and then fled from, King Saul.

What's Special in 1 Samuel 16–31?

1. **David is God's choice** (1 Samuel 16). God sent Samuel to anoint Saul's successor. When Samuel assumed that one of David's impressive-looking brothers was God's choice, the Lord corrected him. "Do not look at his appearance or at his physical stature . . . for man looks at the outward appearance, but the LORD looks at the heart" (1 Samuel 16:7 NKJV). David, who was physically unimpressive, was chosen because he had a heart for God.

2. David vs. Goliath (1 Samuel 17). No story better illuminates David's utter confidence in God than the familiar tale of David's unequal battle with the armored and giant Philistine warrior. The defeat of Goliath (see Illustration #10) demoralized the Philistines and led to a great Israelite victory.

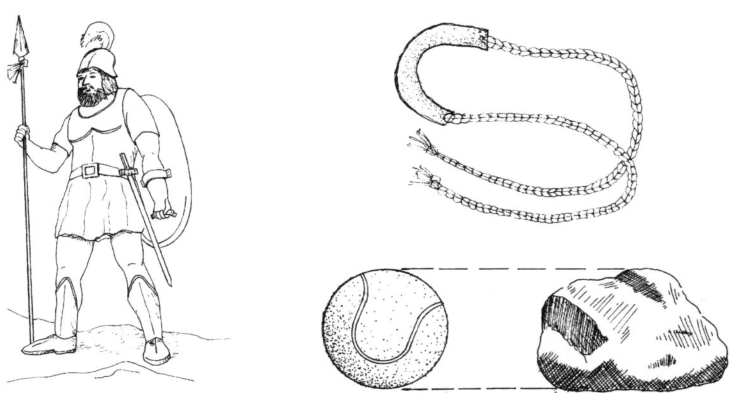

Illustration #10
How tall was Goliath?—at 6 cubits and a span, Goliath was over 9 feet tall.

What did a sling look like?—It looked like a doubled rope with a leather pocket in the center.

How heavy were sling stones?—Sling stones found on Israelite battlefields were the size of tennis balls. Stones were more rounded than rough.

3. Stories of David's early years (1 Samuel 18–31). The increasingly troubled relationship between King Saul and David is traced in the following stories. Reading two or three will provide a good amount of information about the respective characters of both David and Saul.

1 Samuel	The Story
18:1–16	David's successes make Saul jealous and fearful
18:17–30	Saul attempts to trick David into a fatal assault
19:1–18	Saul hurls his own spear at David, then orders his death
20:1–42	Saul's son Jonathan defends David's loyalty
21:1–21	David is forced to flee the country
22:6–23	Saul executes eighty-five priests who unwittingly helped David
23:7–29	David assembles a small army, which Saul pursues
24:1–22	David demonstrates his loyalty by sparing Saul's life
26:1–25	David again spares Saul's life
27:1–12	Discouraged, David leaves Israel and settles among the Philistines
29:1–21	David avoids fighting Saul on the Philistine side
31:1–13	Saul and Jonathan are killed in a battle with the Philistines

2 Samuel

. . . David's forty-year reign

Who	An unnamed author wrote
What	about the origin
Where	of Israel's royal line
When	from 1010 BC to 970 BC
Why	to establish the right of David's descendants to the throne

the big picture

2 Samuel

This book is a record of David's ascent to the throne and his many accomplishments during his forty-year reign. Both David's great strengths and personal failures are depicted for all to read. The book reviews:

- David's rule in Judah (2 Samuel 1–4)
- David's uniting of Israel (2 Samuel 5–24)

1 Chronicles

. . . David's forty-year reign

Who	An unnamed author
What	reviewed David's reign
Where	over a united Israel
When	from 1003 BC to 970 BC
Why	to encourage exiled Jews in the 500s BC

the big picture

1 Chronicles

This book emphasizes David's accomplishments that remind Jewish exiles in Babylon that God has promised to restore the monarchy ruled by a descendant of David, Israel's second king. The book contains:

- Genealogies (1 Chronicles 1–10)
- A record of David's acts (1 Chronicles 11–29)

A King After God's Own Heart

DAVID: First Samuel introduced David as a young, gifted, and persecuted officer in Saul's army and a member of his household. Second Samuel and 1 Chronicles present a mature David who, under God, rules as king of Israel. David's great accomplishments are credited not just to his genius but to his commitment to the Lord. Truly, David's achievements were spectacular.

During his four decades of rule David transformed his people from a loose coalition of tribes to a strong central monarchy. Specifically, David's rule marks the transition

- From government by judges to government by a king.
- From a loose **confederation** of tribes to a united nation.
- From **anarchy** to a strong central government.
- From poverty to an **iron age** economy and wealth.
- From oppression to conquest. Under David Israel occupied ten times as much territory as before.

From worship at local sites to worship at Jerusalem, which David established as Israel's political and worship center.

covenant promisess
Genesis 12:1–3, 7

confederation
closely associated but independent tribes

anarchy
living without laws

iron age
began when people learned to make tools and weapons of iron

Asia Minor
modern Turkey

caste system
a way of classifying people by social groups they remain in for life

transmigration
the belief that after death a person may come back as a bug or animal

What's happening in the world while David is creating a nation? In . . .

Asia Minor	Ionian Greeks establish twelve cities.
China	An advanced mathematics textbook is published.
Europe	Gold is being used in jewelry.
India	The **caste system** is introduced, and the teaching of **transmigration** of souls originates.

What's Special in the Books That Record the Events of David's Reign?

1. **The genealogy** (1 Chronicles 1–10). The seemingly endless list of strange names puzzles people today. But to the Israelites the names were vital. Each name served to anchor in history the fact that, whatever might happen, the Hebrew people would remain God's chosen people. As descendants of Abraham, Isaac, and Jacob, the Jews are God's chosen inheritors of the covenant promises given to Abraham.

2. David's seven-year reign in Judah (2 Samuel 1–4). After Saul's death the tribe of Judah recognized David as king. However, the Northern Hebrew tribes supported a son of Saul named Ishbosheth. Only after seven years, in 1003 BC, was David named king of all the Israelites.

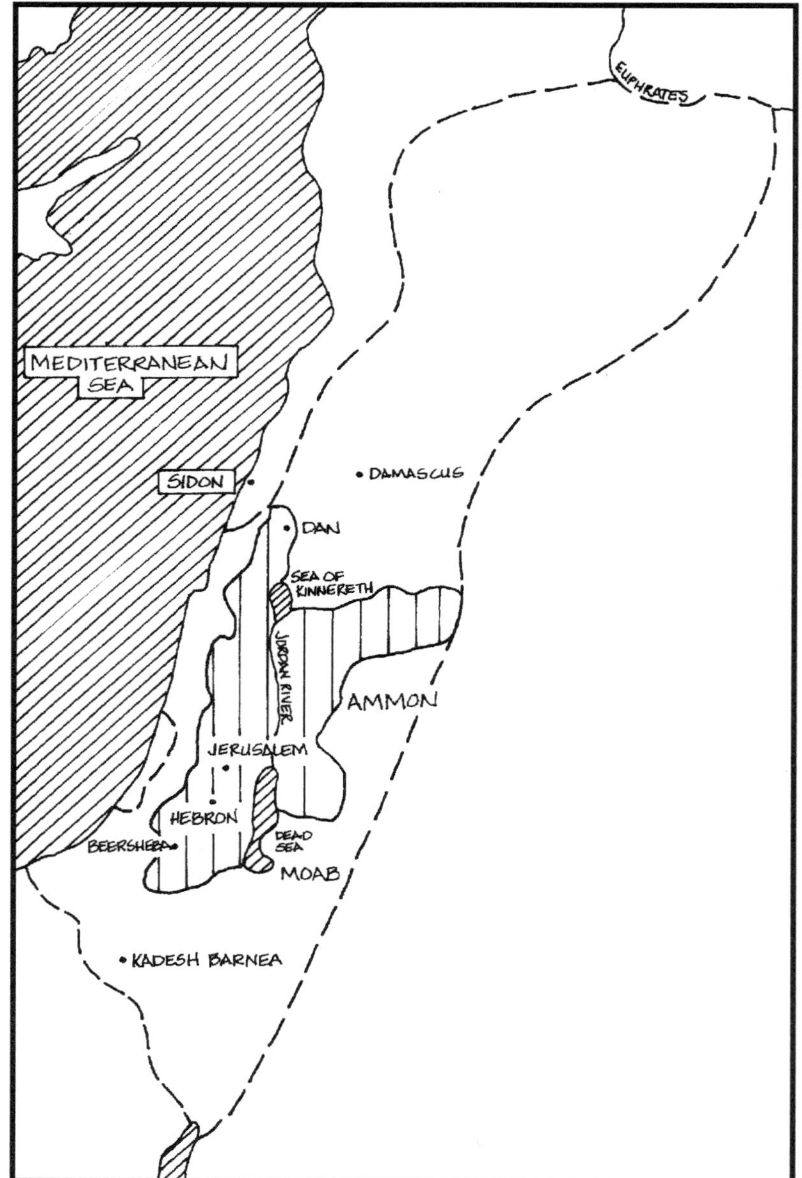

Illustration #11
Israelite Territory Before and After David's Reign—King David expanded Israel's borders to give his people ten times as much land as they occupied when Saul became king. The striped area of land indicates the extent of Israel's kingdom before David's reign. The dashed line indicates the extent of Israel's kingdom at the end of David's reign.

3. David's military victories. Aided and guided by God, David's armies imposed crushing defeats on the nations that surrounded Israel. The victories expanded the territory controlled by Israel (see Illustration #11) by ten times. The victories also gave David control of trade routes, which brought great wealth to Israel. The "war stories" illustrate David's conscious dependence on God; they are found in the following passages:

Davidic covenant
Psalm 89:2–8;
Jeremiah 33:20–22;
2 Samuel 7:1–17;
Isaiah 9:6–7;
Jeremiah 33:14–26;
Matthew 1:1–16

death itself
1 Corinthians 15:20–28

house
here it is both a temple and a dynasty

The War Stories of King David

The Enemy	The War Story
The Jebusites	2 Samuel 5:6–16
The Philistines	2 Samuel 5:17–25; 1 Chronicles 20:4–8
The Moabites	2 Samuel 8:2
The Syrians	2 Samuel 8:3–11; 1 Chronicles 18
The Edomites	2 Samuel 8:13–14
The Ammonites and Arameans	2 Samuel 10:1–19; 1 Chronicles 19

4. The Davidic covenant (2 Samuel 7; 1 Chronicles 17). God had promised Abraham, "In you all the families of the earth shall be blessed" (Genesis 12:3 NKJV), but God did not explain to Abraham how he would keep that promise. The Davidic covenant revealed that God intended to keep his promise through a descendant of David.

King David longed to build a temple in honor of God, but God would not let him. Instead God promised to build David a **house**. God promised there would always be a descendant of David qualified to inherit Israel's throne. God's covenant promise to David concludes, "Your house and your kingdom shall be established forever before you. Your throne shall be established forever" (2 Samuel 7:16 NKJV).

This Davidic covenant is the foundation of much Old Testament prophecy, which describes an era of world-wide peace under David's promised descendant. The New Testament Gospels make it clear that the person the promises refer to is none other than Jesus Christ.

Jesus Christ, the only living descendant of David, will fulfill God's promise and rule an eternal kingdom. The enemy Jesus defeated in his resurrection was death itself. Truly all peoples on earth are blessed by the forgiveness and eternal life Christ makes available to whoever will trust him.

salvation
Romans 5:9–11

responsibility
Psalm 51

5. David's personal failures (2 Samuel 11–18, 24). The annals of other ancient rulers glorify their victories and ignore their defeats or personal flaws, but the Bible graphically describes David's sins and weaknesses. David is no mythical hero; he is a flesh-and-blood human being whose great strengths are matched by great weaknesses. Each story sketched below describes a sin or failure of Israel's greatest king.

The Sins of King David

2 Samuel 11	2 Samuel 13	2 Samuel 14	2 Samuel 24
David seduces Bathsheba, and when she becomes pregnant, David arranges for her husband's death in battle.	When one of David's sons rapes a half sister, David fails to act. The girl's full brother, Absalom, murders the rapist.	David neitherpunishes nor forgives his son Absalom. The alienated Absalom plans a rebellion in which many lose their lives.	David conducts a military census, which displays a lack of trust in God.

Lessons from David's Flaws and Failures

1. Even the greatest saints have inherited Adam's sin nature. We all need the salvation God offers those who trust him.
2. David's sin with Bathsheba robbed him of moral authority in his own family and paralyzed his ability to correct his sons. There are consequences even to forgiven sins.
3. Although Saul and David both sinned, there was a significant difference between them. David took public responsibility for his sins, and openly sought God's forgiveness. Saul made excuses, and pretended all was right between him and the Lord. God can and will forgive our sins, but we must be honest with ourselves, with him, and with others.

what others say

Blaise Pascal

It is equally dangerous to man to know God without knowing his own wretchedness, and to know his own wretchedness without knowing God.[1]

From David's Great Cry of Confession

PSALM 51:1, 3–4, 10, 14 ***Have mercy upon me, O God, according to Your lovingkindness . . . For I acknowledge my transgressions, and my sin is always before me. Against You, You only, have I sinned, and done this evil in Your sight . . . Create in me a clean heart, O God, and renew a steadfast spirit within me . . . Deliver me from the guilt of bloodshed, O God, the God of my salvation, and my tongue shall sing aloud of Your righteousness." (NKJV)***

what others say

Saint Augustine

The confession of evil works is the first beginning to good works.[2]

6. **David's religious reforms** (1 Chronicles 22–26; 28, 29). Early in his reign David had brought the ark of the covenant to Jerusalem. When his military conquests were complete, David focused his attention on worship. He made detailed plans for the temple his son Solomon would build. He contributed vast wealth to the project and collected only the best building materials. David also developed job descriptions for the priests and Levites who would serve at the temple. He hired trained musicians and singers. One of David's greatest accomplishments was to personally write many of the songs and poems to be used in public worship. Many of these songs and poems are recorded for us in Psalms, the nineteenth book of the Old Testament.

When David died in 970 BC, he left a powerful, wealthy, and united Hebrew nation, eager to honor God and to celebrate him.

Chapter Wrap-Up

- First Samuel records the beginning of the Israelites' transition from a loose association of tribes to a nation ruled by kings.
- Samuel, Israel's last judge, anointed Saul king about 1050 BC.
- Saul failed to trust or obey God and was not allowed to found a dynasty.
- David, Saul's successor, succeeded in building Israel into a powerful and dominant nation of the Middle East.
- God gave a promise covenant to David, guaranteeing that a descendant of his would rule forever.

Study Questions

1. What three key figures marked the transition to monarchy?
2. What were conditions like in Israel when Samuel was born?
3. How had conditions changed by the time David died?
4. What were the most important differences between Saul and David? Why did one fail and the other succeed?
5. What were at least three of David's major accomplishments?
6. How did God's promise to David in 2 Samuel 7 relate to the covenant promises God made to Abraham?
7. What are some of the things that people today might learn from a study of David's life?

1 Kings 1–11 • 2 Chronicles 1–9 • Job • Psalms Proverbs • Ecclesiastes • Song of Solomon

Let's Get Started

David's kingdom dominated the Middle East through the reign of David's son, Solomon. The eighty years that David and Solomon ruled were Israel's golden age. The nation was prosperous and powerful. The two kings initiated great literary works, and a magnificent temple was erected in Jerusalem. The golden age would soon pass, but its glories would be remembered.

thousands of proverbs and over a thousand songs
1 Kings 4:29–30

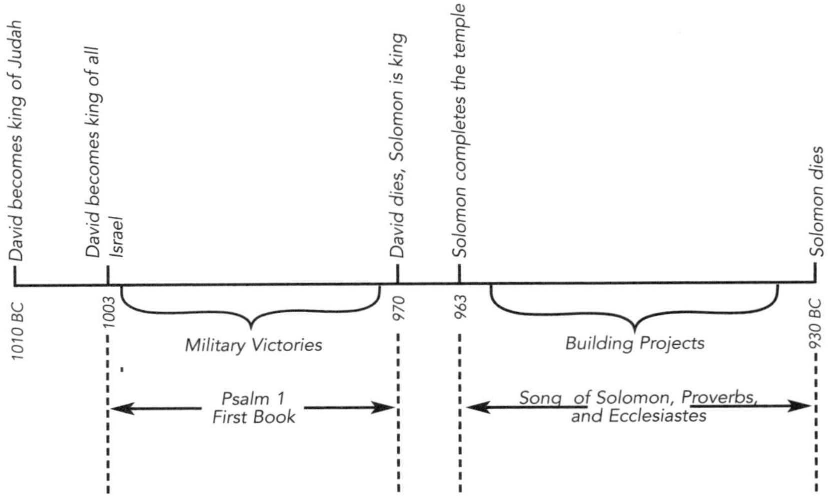

Time Line #5
During these eighty years, the normally dominant powers, Egypt to the South, and the Hittites and Assyrians to the North, were weak and unable to threaten Israel.

Even the Wisest May Fall

SOLOMON: Solomon succeeded David as king of Israel. Solomon was famous for his intellectual achievements. He wrote thousands of proverbs and over a thousand songs. He also became a botanist, cataloging plant life, and a zoologist, researching the habits of animals. Solomon found time to carry out many building projects, including construction of the magnificent Jerusalem temple, which was one of the wonders of the ancient world. Solomon's wealth, like his wisdom, was legendary. Solomon's personal income, not including monies from taxes and trade, was an annual twenty-five tons of gold.

twenty-five tons of gold
2 Chronicles 9:13

disobedience
1 Kings 9:6–9

What's Special About Solomon's Reign?

1. **God appeared to Solomon** (1 Kings 3; 9; 2 Chronicles 1; 7). God spoke to Solomon twice. At the beginning of Solomon's reign the young king asked for a discerning heart to govern your people and to distinguish between right and wrong (1 Kings 3:9). This unselfish request pleased God, who promised Solomon wisdom, wealth, and a long life.

Later in Solomon's reign God spoke to Solomon again. The Lord encouraged Solomon to "walk before Me as your father David walked, in integrity of heart and in uprightness" (1 Kings 9:4 NKJV) and warned Solomon about the danger of disobedience.

2. **Solomon constructed the Jerusalem temple** (1 Kings 5–8; 2 Chronicles 2–7). Ten of the twenty chapters that feature Solomon are devoted to the construction and dedication of the Jerusalem temple (see Illustration #12). Clearly the temple was important. But why? First, the temple was the place where God met with his people. It was the only place where sacrifices could be offered, and prayers to God were to be made facing toward the temple. Second, during the entire kingdom period the spiritual state of God's people was reflected in either their neglect of or their devotion to temple worship.

Solomon's temple was destroyed by the Babylonians in 586 BC, but another temple was later built on the same spot. That temple was expanded and beautified in the time of Christ. It too was destroyed, by the Romans in AD 70.

3. **Solomon turned from God** (1 Kings 11). Solomon's early promise was never fulfilled. Despite his youthful dedication to God, Solomon turned away from the Lord in his later years. In disobedience to God's Law, he cemented treaties with many nations by marrying women of foreign royal families. That choice led directly to tragedy.

Illustration #12
Solomon's Temple—Solomon lavished tons of gold on the magnificent temple he built to honor God. At today's prices, it would be worth five billion dollars!

Poetry—Who Reads That?

It's appropriate to pause here in our study of the Bible, and to explore the Old Testament's five fascinating books of poetry.

Israel's golden age was a time of great literary achievement. A collection of praise poems, the book of Psalms, was begun by David, who wrote many of them himself. His son Solomon recorded many of the brief sayings found in the book of Proverbs. Solomon also wrote a dark philosophical treatise (Ecclesiastes) and a **lyric poem** celebrating married love (**Song of Solomon**).

These books, with Job, are poetry. But Hebrew poetry is unusual. Rather than depending on **rhyme and meter**, Hebrew poetry depends on setting ideas side by side, in a pattern called "parallelism."

Poetry that depends on rhyme or rhythm is difficult to translate. But Hebrew poetry can be rendered effectively in any language. The vivid power of Hebrew poetry was often used by the prophets to enhance their message. Such power is reflected in the five poetic books of the Old Testament: Job, Psalms, Proverbs, Ecclesiastes, and Song of Solomon.

lyric poem
having the form and general effect of a song

Song of Solomon
also called the Song of Songs

rhyme and meter
placing emphasis on syllables

The Basic Forms of Poetic Parallelism

Form of Parallelism	Characteristic	Example in Scripture
Synonymous parallelism	The thought in the first and second lines is the same	"Then our mouth was filled with laughter, and our tongue with singing" (Psalm 126:2 NKJV)
Antithetical parallelism	The thought in the first line is emphasized by its opposite	"The merciful man does good for his own soul, but he who is cruel troubles his own flesh" (Proverbs 11:17 NKJV)
Synthetic parallelism	The thought in the first line is developed or completed by thoughts in following lines	"I will both lie down in peace, and sleep; for You alone, O LORD, make me dwell in safety" (Psalm 4:8 NKJV)

Job

. . . the mystery of suffering

Who	An unknown author
What	related the story of Job
Where	in Mesopotamia
When	some two thousand years before Christ
Why	to explore faith's response to human suffering

Oh, Woe Is Me — The Story of Job

1. **Job 1, 2.** Job is a man singled out by God himself as blameless and upright. When Satan argues that this is only because God has blessed Job and protected him from harm, God permits Satan to attack Job. In a single day sudden tragedies strip Job of his wealth and family, but Job remains true to God. Even when Satan afflicts Job with agonizing open sores, Job remains faithful. Satan, proven wrong, is not heard from again. But Job's suffering continues.

2. Job 3–31. Three friends come to console Job and are stunned at his condition. Job, near despair, finally tells the three that he wishes he'd died at birth. The three friends begin a dialogue with Job. Each of the three is convinced that God is just and righteous, and that God punishes sin. They conclude Job must have sinned. The friends urge Job to confess the hidden sin that God is punishing and to appeal for mercy. But Job's conscience is clear: there is no hidden sin. He can't explain why God is making him suffer, but he refuses to confess sins he is not aware of.

suffering
1 Peter 2:18–25; Romans 5:3–5

restores
James 5:10–12

As the dialogue continues, Job's three friends press harder and harder. Job must have sinned, and sinned terribly. Job argues back that he has not sinned and that God isn't being fair.

3. Job 32–37. Job and his friends are at an impasse. Then a younger man named Elihu speaks up. He points out that suffering need not always be punishment. God may use suffering to teach and to get a person's attention. So Job's friends are wrong to attack him as a sinner, and Job is wrong to say God isn't being fair.

4. Job 38–41. Then God himself speaks to Job. God does not tell Job why he permitted the suffering. He simply reminds Job of two basic truths: God is great beyond human comprehension, and human beings are weak and limited.

5. Job 42. Job realizes it is not a creature's place to explain the Creator's doings. God rebukes the three friends, and then restores all Job has lost and more.

Thinking About Job

The book of Job does not tell us why God allows good people to suffer. It does remind us that people of faith respond to suffering differently from those without faith. Some, like the three friends, feel driven to ask "Why?" Others, like Job, learn to simply trust God no matter what comes.

The New Testament book of James notes, "You have heard of the perseverance of Job and seen the end intended by the Lord—that the Lord is very compassionate and merciful" (James 5:11 NKJV). Even when God permits suffering, his ultimate intent is to bless.

Psalms

. . . the book of praises

Who	David and others
What	penned these poems
Where	in ancient Israel
When	over a span of centuries
Why	as an aid to private and congregational worship

Let Us Praise the Lord

1. **The five "books" within the book of Psalms. Each book represents a collection of poems.** The first book (Psalms 1–41) was collected in the time of David. The last book (Psalms 107–150) was collected around the time of Ezra, some six hundred years later. Many of the psalms were used in worship before being included in one of the official collections.

2. **One of the most striking features of the psalms is the depth of emotion they display.** The psalms remind us that whatever we may feel—anger or pain, thankfulness or joy—we can freely pour out our hearts to the Lord. As we share our innermost emotions with the Lord, we can be confident that he hears and cares, and that God will work within our hearts as well as in our circumstances.

Psalms That Touch Our Hearts

How do we deal with strong emotions? What is the value of expressing our feelings freely in conversation with God? Below is a list of emotions along with a list of pairs of psalms. Reading at least two of the psalms will provide an introduction to how the psalms express emotion.

3. **Classification of psalms.** While we can describe the psalms by the emotions they express, these wonderful poems can also be classified by theme as shown on the next page.

Expressions of Emotion

The Emotion	Scripture
Anger at others	Psalms 7, 36
Guilt over sins	Psalms 32, 51
Anxiety or fear	Psalms 23, 64
Discouragement	Psalms 42, 107
Joy	Psalms 33, 98
Loneliness	Psalms 25, 91
Stress	Psalms 31, 89
Troubled	Psalms 10, 126
Weakness	Psalms 62, 102
Envy	Psalms 16, 73

What's to Talk About?

Type of Psalm	Theme	Examples (Psalms)
Penitential	Confess sins	6, 32, 51, 102, 130
Wisdom	Consider right choices	1, 37, 49, 73, 127
Messianic	Anticipate Christ	22, 89, 110
Imprecatory	Call on God to judge	35, 58, 109, 137
Lament	Complain to God	4, 12, 26, 57, 88
Praise	Thanks for deliverance	18, 30, 34, 116, 138
Praise	Praise for God himself	103, 113, 117, 146

4. **The book of Psalms' life-changing impact.** More than any other book of the Bible, the book of Psalms explores the personal nature of our relationship with God. Anyone who wants to grow to know God better will find the Psalms an unmatched help and guide.

what others say

Albert H. Baylis

Innumerable saints and sinners through centuries of time have been uplifted, consoled, inspired, and radically changed by reading and meditating on the Psalms.[1]

Proverbs

. . . guidelines for daily life

Who	Solomon and others
What	contributed wise sayings
Where	in Israel
When	some nine hundred years before Christ
Why	to help readers make good decisions

Wisdom for Today

A proverb is a brief saying that makes a practical point, usually by comparing or contrasting an idea with something familiar. The Hebrew term translated *proverb* means "to represent" or "to be like." The Old Testament book of Proverbs is a collection of sayings, intended to give the reader the wisdom needed to make wise choices in daily life.

The book of Proverbs begins with a Statement of Purpose. The proverbs are

- To know wisdom and instruction,
- To perceive the words of understanding,
- To receive the instruction of wisdom,
- Justice, judgment, and equity. (Proverbs 1:2–3 NKJV)

What's Special About Proverbs?

1. **The book of Proverbs states general principles.** These principles are applicable to all people everywhere, not just to believers. The proverbs are not promises given by God. They describe what will usually happen when a person makes a right choice, not what God guarantees will happen.

2. **The book of Proverbs is about choices.** The writers are not trying to convey information, but to guide decisions. The writers are concerned that we do the right thing, and avoid the harmful consequences of bad decisions.

3. **"Fear of the Lord" is critical.** The book of Proverbs clearly states

that "the fear of the LORD is the beginning of knowledge, but fools despise wisdom and instruction" (Proverbs 1:7 NKJV). Fear of the Lord is not terror but a reverential acknowledgment of his power and his presence. Only a firm belief in God will keep human beings on the wise moral pathway described in Proverbs.

4. **Many topics are explored in the book of Proverbs.** The chart below lists proverbs on a variety of topics.

Topic	Selected Proverbs
Adultery	Proverbs 5:1–6; Proverbs 6:24–32; Proverbs 7:6–27; Proverbs 22:14; Proverbs 23:26–28; Proverbs 29:1; Proverbs 30:7
Alcohol	Proverbs 20:1; Proverbs 23:20–21; Proverbs 29–35; Proverbs 31:4–7
Crime	Proverbs 6:30–31; Proverbs 10:9–16; Proverbs 13:11; Proverbs 15:6, 27; Proverbs 16:8–19; Proverbs 17:15, 23
Discipline	Proverbs 3:11–12; Proverbs 5:12–14; Proverbs 9:7–10; Proverbs 13:18, 24; Proverbs 19:18; Proverbs 22:15; Proverbs 27:5
Friendship	Proverbs 12:26; Proverbs 13:20; Proverbs 16:28; Proverbs 17:17; Proverbs 18:1, 24; Proverbs 19:17; Proverbs 22:10
Gossip	Proverbs 11:13; Proverbs 16:28; Proverbs 18:8; Proverbs 20:19; Proverbs 26:22
Government	Proverbs 8:15–16; Proverbs 14:28; Proverbs 34–35; Proverbs 16:12–15; Proverbs 18:17; Proverbs 24:24–25; Proverbs 25:5
Laziness	Proverbs 6:9–11; Proverbs 12:24–27; Proverbs 13:4; Proverbs 15:19; Proverbs 19:15; Proverbs 20:4, 20; Proverbs 24:30–34
Lies	Proverbs 6:16–17; Proverbs 12:17–19, 22; Proverbs 14:5, 24; Proverbs 17:4, 20; Proverbs 24:28–29; Proverbs 30:8
Love	Proverbs 10:12; Proverbs 15:17; Proverbs 16:6; Proverbs 17:9, 17; Proverbs 19:22; Proverbs 20:6
Neighbors	Proverbs 3:29–30; Proverbs 6:16–19; Proverbs 11:9; Proverbs 14:20-21; Proverbs 26:17–20; Proverbs 29:5
Parent/Child	Proverbs 6:20–23; Proverbs 10:1; Proverbs 15:20; Proverbs 17:6, 21, 25; Proverbs 22:6; Proverbs 23:13–14, 22, 24
The Poor	Proverbs 13:8, 18, 23; Proverbs 14:20, 31; Proverbs 17:5; Proverbs 19:1, 4, 7, 17, 22; Proverbs 30:11–14

Topic	Selected Proverbs
Pride	Proverbs 6:16–17; Proverbs 8:13; Proverbs 11:2; Proverbs 15:25; Proverbs 18:5, 18; Proverbs 18:12; Proverbs 25:6–7
Temper	Proverbs 14:17, 29; Proverbs 15:1, 18; Proverbs 16:32; Proverbs 19:19; Proverbs 22:24–25; Proverbs 29:11, 22
Wealth	Proverbs 10:2, 4, 15, 22; Proverbs 11:4, 28; Proverbs 13:8, 21–22; Proverbs 14:24; Proverbs 20:21; Proverbs 23:4–8
Work	Proverbs 12:11, 14, 24, 27; Proverbs 14:23; Proverbs 16:26; Proverbs 18:9; Proverbs 22:29; Proverbs 27:18, 23–27

Ecclesiastes

. . . searching for life's meaning

Who	Solomon
What	wrote this book
Where	as king in Jerusalem
When	near the end of his life
Why	to ask whether human life has meaning apart from a personal relationship with God

Searching for a Meaning Without God

Near the end of his life, Solomon lost his spiritual moorings and began to worship the gods of his foreign wives. During this time Solomon decided to search for life's meaning. He wrote, "I set my heart to seek and search out by wisdom concerning all that is done under heaven" (Ecclesiastes 1:13 NKJV). Solomon would use his great intelligence to test and explore human experience. But he would limit himself to all that is done under heaven. Solomon would not consider truth revealed by God! He would search for meaning in the brief years human beings have to live here on earth. And Solomon failed! Despite the fact that he had access to every pleasure, wealth beyond counting, and achievements that won the acclaim of all, Solomon summed up his findings in a few tragic words:

Ecclesiastes 1:2 ***"Vanity of vanities," says the Preacher; "Vanity of vanities, all is vanity."*** *(NKJV)*

Try as we will to find meaning apart from God, we will fail. For apart from God and his loving purpose for us, human life is meaningless.

inspired
God makes sure that the message communicates what he wants it to

revelation
God himself unveils truth we could not otherwise know

What's Special About Ecclesiastes?

1. Ecclesiastes is a book of inspired scripture, but not of revelation. Ecclesiastes is an accurate report of Solomon's reasoning. But not everything Solomon writes is true. This book is in the Bible to remind us of an important truth.

Some of the sayings in this book are disturbing, for they seem to contradict other teachings in the Bible. It's important to remember that not every word in Ecclesiastes is intended to reveal truths from God. Instead, Ecclesiastes is intended to accurately report the musings of Solomon and to compellingly convey a vital message needed by all human beings. The message is that apart from God and the perspective his Word conveys, human life truly is meaningless. Those who struggle to find meaning for their lives apart from God are doomed to failure—an overarching truth that Solomon, the wisest of humans, learned too late.

2. Where did Solomon look for meaning? (Ecclesiastes 1:12–6:12) The first half of Ecclesiastes, chapters 1 through 6, contains a report of where Solomon searched for the elusive answer. Here are his conclusions:

Solomon's Search for Meaning	Scripture
Introduction	Ecclesiastes 1:1–11
Can knowledge provide meaning?	Ecclesiastes 1:12–18
Can pleasure provide meaning?	Ecclesiastes 2:1–11
Can accomplishments provide meaning?	Ecclesiastes 2:17–26
Can human beings make any real changes in the way things are?	Ecclesiastes 3:16–22
Man's fate suggests that life is meaningless	Ecclesiastes 4:1–16

Solomon's Search for Meaning	Scripture
Man's inability to affect God's works suggests that life is meaningless	Ecclesiastes 5:1–7
Can possessions give meaning to life?	Ecclesiastes 5:8–6:2
Man's inability to control his future suggests that life is meaningless	Ecclesiastes 6:3–12

3. **How can we make the best of meaningless lives** (Ecclesiastes 7:1–12:8)? Solomon found that human life—if this life is all there is—can have no meaning. But he couldn't resist pointing out that even under the circumstances, some courses of action are better than others.

4. **Solomon's epilogue** (Ecclesiastes 12:9–14). As the book concludes, we can sense Solomon looking back over the years to the bright promise of his youth. Here are his recommendations:

ECCLESIASTES 12:13–14

Let us hear the conclusion of the whole matter:
Fear God and keep His commandments,
For this is man's all.
For God will bring every work into judgment,
Including every secret thing,
Whether good or evil. (NKJV)

To Make the Best of a Meaningless Life	Scripture
Make the best choices you can	Ecclesiastes 7:1–12
Adopt a fatalistic attitude	Ecclesiastes 7:13–14
Avoid extemes	Ecclesiastes 7:15–22
Be wise, avoid folly	Ecclesiastes 7:23–8:1
Submit to authorities	Ecclesiastes 8:2–10
Be God-fearing	Ecclesiastes 8:11–13
Enjoy the good things life offers	Ecclesiastes 8:14–15
Enjoy life while you can: death awaits	Ecclesiastes 9:1–12
Follow wisdom	Ecclesiastes 9:13–10:20
Prepare for the future	Ecclesiastes 11:1–6
Enjoy your youth—old age is creeping up	Ecclesiastes 11:7–12:8

Song of Solomon

. . . the celebration of love

Who	A young Solomon
What	wrote this love poem
Where	in Jerusalem
When	during his early reign
Why	as a celebration of married love

allegory
a story used to make a point

monogamous
a lifelong commitment to a single spouse

The Love of a Lifetime

Is this the story of Solomon's attempt to woo a young woman, the Shulamite, away from her rural lover? Or does the poem grow out of Solomon's one early experience of true love? Or is it simply an **allegory,** intended to depict the love of God for Israel, or of Christ for the believer? Charles Swindoll and many others think this poem is about true love, a love that was lost as Solomon abandoned **monogamous** marriage for politically motivated multiple marriages.

what others say

Bruce Wilkinson

Solomon's relationship with the Shulamite was the only pure romance he ever experienced. The bulk of his marriages were political arrangements. It is significant that the Shulamite was a vineyard keeper of no great means. This book was also written before Solomon plunged into gross immorality and idolatry.[2]

What's Special About the Song of Solomon?

1. **The poem is written in three voices.** The voice of the Lover is Solomon's. The voice of the Beloved is the Shulamite. The other voice is a chorus of the Shulamite's friends.

2. **The poem is divided into three sections.**
   1. The Courtship (Song of Solomon 1:2–3:5)
   2. The Wedding (Song of Solomon 3:6–5:1)
   3. The Deepening Relationship (Song of Solomon 5:2–8:14)

what others say

Charles Swindoll

What an ideal we have in Solomon's Song for Christian marriages! What freedom to be wildly in love, romantic, tender, and sensual. To be committed, secure, [and] happy.[3]

3. The Song of Solomon, by its positive example, can disclose at least four things our marriages need.

A. **Personal attention.** Physical love is an art that cannot grow without being nurtured. It requires emotional intimacy, the enjoyment of being with one another.

B. **Leisure.** Creativity, enjoyment, and playfulness only blossom in a relationship when they are cultivated in the soil of time.

C. **Meaningful getaways.** Special times away from the clutter and clamor of constant demands can refresh a relationship.

D. **Security.** Reaching the deepest level of secure, peaceful love takes commitment.

Chapter Wrap-Up

- The years 1010 BC to 930 BC were Israel's golden years, marked by power, prosperity, and literary production.
- David and Solomon were the two kings who ruled during the golden years.
- The construction of the Jerusalem temple was the most notable achievement of King Solomon.
- The period also witnessed the initiation of great poetic, literary productions.
- The book of Job, from an earlier era, explores how a person of faith can respond to suffering.
- Psalms, much of which was written by King David, is a guide to worship and a personal relationship with God.
- Proverbs, much of which was written by Solomon, gives practical advice on making wise and right choices.

- Ecclesiastes, written after Solomon was estranged from God, is a search for meaning in life apart from God.
- The Song of Solomon is a poem exploring the joys of married lovers.

Study Questions

1. Who were the two kings who ruled during Israel's golden age?
2. What accomplishments marked Israel's golden age?
3. What four books of Bible poetry were written or begun during the golden age?
4. What characteristic of Hebrew poetry makes it possible to easily translate it into any language?
5. What is the theme of each of the following books of Bible poetry?

   Job ______________________________

   Psalms ______________________________

   Proverbs ____________________________

   Ecclesiastes __________________________

   Song of Solomon ________________________

1 Kings 12–22 • 2 Kings • Jonah • Amos • Hosea

Let's Get Started

When Solomon died in 930 BC (see Time Line #6 on page 117) the unified Hebrew kingdom was torn apart. Two tribal groups to the south remained committed to rulers from David's family line. This Southern Kingdom was known as Judah. The ten northern Hebrew tribes set up a rival kingdom, which kept the old name of Israel. From the beginning the kings of Israel abandoned God's Law in favor of a counterfeit religion. Despite the ministry of prophets sent to call Israel back to God, the Northern Kingdom continued on its fatal course. In 722 BC Israel fell to the Assyrians. Its citizens were taken captive and dispersed across the Assyrian Empire.

1 and 2 Kings

. . . a historical account

Who	An unnamed author
What	evaluated the reigns of kings
Where	from Israel and Judah
When	between 970 BC and 586 BC
Why	to demonstrate the value of obeying and the danger of disobeying God

We Don't Need Them

When Solomon died, the people appealed to his son Rehoboam for tax relief. The foolish young king refused. The ten northern tribes rebelled and crowned Jeroboam as their king. Jerusalem, the site of Solomon's temple, lay in the South. That worried Jeroboam. If the people of the North went to Jerusalem to worship, as God's Law required, how long would they remain loyal to him? So Jeroboam created his own religion, one that mimicked the faith God

counterfeit religion
1 Kings 12:26–33; Amos 4:1–5

apostate
one who has rebelled against what one has believed

had revealed to Moses. Jeroboam appointed his own priests, set up calf idols at worship centers in Bethel and Dan, and established his own religious holidays. While claiming that this religion was a vehicle for worship of the Lord, every act of "worship" was in direct violation of God's Law.

Every ruler of the Northern Kingdom supported this counterfeit religion and did evil in God's sight. There was no way that **apostate** Israel could survive or avoid God's judgment.

Overview

The chart identifies the kings and prophets of the Northern Hebrew Kingdom. Not one of these kings sought to honor God. For fascinating insight into the lives of the evil rulers who governed Israel, read the stories told of King Ahab.

Prophetic Voices

God did not abandon Israel during the two hundred years (930–722 BC) that the Northern Hebrew Kingdom existed. Again and again God sent prophets who warned the Israelites and urged them to return to him.

Two categories of prophets are found in the Bible. Some were speaking prophets, whose stories are woven into a historical narrative. Others were writing prophets, whose messages are recorded as books of the Bible. Elijah and Elisha were speaking prophets whom God sent to Israel. Jonah, Amos, and Hosea were writing prophets who preached in the North.

The books of the writing prophets are collected together at the end of the Old Testament. But to best understand the writing prophets, we need to understand the historical context in which their messages were given.

What was the message of the prophets God sent to the Northern Kingdom? And how are their messages important to us today?

Kings and Prophets of the Northern Kingdom

King	Prophets	Years Reigned	Scripture
Jeroboam I	—	22	1 Kings 12–14
Nadab	—	2	1 Kings 15
Baasha	—	24	1 Kings 15–16
Elah	—	2	1 Kings 16
Zimri	—	7 days	1 Kings 16
Omri	—	12	1 Kings 16
Ahab	Elijah	22	1 Kings 16–22
Ahaziah	Elijah	2	1 Kings 22; 2 Kings 1
Jehoram (Joram)	Elisha	12	2 Kings 3–8
Jehu	Elisha	28	2 Kings 9–10
Jehoahaz (Joahaz)	Elisha	17	2 Kings 13
Jehoash (Joash)	Elisha	16	2 Kings 13
Jeroboam II	Jonah and Amos	41	2 Kings 14
Zechariah	Hosea	6 months	2 Kings 15
Shallum	Hosea	1 month	2 Kings 15
Menahem	Hosea	10	2 Kings 15
Pekahiah	Hosea	2	2 Kings 15
Pekah	Hosea	20	2 Kings 15
Hoshea	Hosea	9	2 Kings 17

motivate us
1 Thessalonians 4:13–18;
2 Peter 3:10–13

Many people today assume that the prophets were only concerned with the future. It's true that the Old Testament books of prophecy do contain many predictions about what God intended to do at some future time. But to understand the prophets we need to realize that their primary mission was to the rulers and the people of their own day. The warnings of future judgment are meant to confront issues such as injustice, materialism, empty religion, and the oppression of the helpless by the powerful. Predictions of future blessings are meant to encourage the sick and the suffering and to reassure victims of injustice that God does care and that he intends to right every wrong. We may be fascinated by the portrait of what lies ahead to be found in the writings of the prophets. But we must never overlook the fact that visions of God's action in the future are intended to motivate us to godly living in our own time.

Preach It!

Most people know that the Bible contains miracle stories, but few are aware that hundreds of years of Bible history might pass without

authenticated
provided proof

Baal
a Canaanite term for"god"

any miracles at all. In fact, most of the miracles recorded in Scripture took place in three relatively brief periods!

The first age of miracles spanned just fifty years. It included the cluster of miracles God performed through Moses to force Pharaoh to free his Israelite slaves, and additional miracles as Israel traveled to the Promised Land.

The second age of miracles also lasted about fifty years, during the time of Elijah and Elisha. The miracles performed by these two prophets served as a fresh revelation of God's power and grace at a critical moment when the Northern Hebrew Kingdom seemed about to adopt a pagan religion as its official faith.

The third age of miracles was inaugurated by Jesus, whose many miracles authenticated his claim to be God's Son. Christ's apostles also performed miracles in Jesus' name in the early days of the Christian church.

While the Bible reports that God does work miracles, people who assume that miracles were everyday occurrences in Bible times are wrong. Miracles were unusual events, and were reserved for critical moments in history when God had fresh revelations for his people.

Three Ages of Miracles

First Age	Second Age	Third Age
Moses	Elijah, Elisha	Christ, apostles
1446–1306 BC	860–810 BC	AD 27–75
Revealed God as Lord	Proved the Lord is the true God	**Authenticated** Christ as God's Son
Introduced the Old Testament		Introduced the New Testament

Elijah

Elijah was sent to Israel at a critical time. King Ahab had married Jezebel, the daughter of a pagan king. Together Jezebel and Ahab set out to replace worship of the Lord with the worship of **Baal** (see Illustration #3, page 10). The royal couple executed God's prophets and imported hundreds of false prophets from Jezebel's homeland. The effort seemed about to succeed when God sent Elijah to confront the king and demonstrate his power.

Fire from Heaven

Elijah called on God to stop the rains. For three terrible years no rain fell, and the land of Israel dried up. Ahab's powerful military was devastated as no fodder was available for his chariot horses. Then Elijah reappeared, and challenged Ahab to a duel between himself and four hundred prophets of Baal. The contest took place on Mount Carmel, and was witnessed by thousands of Israelites. Baal's prophets cried out all day for their god to send fire and burn up a sacrifice they had laid out. But nothing happened. Then when Elijah called on the Lord to act, fire from heaven burned up the sacrifice and even the stone altar on which it lay. The people were convinced that the Lord, he is God. At Elijah's command, the people killed the prophets of Baal. The threat of Israel's paganization was turned back!

Stories of Elijah	Reference
Elijah is fed by ravens	1 Kings 17:1–6
Elijah multiplies a widow's food	1 Kings 17:7–16
Elijah raises the widow's dead son	1 Kings 17:17–24
Elijah defeats the prophets of Baal	1 Kings 18:16–48
Elijah defeats the prophets of Baal	1 Kings 19:1–18
Elijah announces Ahab's doom	1 Kings 21:1–28
Elijah is taken up alive into heaven	2 Kings 2:1–18

Elisha

Elisha was the apprentice and then the successor of Elijah. He ministered after the death of Ahab, through the reigns of Ahab's descendants Ahaz and Jehoram.

During the years Elisha prophesied, Israel was threatened by a powerful Syrian (or Aramean) kingdom led first by Ben-Hadad and then by Hazael. While Elijah had confronted Ahab and displayed the power of God, Elisha's ministry displayed God's grace and willingness to support his people. Despite the miracles Elisha performed on Israel's behalf, there was no great national return to God. Later Elisha anointed a military commander, Jehu, as the next king of Israel. Jehu wiped out Ahab's remaining family and purged Israel of the worship of Baal which Ahab and Jezebel had tried to establish. But Jehu continued to support the false worship system installed by Jeroboam decades before.

Stories of Elisha	Reference
Elisha divides the Jordan River	2 Kings 2:1–14
Elisha purifies bad waters	2 Kings 2:19–22
Elisha curses jeering young men	2 Kings 2:23–25
Elisha predicts a miracle victory	2 Kings 3:1–25
Elisha multiplies a widow's oil	2 Kings 4:1–7
Elisha promises a pregnancy	2 Kings 4:8–17
Elisha raises a dead son	2 Kings 4:18–37
Elisha makes poison stew harmless	2 Kings 4:38–41
Elisha multiplies loaves of bread	2 Kings 4:42–44
Elisha curses Gehazi with leprosy	2 Kings 5:1–27
Elisha makes an ax-head float	2 Kings 6:1–7
Elisha traps a Syrian army	2 Kings 6:8–23
Elisha shows his servant an angel army	2 Kings 6:13–17
Elisha predicts food for a besieged city	2 Kings 6:24–7:20

Write It Down!

Jonah

. . . God's reluctant messenger

Who	Jonah
What	announced judgment
Where	in Nineveh
When	when Jeroboam II ruled Israel
Why	and he gave the city an opportunity to repent

Swallowed Up

the big picture

Jonah

This book contains four brief chapters.

- Jonah runs away and is swallowed by a great fish.
- Jonah thanks God for saving his life.
- Jonah goes to Nineveh, and the city repents!
- Jonah sulks, and is rebuked by God for his lack of compassion.

Jeroboam II was an evil but vigorous and successful ruler. During his forty-one-year reign, the Northern Kingdom became a power in the Middle East. Second Kings 14:25 (NKJV) tells us that "he restored the territory of Israel from the entrance of Hamath to the Sea of the Arabah," expanding Israel's borders almost to the extent achieved under David and Solomon. Jeroboam II's victories had been in accordance with the "word of the LORD God of Israel" given by a patriotic prophet, Jonah the son of Amittai, "the prophet who was from Gath Hepher" (2 Kings 14:25 NKJV).

repentance
Jeremiah 15:19; Isaiah 30:15

But when God called this same Jonah to go and preach against Nineveh (see Illustration #4), the capital of the Assyrian Empire, Jonah hurriedly took a ship heading in the opposite direction—to Spain, not north to Assyria! In the book that bears his name, Jonah explains why he acted as he did

repentance
Not just sorrow for sin, but a commitment to change

sackcloth
a very coarse material similar to burlap

JONAH 4:2 ***I know that You are a gracious and merciful God, slow to anger and abundant in lovingkindness, One who relents from doing harm.*** *(NKJV)*

Assyria was the great enemy of Jonah's people. Jonah wanted God to destroy Nineveh. He was afraid that if he warned the Assyrians they might repent, and God would not destroy them after all.

It is against this background that we read the adventures of Jonah, and ponder the significance of his familiar but misunderstood little book.

What's Special About Jonah?

1. **No whale tale** (Jonah 1:17). Early English versions translated a Hebrew word that means a "great fish" as a "whale." The text makes it clear that God had to specially prepare the great fish that swallowed Jonah so that Jonah would not drown.
2. **Jonah's second chance** (Jonah 3:1–4). The Lord gave the disobedient Jonah a second chance to obey him. This time Jonah delivered God's message: "Yet forty days, and Nineveh shall be overthrown!" (Jonah 3:4 NKJV).

3. **The Ninevites** "believed God" (Jonah 3:5–9). The people of Nineveh believed God and displayed **repentance** by fasting and wearing **sackcloth**. The king himself demanded that all give up their evil ways and their violence.
4. **Nineveh survived** (Jonah 3:10)! The book of Jonah introduces a vital principle. Most Bible prophecies of coming judgment are

conditional. They describe what will surely happen—if the nation or individuals addressed fail to repent. But God is "gracious and merciful." He will delay or withhold judgment if people only turn to him.

5. **Jonah contained a powerful message for Israel** (Jonah 4:2). Jonah preached in Nineveh, but the message of the book of Jonah was for Israel, not the Assyrians. Prophets had long called on the people of Israel to repent and turn to God. Nineveh's survival was an object lesson for Israel. If God withheld judgment on repentant Nineveh, surely God would forgive his own people—if only they too would repent.

key point

God's goodness to others reminds us that he yearns to be good to us too.

. . . judgment coming

Who	God sent a rancher from Judah
What	to announce judgment
Where	on Israel
When	during the reign of Jeroboam II
Why	because of the injustice and oppression that existed in the Northern Kingdom

The Day of the Lord

the big picture

Amos

The book of Amos contains a series of Amos's sermons to Israel. The topics of the sermons serve as an outline of the book.

- God will judge Israel's neighbors (Amos 1:1–2:5)
- God will judge Israel (Amos 2:6–16)
- Israel's sins identified (Amos 3:1–6:14)
- Five visions of doom related (Amos 7:1–9:10)
- Israel's ultimate restoration assured (Amos 9:11–15)

Amos was a rancher who lived in Judah when God called him to deliver his Word across the border in Israel during the reign of Jeroboam II. The Northern Kingdom was unusually prosperous at the time, but the very wealthy oppressed the very poor. Amos boldly took his message of coming judgment to the retreat of the rich at Bethel, one of the worship centers established long before by Jeroboam I. There the priest Amaziah threatened Amos's life and ordered him not to prophesy. But Amos boldly announced God's judgment on the priest, and finished his message of Israel's impending doom before returning to his ranch in Judah.

sins of Israel
Amos 2:6–8; 4:1–6; 5:4–7,11–12, 21–24; 6:4–7

About forty years after Amos preached God's Word to an unrepentant Israel, the Assyrians under Sargon II crushed that nation and scattered its population throughout the Assyrian Empire.

What's Special in Amos?

1. **God's complaints against Israel.** Amos powerfully describes the sins of Israel that cry out for judgment. Israel shows contempt for God by following the counterfeit religion instituted by Jeroboam I and by constantly violating God's moral Law. The wealthy in Israel show contempt for God by their systematic oppression of the poor. False religion, immorality, and raw material: all reveal how far the hearts of God's people are removed from him.

what others say

Billy Graham

From the beginning of time until the present moment, man's ungodly quest for power, his determination to use his gift of free choice for his own selfish ends, has brought him to the brink of doom. The rubble and ruins of many civilizations lie scattered over the earth's surface—mute testimony to man's inability to build a lasting world without God.[1]

What's Special in Amos?

False religion	Immorality	Injustice
I hate, I despise your feast days, and I do not savor your sacred assemblies. Though you offer Me burnt offerings and your grain offerings, I will not accept them.	A man and his father go in to the same girl, to defile My holy name. They lie down by every altar on clothes taken in pledge, and drink the wine of the condemned in the house of their god.	They sell the righteous for silver, and the poor for a pair of sandals. They pant after the dust of the earth which is on the head of the poor, and pervert the way of the humble.
Amos 5:21–22 NKJV	Amos 2:7–8 NKJV	Amos 2:6–7 NKJV

Day of the Lord
a time of terrible judgment

Tribulation Period
seven years of God's judgment at history's end

2. **The "Day of the Lord"** (Amos 5:18–27). The Old Testament prophets speak often of a Day of the Lord or refer to that day. These phrases have a special meaning. The **Day of the Lord**, another name for the **Tribulation Period**, is a future moment in time when God will personally intervene in human history.

In most prophetic passages, as here in Amos, references to the Day of the Lord picture God acting to punish sin. As Amos warns, "Is not the day of the LORD darkness, and not light? Is it not very dark, with no brightness in it?" (Amos 5:20 NKJV). For sinning Israel, the coming Day of the Lord would be dark indeed. For "'I will send you into captivity beyond Damascus,' says the LORD, whose name is the God of hosts" (Amos 5:27 NKJV).

3. **Five visions of doom** (Amos 7:1–9:10). Amos relates five visions that God showed him. The visions reveal that while God has withheld punishment in the past, he will do so no longer. "The end has come upon My people Israel; I will not pass by them anymore" (Amos 8:2 NKJV).

4. **A promise of future restoration** (Amos 9:11–15). The defeat of the Northern Kingdom by the Assyrians and the exile of the ten northern Hebrew tribes did not mean that God had voided the covenant promises given to Abraham over a thousand years before. While that generation of Israelites would be torn from the land, by history's end God would bring their descendants back to the Promised Land.

Each of the Old Testament prophets who predict divine judgment on God's sinful people includes the same reassuring message. Whatever happens, ultimately God's promises to Abraham will be kept, and God's people will be blessed. Amos's last words, spoken in God's name, are:

AMOS 9:14–15

"I will bring back the captives of My people Israel;
They shall build the waste cities and inhabit them;
They shall plant vineyards and drink wine from them;
They shall also make gardens and eat fruit from them.
I will plant them in their land,
And no longer shall they be pulled up
From the land I have given them,"
Says the LORD your God. (NKJV)

Hosea

. . . covenant love

Who	The prophet Hosea
What	contrasted Israel's ungratefulness with God's covenant love
Where	in Israel
When	during the last thirty years of Israel's existence
Why	to explain the reason for Israel's imminent destruction by Assyria

Keep on Loving

the big picture

Hosea

The book has two stories to tell: the story of Hosea and his wife Gomer, and the story of the Lord and his people Israel.

1. The unfaithful wife	**Hosea 1–3**
2. The unfaithful nation	**4–14**
A. Israel's sins denounced	**4–8**
B. Israel's doom announced	**9–10**
C. God's love affirmed	**11**
D. Discipline first	**12–13**
E. Then blessing	**14**

Hosea the prophet was married to an unfaithful wife. Yet he continued to love her deeply. Even though she abandoned him and her children for lovers, Hosea provided for her and ultimately brought her back home. Hosea's personal experience mirrored the experience of God with Israel. Although God loved Israel as a husband loves his wife, Israel had taken his many gifts and turned to idolatry.

Hosea shares his personal story first. Then he recounts God's complaint against unrepentant Israel and expresses God's deep, continuing love for his unfaithful people.

What's Special in Hosea?

1. Hosea's commitment to his wife (Hosea 3:1–4). The commitment that Hosea displayed to his marriage is remarkable, especially in our day when divorce is so common. Hosea's willingness to keep on loving despite his deep hurt reminds us that marriage is a commitment that is not to be quickly set aside.

powerful love
Romans 5:5–11

2. **God's indictment of sinful Israel** (Hosea 4:1–19). Like the other prophets whom God sent to his people, Hosea spoke plainly about the sins that called for divine judgment. In unequivocal terms Hosea announced, "The LORD brings a charge against the inhabitants of the land," and he went on to spell that charge out:

HOSEA 4:1–2

There is no truth or mercy
Or knowledge of God in the land.
By swearing and lying,
Killing and stealing and committing adultery,
They break all restraint,
With bloodshed upon bloodshed. *(NKJV)*

3. **God's love is unshakable** (Hosea 11). In one of Scripture's most eloquent passages, God expresses his boundless love for Israel. From infancy God has cared for his people, like a parent teaching them to walk, protecting and caring for them. God's love is so deep that whatever the provocation, God simply will not let his people go.

It's important to remember that God's love does not fail. The book of Hosea reminds us that in the end God brings the wanderer back to himself. Ahead there remained a day for Israel when God "will heal their backsliding [and] love them freely" and Israel will "grow like the lily" (Hosea 14:4–5). That powerful love can tame sinners today as well, healing us and enabling us to blossom.

Chapter Wrap-Up

- After the death of Solomon the united Hebrew Kingdom was divided, with the Southern Kingdom called Judah, and the Northern Kingdom Israel.
- The Northern Kingdom, Israel, was ruled by a succession of evil kings.
- Even though God sent prophets to warn Israel and turn the nation back to him, the people did not listen, and Israel fell to the Assyrians in 722 BC.
- Among the prophets that God sent to Israel were the speaking prophets Elijah and Elisha.
- The ministry of Elijah and Elisha is notable because it occurred during one of three periods in which miracles were common.
- Jonah was an Israelite prophet whose mission to Nineveh provided proof that God would withhold judgment if a people repented of their sins.
- Amos was a writing prophet whose book contains sermons warning Israel that God would judge them for their idolatry and social injustice.
- Hosea was a writing prophet whose commitment to his unfaithful wife mirrored God's love for and commitment to unfaithful Israel.

Study Questions

1. What sin fixed the destiny of Israel when the Northern Kingdom was first established?
2. In what way were the kings of Israel alike?
3. What two speaking prophets are associated with the Bible's seond age of miracles?
4. What two prophets ministered to Israel during the reign of Jeroboam II? What was the message of each to Israel?
5. What is the Day of the Lord?
6. What sins in Israel called for God's judgment? In what ways is our country today like ancient Israel?

1 and 2 Kings • 2 Chronicles Obadiah • Joel • Micah • Isaiah

Let's Get Started

Solomon died in 930 BC (see Time Line #6). When he died the ten northern Hebrew tribes broke away to establish an independent kingdom, Israel (see chapter 8), whose capital would be Samaria. In the South, or Judah, descendants of David continued to rule from Jerusalem. Many in the North, unhappy with Jeroboam's decision to establish a counterfeit religion, moved south to continue to worship God at the temple Solomon had constructed.

The two rival Hebrew kingdoms existed side by side for more than two hundred years, sometimes at war, sometimes cooperating against common enemies. When the Northern Hebrew Kingdom fell to Assyria in 722 BC, Judah survived. Judah continued to be ruled by David's descendants until 586 BC, when the nation fell to the Babylonians and its citizens were also sent into exile.

1 and 2 Kings

. . . a historical account

Who	Unknown authors
What	evaluated the kings
Where	of Israel and Judah
When	from 970 BC to 586 BC
Why	to demonstrate the value of obeying God and the danger of disobeying him

2 Chronicles

. . . a commentary on history

Who	Unknown authors
What	highlighted godly kings
Where	of Judah
When	from 970 BC to 586 BC
Why	to show that when God was honored and wor

Overview

The chart below identifies the kings and the writing prophets of the Southern Hebrew Kingdom, Judah, from the division of the Hebrew Kingdom in 930 BC until the fall of Israel in 722 BC. Note that most of 2 Chronicles is devoted to the rule of Judah's godly kings.

Kings and Prophets of the Southern Kingdom

Kings	Evaluation	Prophetic Books	Years reigned	Scripture
Rehoboam	Evil	—	17	1 Kings 12–14; 2 Chronicles 11, 12
Abijah	Evil	—	—	1 Kings 15; 2 Chronicles 13
Asa	Godly	—	41	1 Kings 15; 2 Chronicles14–16
Jehoshaphat	Godly	—	25	1 Kings 22; 2 Chronicles 17–20
Jehoram	Evil	Obediah	8	2 Kings 8; 2 Chronicles 21
Ahaziah	Evil	—	1	2 Kings 8; 2 Chronicles 22
Queen Athaliah	Evil	—	6	2 Kings 11; 2 Chronicles 22, 23
Joash	Godly	Joel	40	2 Kings 12; 2 Chronicles 24
Amaziah	Godly	—	29	2 Kings 14; 2 Chronicles 25
Uzziah	Godly	—	52	2 Kings 15; 2 Chronicles 26
Jotham	Godly	Micah and Isaiah	16	2 Kings 15; 2 Chronicles 27
Ahaz	Evil	Micah and Isaiah	16	2 Kings 16; 2 Chronicles 28
Hezekiah	Godly	Micah and Isaiah	29	2 Kings 18–20; 2 Chronicles 29–32

Now for the Southern Kingdom

While Israel and Judah struggled to survive, in . . .	
India	Medical schools used anatomical models.
Europe	Wheels with spokes began to be used.
Greece	The first recorded Olympic games took place.
England	Celtic peoples began to arrive.
Asia Minor	People began to use iron in utensils.

Moral Leadership

The kings of Judah were more than political leaders. They provided moral and spiritual leadership as well. The spiritual and political well-being of the nation was closely linked. In general the nation prospered under godly kings and suffered under ungodly kings.

A look at passages in 2 Chronicles, which describe the rule of two of Judah's godly kings (Asa and Jehoshaphat), provides a clear picture of what rulers did to encourage personal and national spiritual **revival**.

revival
heartfelt return and commitment to God

high places
hilltops where pagan deities were worshiped

Asherah poles
wooden symbols of a pagan goddess

How Asa Led . . . (2 Chronicles)	How Jehoshaphat Led . . . (2 Chronicles)
Did what was right and good (14:2)	Sought God personally (17:4)
Removed foreign altars from **high places** (14:3)	Followed God's commandments (17:4)
Commanded the people to seek the Lord (14:4)	Removed high places and **Asherah poles** (17:6)
Commanded the people to obey Gods laws and commandments (14:4)	Sent Levites throughout Judah to teach God's Law (17:9)
Relied on God when war came (14:11)	
Repaired the altar and offered sacrifices (15:8)	
Led a ceremony of covenant renewal (15:11)	
Deposed the queen mother for idolatry (15:16)	

Godly leaders can still influence nations for good. Ungodly leaders still erode the moral and spiritual fiber of a nation.

what others say

King Solomon

Righteousness exalts a nation, but sin is a disgrace to any people.[1]

Those Prophets Again

One of the most significant roles in the Old Testament was that of the prophet. A number of speaking prophets are mentioned in the

oracle
a prophet's utterance

entrails
internal organs

mediums
one possessed by or consulting a ghost or spirit of the dead, especially for information about the future

occult
anything dealing with the mystic arts like Satanism, black magic, witchcraft, etc.

witchcraft
trying to predict the future through omens sorcery: black magic omens: something that seems to be a sign of things to come

horoscopes
diagrams of the heavens, showing the relative positions of planets and the signs of the **zodiac**, used to predict events in people's lives

zodiac
the twelve imaginary signs in heaven

Old Testament books of history. No less than seventeen of the thirty-nine Old Testament books are composed completely of the messages given by writing prophets.

What was the mission of the prophets, and why were they so important? The answer is found in the way ancient peoples sought supernatural guidance.

Stay Away from the Occult

The Greeks went to Delphi to consult the **oracle** there. The Romans looked for signs in the **entrails** of a slaughtered pig, or in the direction taken by a flight of birds. The peoples of the ancient Middle East consulted **mediums** or spiritists who claimed to contact the dead or some spirit. The religions of all ancient peoples involved some aspect of the **occult**, some search for supernatural guidance.

When the Israelites were about to enter Canaan, God warned them against all occult practices. The Bible forbids every kind of occult practice, labeling all of them abominations to the Lord.

> DEUTERONOMY 18:9–12 *When you come into the land which the LORD your God is giving you, you shall not learn to follow the abominations of those nations. There shall not be found among you anyone who makes his son or his daughter pass through the fire, or one who practices* ***witchcraft****, or a soothsayer, or one who interprets omens, or a sorcerer, or one who conjures spells, or a medium, or a spiritist, or one who calls up the dead. For all who do these things are an abomination to the LORD, and because of these abominations the LORD your God drives them out from before you. (NKJV)*

God's answer for his Old Testament people was the prophet: a person commissioned to speak in God's name and convey God's will to his own. God himself would provide all the guidance his people needed in order to know and to do his will.

Today people look for guidance in **horoscopes**, call the psychic networks, and consult spiritists. These practices are still abominations to the Lord. God wants us to rely on him, not on the occult.

A Need for Special Guidance

God had given his people a written Law to guide them. But there were situations in which the nation or individuals faced uncertain choices and needed to know God's will. There were times when God's people strayed and needed to be warned and called back to his ways.

True vs. False Prophets

But how could God's Old Testament people distinguish a true messenger of God from a pretender? Deuteronomy identifies four tests, and a true prophet could pass them all.

1. A true prophet will urge people to follow the Lord (Deuteronomy 13:1–4).
2. A true prophet will be an Israelite, not a foreigner (Deuteronomy 18:15).
3. A true prophet will speak God's Word in God's name (Deuteronomy 18:19).
4. A true prophet will make predictions that come true (Deuteronomy 18:21–22).

Today we can be sure that the prophets of the Bible truly were God's messengers, for we have hundreds of their predictions in Scripture which have been fulfilled. But when a prophet delivered a message in his own generation, all four of these tests were needed to authenticate him or her as God's messenger.

An Example from Scripture

God sent the prophet Jeremiah to urge the people of Jerusalem to submit to the Babylonians. One morning at the Jerusalem temple, a prophet named Hananiah contradicted Jeremiah. Hananiah loudly announced in the name of the Lord that within two years the power of Babylon would be broken and Judah's captive king and nobles would be returned to Jerusalem. Hananiah passed some of the tests: he was a Jew, and he had spoken in the name of the Lord.

Jeremiah, a patriot, was delighted. But shortly after, God sent Jeremiah back to confront Hananiah. Hananiah had made up the message he delivered in God's name. Boldly Jeremiah said, "Hear now, Hananiah, the LORD has not sent you, but you make this people trust in a lie" (Jeremiah 28:15 NKJV). Then Jeremiah announced God's sentence: "This year you shall die, because you have taught rebellion against the LORD" (Jeremiah 28:16 NKJV).

Two months later, Hananiah was dead. Jeremiah's words had come true. Jeremiah, not Hananiah, was God's prophet. The people of Judah were responsible for listening to and obeying God's words given through Jeremiah.

When we read the writings of the prophets recorded in the Bible, we need to remember that each prophet had a message for his or her own generation. Yet that message will contain truths we can apply to our own lives today.

With this in mind, we can look at Bible books written by the prophets, who brought God's Word to the people of the Southern Hebrew Kingdom, Judah.

Obadiah

. . . Edom's doom

Who	The prophet Obadiah
What	announced that because
Where	Jerusalem
When	was plundered by the Edomites
Why	God would destroy Edom for attacking his people

Okay, That's Enough

At least four times in history the Edomites, a neighboring nation, attacked Judah and plundered Jerusalem. After one of these invasions, the prophet Obadiah announced that God would destroy Edom. In his covenant with Abraham God had promised, "I will bless those who bless you, and I will curse him who curses you" (Genesis 12:3 NKJV).

Obadiah's brief, one-chapter book contains God's announcement that he will keep this pledge. The Edomites had marched through the gates of God's people, seized their wealth, and waited at the crossroads to cut down their fugitives (Obadiah 1:13–14). Therefore

God would see to it that the house of Esau (a synonym for Edom, which was founded by Esau) was consumed. "No survivor shall remain of the house of Esau" (Obadiah 1:18 NKJV).

Esau
Genesis: 36:8–9

a great swarm of locusts
Revelation 9:3–11

Joel

. . . final judgment coming

Who	The prophet Joel
What	shared his vision of near and final judgment
Where	in Judah
When	possibly around 825 BC
Why	as a warning and call to repentance

Buzzzzzz . . .

the big picture

Joel

This three-chapter book is divided into two sections. The first section (Joel 1:1–2:27) concerns the locusts that swarmed Judah from the North, which was unusual because most locust swarms were blown into the Holy Land from the South. The second section (Joel 2:28–3:21) is a vision of the coming Day of the Lord, a description of events that lie far in the future.

Joel writes just after a great swarm of locusts had stripped Judah of all vegetation. He announced that God sent the locusts to call Judah to repentance. But as Joel contemplated the locusts, God gave him a vision of another invasion of the Promised Land at history's end. This hoard is a vast human army, which would also devastate the land and its people. At that time God himself would intervene. He would punish the nations and rescue his own.

How are the people of Judah to respond to this message from God? They are to return to the Lord with all their hearts, for who knows? He may turn and have pity and leave behind a blessing (Joel 2:14) for Joel's generation.

What's Special in Joel?

repentance
2 Corinthians 7:8–11

ashes
Job 2:7–8

1. **The call to repentance** (Joel 1:13–15). Joel interprets the locust invasion as punishment for Judah's sins. He calls on God's people to turn to the Lord quickly, lest something worse happen.
2. **True repentance** (Joel 2:12–14). In Bible times people openly displayed grief and sorrow. To show repentance they tore their clothing, smeared dirt on their faces, and wept loudly as they sat in ashes. Joel reminds Judah that God demands true repentance when he says, "Rend your heart, and not your garments" (Joel 2:13 NKJV).
3. **God's response to true repentance** (Joel 2:18–27). Through Joel, God promises to bless and protect his people when they repent and turn to him. "I will restore to you the years that the swarming locust has eaten," God says (Joel 2:25 NKJV).
4. **History's end** (Joel 2:28–3:21). By seeing the locust plague Joel catches a glimpse of an overpowering human army that will invade the Holy Land in the distant future. God would use that occasion to bless his people, for he would judge the nations who invade it. "Judah shall abide forever, and Jerusalem from generation to generation" (Joel 3:20 NKJV).

The Message of Joel

Joel had an important message for his generation. God is sovereign and speaks through events. The prophet rightly interpreted the locust plague as a call to Judah to repent.

Like Judah, we are to remember that God is in control of the events of our lives. How often are our troubles invitations to draw closer to God, that he might bless us.

what others say

John Alexander

To deny sin is bad news, indeed. The only good news is sin itself. Sin is the best news there is, the best news there could be in our predicament. Because with sin, there's a way out. There's the possibility of repentance. You can't repent of confusion or psychological flaws inflicted by your parents—you're stuck with them. But you can repent of sin. Sin and repentance are the only grounds for hope and joy. The grounds for reconciled, joyful relationships. You can be born again.[2]

Both physical life and spiritual life have beginnings. One began when our mothers gave birth. The other begins when a person trusts Jesus Christ as Savior. God gives those people a spiritual life that lasts forever, guaranteeing that the believer will live eternally in heaven with God. This is what we call being born again—being born a second time, spiritually.

Jesus Christ
John 3:16–18

A ruler would be born in Bethlehem
Micah 5:2;
Isaiah 9:2–7;
Luke 1:39–55

Micah

. . . judgment coming

Who	The prophet Micah, prophesying,
What	warned of the destruction of both Samaria and Jerusalem
Where	in Israel and Judah
When	just before Assyria invaded
Why	because of the sins of both Hebrew kingdoms

Repent or You'll Regret It

the big picture

Micah

God was about to step into history to judge his idolatrous people. Micah portrays the anguish his actions would cause. While God's sinful people lay awake plotting wickedness, God had set his own plan in motion. The present civilization would be destroyed, but a remnant of the people would be preserved. Leaders and prophets alike had led God's people astray; the nation must fall. But however devastating, this judgment would not be the end.

One day God would bring back the exiles and raise a new temple in Jerusalem. A ruler would be born in Bethlehem who would shepherd God's flock and bring peace to all the earth.

Micah was a prophet who ministered in Judah during the reigns of Jotham, Ahaz, and Hezekiah. These were critical years for both Hebrew kingdoms, as an aggressive Assyria loomed just over the horizon, threatening their independence. Micah had a similar message for both Israel and Judah, which he delivered to their capital cities, Samaria and Jerusalem. That message was one of impending doom, for each society was corrupt. In clear and unmistakable words

indictment
an official charge of wrongdoing

Micah presented God's **indictment** spelling out the sins that called for judgment.

Micah's warnings to Israel fell on deaf ears. He lived to see Israel fall to Assyria, and to see its population taken away. But Micah also saw a godly king, Hezekiah, replace the evil Ahaz in the South. Through the influence of Hezekiah and the prophets Micah and Isaiah, Judah turned back to the Lord. While the Assyrians did invade Judah, Jerusalem and the Southern Kingdom survived.

For a time, however, Israel must lose its national identity because of the people's many sins. But at history's end God would restore Israel and would forgive his people's sins, as he had pledged to Abraham long ago.

What's Special in Micah?

1. **Sins demand judgment** (Micah 3:1–7; 6:7–16). God is a moral Judge who is responsible for punishing sin. Micah draws a picture of political leaders who exploit citizens and of religious leaders who pretend that nothing is amiss. He goes on to describe a materialistic society in which the average person is dishonest and deceitful, practicing "religion" but unconcerned with justice.

Through Micah God makes it unmistakably clear that he will judge:

MICAH 5:12–15

I will cut off sorceries from your hand,
And you shall have no soothsayers.
Your carved images I will also cut off,
And your sacred pillars from your midst;
You shall no more worship the work of your hands;
I will pluck your wooden images from your midst;
Thus I will destroy your cities.
And I will execute vengeance in anger and fury
On the nations that have not heard. *(NKJV)*

2. **Salvation depends on a Savior** (Micah 5:2–5; 7:19–20). Like other prophets who warned of coming judgment, Micah looked beyond the coming disaster to a day when God would save his people. In this book, written more than seven hundred years before Christ, Micah identified the town where the promised Savior would be born!

In one of the clearest of the Old Testament's **messianic prophecies**, Micah wrote:

messianic prophecies
information about Christ revealed in the Old Testament

MICAH 5:2–5

But you, Bethlehem Ephrathah,
Though you are little among the thousands of Judah,
Yet out of you shall come forth to Me
The One to be Ruler in Israel,
Whose goings forth are from of old,
From everlasting . . .
And He shall stand and feed His flock
In the strength of the LORD,
In the majesty of the name of the LORD His God;
And they shall abide,
For now He shall be great
To the ends of the earth;
And this One shall be peace. *(NKJV)*

Jesus' birth some 2,000 years ago culminated in his death and resurrection, winning peace with God for those who trust in him. But the Bible also speaks of a second coming of Jesus, not to die again but to rule. This prophecy of Micah describes one of the outcomes of his return to earth. He comes to rule, and will rescue his people and bring universal peace.

Isaiah

. . . the Old Testament gospel

Who	The prophet Isaiah
What	warned of judgment
Where	to the people of Judah
When	between 740 BC and 690 BC
Why	and conveyed hope linked to the coming Messiah, who will win salvation for individuals and the whole world

A Coming Messiah

sovereign
God is in control of all that happens

Savior
one who delivers from danger and death

the big picture

Isaiah

The prophet's name means "Yahweh is salvation." No other Old Testament prophet pictures so clearly God's firm intention to save his people or describes more distinctly the coming Savior. The sixty-six chapters in Isaiah can be divided into three major sections, with subsections developing their themes.

1. Words of Condemnation — Isaiah 1–35
   - A. God's case against Judah and Israel 1–12
   - B. God's case against the surrounding nations 13–23
   - C. God's case against all the nations 24–35
2. Agents of God's Wrath — Isaiah 36–39
   - A. Looking back at the Assyrians 36–37
   - B. Looking ahead to the Babylonians 38–39
3. Words of Comfort and Hope — Isaiah 40–66
   - A. The Sovereign God will deliver 40–48
   - B. God's Servant-Savior will be the deliverer 49–57
   - C. God's deliverer will save completely 58–66

Isaiah also lived under the threat of Assyria and witnessed the fall of Israel. Like Micah, Isaiah urgently warned Judah to turn back to God. Isaiah supported godly King Hezekiah's efforts to bring about a spiritual revival. God honored the king's faith by turning back the invading Assyrians. Yet Isaiah's early ministry was devoted to continually exposing the sins of God's people, and to warning that God must and would judge them.

The theme of Isaiah's messages changed radically in the latter part of his ministry, as reflected in chapters 40–66. His visions carry him beyond the time of Judah's future defeat by another northern enemy, Babylon, to portray a **sovereign** God who is committed to deliver his people and to bless all mankind. Isaiah promises that in God's own time he will send his Messiah. Through this promised **Savior** God will deliver individuals who trust in him, and purge the whole world of sin's corruption.

What's Special in Isaiah?

1. **God's weariness with sin** (Isaiah 1). The Lord put up with the sinful behavior of Israel and Judah far too long. Even the revivals led by godly kings in the South had not touched the hearts of God's people. Any society that is satisfied with a "religion" but fails to produce a just society is doomed.

2. **God's use of human agents** (Isaiah 10:1–12). Isaiah identifies Assyria as the rod of (God's) wrath. The Assyrian invasion was not a random event, but something God allowed to punish the sins of Israel and Judah. God is in control of history, and the rise and fall of nations accomplished his purposes.

3. **Hope shines through the darkest of Isaiah's prophecies**. Although Isaiah 1–35 contains repeated images of judgment and coming doom, Isaiah frequently assures his hearers that God is committed to them, and he will keep his covenant promises to Abraham and David. Isaiah reveals that God's promises will be fulfilled through the gift of God's Son, who will be born as a human child.

Isaiah 9:6–7

For unto us a Child is born,
Unto us a Son is given;
And the government will be upon His shoulder.
And His name will be called
Wonderful, Counselor, Mighty God,
Everlasting Father, Prince of Peace.
Of the increase of His government and peace
There will be no end,
Upon the throne of David and over His kingdom,
To order it and establish it with judgment and justice
From that time forward, even forever.
The zeal of the Lord of hosts will perform this. (NKJV)

This is just one of many prophecies in Isaiah about the coming Savior. As we will see later, these Old Testament prophecies unmistakably refer to Jesus Christ!

4. **Isaiah emphasizes God's sovereign power** (Isaiah 40–48). The comfort and hope that Isaiah offers to Judah are based on his understanding of the nature of God. The God of Israel and Judah is the Creator, who made and governs the universe. God is the

covenant promises
Genesis 12:1–3, 7

future
Isaiah 60:15–22; 65:17–25

sovereign control
Isaiah 46:9–11

One who has made covenant promises and who will surely keep them. He is the One who knows the future and who reveals it, for he controls the future. The idols men worship are nothing. The God of Israel and Judah is the almighty, sovereign Lord.

5. **There's a glorious future for the people of God** (Isaiah 58–66). The history of Israel and Judah had been marked by alternating periods of blessing and devastating tragedy. Isaiah looked beyond history and described a future of endless blessing after the Savior punished sin and established God's rule in the hearts of human beings.

The Message of Isaiah

Isaiah's message to the people of Judah was both timely and timeless. He warned his contemporaries about coming judgment, yet reminded them that in the end God would rid the universe of sin and usher in a time of endless blessing for all who trust in him.

The timeless message of Isaiah is reflected in the prophet's emphasis on God's sovereign control of history and in his many predictions describing the ministry of the Savior that God would send to deliver his people. The Savior, Jesus Christ, described so powerfully by Isaiah, has appeared with the offer of salvation for all. Ultimately Jesus will return to earth, and then all things truly will be set right.

Chapter Wrap-Up

- When Solomon died in 930 BC his kingdom was divided, with the Southern Kingdom renamed Judah.
- Judah was ruled by descendants of David from its beginning to its fall to the Babylonians in 586 BC.
- Many of the kings of Judah were godly and helped to begin religious revivals.
- God also sent both speaking and writing prophets to the kings and people of the South as his spokesmen.
- The prophet Obadiah predicted the doom of the Edomites, who had plundered God's people.

- The prophet Joel was given a vision of a terrible judgment to come at history's end before God fully restored his people to himself.
- The prophet Micah ministered during the years Israel fell. He not only warned Judah of coming judgment but also predicted the appearance of the promised messianic King.
- The book of the prophet Isaiah contains both warnings and promises. Many passages predict the coming of a king who would also be the Savior.

Study Questions

1. What Bible books record the history of Judah after Solomon's kingdom was divided?
2. Why was it important that Judah be ruled by godly rather than evil kings?
3. Why did all pagan peoples adopt occult practices? What was God's alternative to the occult for his people?
4. What were the four tests of a true prophet?
5. Match each of these four prophets to one of the following:

Obadiah	The Savior to be born in Bethlehem
Joel	God's sovereign rule
Micah	Judgment on Edom
Isaiah	A plague of locusts

2 Kings 15–25 • 2 Chronicles 29–36 • Nahum Zephaniah • Habakkuk • Jeremiah • Ezekiel

Let's Get Started

The Southern Hebrew Kingdom, Judah, survived the Assyrian invasion that destroyed Israel in 722 BC. God answered the prayers of godly King Hezekiah and threw back the invaders. But the sins that led to Israel's defeat were deeply entrenched in Judah as well. Despite revivals under King Hezekiah and later under King Josiah, Judah experienced a spiritual and moral descent that demanded divine judgment.

Time Line #6
A Divided Kingdom

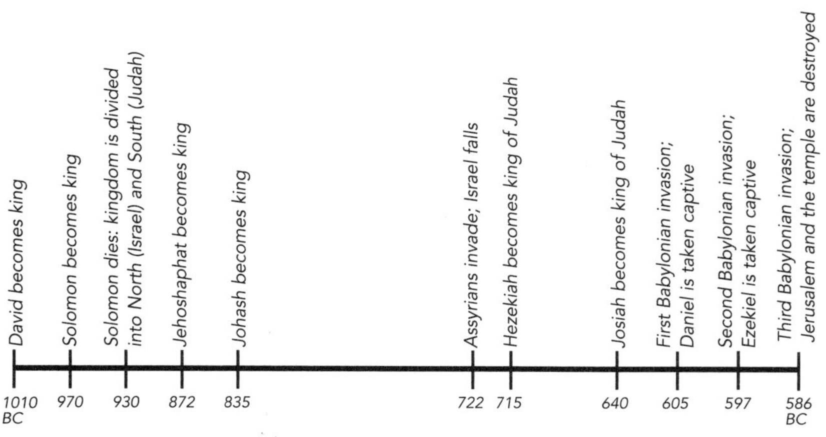

2 Kings

. . . a historical account

Who	Unknown authors
What	evaluated the kings
Where	of Israel and Judah
When	from 970 BC to 586 BC
Why	to demonstrate the value of obeying God and the danger of disobeying him

2 Chronicles

. . . a commentary on history

Who	Unknown authors
What	highlighted godly kings
Where	of Judah
When	from 970 BC to 586 BC
Why	to show that when God was honored and worshiped, Judah was blessed

And One Kingdom Remains

If God's people are fully dedicated to him, the Lord will protect and bless them.

When the Assyrian armies crushed Israel, Judah was ruled by Hezekiah. As soon as he became king, Hezekiah set out to revive Judah's faith in the Lord. That proved to be the key to Judah's survival. The Assyrian armies that crushed Israel also invaded Judah. They destroyed the fortified cities that guarded Judah's borders and threatened Jerusalem itself.

When an Assyrian envoy appeared outside the capital and ridiculed the idea of reliance on God, King Hezekiah and the prophet Isaiah appealed to the Lord. God answered their prayers with a sudden plague that killed thousands of Assyrian soldiers, forcing King Sennacherib to return home. This pivotal event is recounted three times in the Old Testament, in 2 Kings 18, 19, in 2 Chronicles 32, and in Isaiah 36–39. The lesson for future generations was clear. If God's people were fully dedicated to him, the Lord would protect and bless them.

But the lesson was not taken to heart. Seven kings succeeded Hezekiah of Judah. Only one of the seven, Josiah, was dedicated to the Lord. The nation drifted further into idolatry, and its society became increasingly immoral and unjust. In 605 BC the first of a series of Babylonian invasions into Judah marked the beginning of Judah's end. Finally, in 586 BC, Jerusalem was totally destroyed and its population was deported to Babylon.

Overview

The following chart identifies the kings and the writing prophets of the surviving kingdom, from the fall of Israel in 722 BC to the fall of Judah in 586 BC.

vision
Ezekiel 8–11

The Kings and Prophets of the Southern Kingdom

Kings	Evaluation	Years of Reign	Writing Prophets	Scripture
Hezekiah	Godly	29	Isaiah Micah	2 Kings 18–20 2 Chronicles 20–32
Manasseh	Evil	55	Nahum	2 Kings 21 2 Chronicles 33
Amon	Evil	2	—	2 Kings 21 2 Chronicles 33
Josiah	Godly	31	Zephaniah Habakkuk Jeremiah	2 Kings 22–23 2 Chronicles 34–35
Jehoahaz	Evil	3 months	Jeremiah	2 Kings 23 2 Chronicles 36
Jehoiakim	Evil	11	Jeremiah Ezekiel	2 Kings 24 2 Chronicles 36
Jehoiachim	Evil	3 months	Jeremiah Ezekiel	2 Kings 24 2 Chronicles 36
Zedekiah	Evil	11	Jeremiah Ezekiel	2 Kings 24, 25 2 Chronicles 36

Have It Your Way

When we read the accounts of godly kings like Hezekiah and Josiah, we cannot understand why Judah fell. But the revivals they led were superficial and brought about no permanent change of heart. Ezekiel, who was taken to Babylon as a captive in 597 BC and prophesied to the Jewish community there, was given a vision of Judah's sins. In his vision Ezekiel saw God's people worshiping pagan deities. As Ezekiel watched, God's glory (his visible presence) rose from the inner room (the Holy of Holies) of the temple and withdrew from the Holy City. God's people had abandoned them. He would no longer protect them from their enemies.

What Ezekiel Saw

- An idol by the altar of sacrifice. (Ezekiel 8:3–5)
- Judah's elders worshiping Egyptian deities. (Ezekiel 8:9–13)

his patience
Romans 2:2–6

- Women worshiping a nature goddess. (Ezekiel 8:14–15)
- Men praying to the sun, facing away from rather than toward God's temple. (Ezekiel 8:16)

What God Said

EZEKIEL **8:17–18** ***Is it a trivial thing to the house of Judah to commit the abominations which they commit here? For they have filled the land with violence; then they have returned to provoke Me to anger. Indeed they put the branch to their nose. Therefore I also will act in fury. My eye will not spare nor will I have pity; and though they cry in My ears with a loud voice, I will not hear them.*** *(NKJV)*

God is exceedingly patient. Don't mistake that patience for indifference to sin. Even his patience has limits. There comes a time when the invitation to respond to his love and his offer of forgiveness is withdrawn and judgment follows. That time had come for the men and women of Ezekiel's day. Babylonian armies gathered just over the horizon, and soon Judah and Jerusalem would lie in ruins, and the survivors would be deported to the land of their conquerors.

Voices, Voices, Voices

God promised to send prophets to guide his people, and God kept his promise. At every critical point in the history of the surviving Southern Kingdom, prophets urged and warned God's people to turn to him. But their words fell on deaf ears. As we study the messages of the prophets, we can only wonder at his patience and at what appears to be Judah's determined pursuit of God's judgment.

Nahum

. . . consolation and warning

Who	The prophet Nahum
What	described the fall of Nineveh
Where	in the Middle East
When	while Assyria was still dominant
Why	to affirm God's intent to judge wickedness

God Plays No Favorites

> **the big picture**
>
> **Nahum**
>
> The prophet teaches that divine judgment of the wicked is certain. His brief book is divided into three parts:
>
> - God's anger against Nineveh is expressed (Nahum 1:1–15)
> - Nineveh's imminent fall is described (Nahum 2:1–13)
> - The carnage is graphically portrayed (Nahum 3:1–19)

Nineveh, the capital of Assyria, had repented in the time of Jonah. But before long the success of the Assyrian armies replaced humility with an arrogant pride. The subsequent Assyrian assaults on Israel and Judah had been pitiless, marked by unusual brutality. The prophet Nahum, the exact time of whose life is uncertain, arose to announce that Nineveh was about to be judged by God. Bluntly Nahum proclaimed, "God is jealous, and the LORD avenges; the LORD avenges and is furious. The LORD will take vengeance on His adversaries, and He reserves wrath for His enemies" (Nahum 1:2 NKJV).

What's Special About Nahum?

1. **A basic principle is stated** (Nahum 1:1–15). Nahum states his thesis succinctly: "The LORD . . . will not at all acquit the wicked" (Nahum 1:3 NKJV). In view of this reality Nahum urges the people of Judah, "Keep your appointed [religious] feasts, perform your vows" (Nahum 1:15 NKJV). The God who is about to judge Nineveh will not hesitate to judge the guilty of Judah.
2. **Details of the fall of Nineveh are predicted** (Nahum 2:6; 3:8–15). The prophet describes a flood that will collapse palaces and open river gates to the enemy. Nahum foretells details about the fall of the city decades before the actual event.
3. **Consolation.** The name Nahum means "consolation." God wanted his people to know that he remained in charge of his universe, and that he would surely punish their oppressors.

But the book of Nahum can also be read as a warning. God plays no favorites. He will punish his own people if they also prove to be wicked.

Josiah
2 Kings 22–23

hear readings of God's Word
1 Chronicles 34:29–31

Zephaniah

. . . judgment on Judah

Who	Zephaniah
What	prophesied judgment
Where	in Judah and Jerusalem
When	during the reign of Josiah
Why	for the purpose of urging repentance

Hear the Word!

the big picture

Zephaniah

His mission was to warn Judah of a coming judgment that would sweep away Judah and her neighbors. Yet Zephaniah concluded with a word of hope. After judgment God would bring his people home. The book has three parts:

- Announcement of judgment on Judah (Zephaniah 1:1–2:3)
- Announcement of judgment on the nations (Zephaniah 2:4–15)
- The promise of a future for Jerusalem (Zephaniah 3:1–20)

Josiah was Judah's last godly ruler. He became king when he was only eight, succeeding his grandfather Manasseh and his father, Amon. These two kings, whose combined rule extended more than fifty-seven years, had completely corrupted biblical religion, and Judah was filled with idolatry and injustice. In Josiah's eighteenth year a lost book of the Law, probably Deuteronomy, was recovered. When Josiah read it, he realized how far the nation had strayed from God's ways and set out to revive the true faith. Josiah restored worship in the temple, tore down and burned the idols that infested the land, and got rid of practitioners of the occult. He called all the people together to hear readings of God's Word and urged them to follow it.

Despite the piety and zeal of the king, it was too late to reverse the national spiritual decline. While the nation would be preserved as long as Josiah lived, its sins called out for divine judgment, and judgment would surely come.

What's Special in Zephaniah?

1. **Judgment on Judah** (1:1–2:3). Zephaniah describes a coming great Day of the Lord that is fast approaching Judah. God will judge his own people as well as the nations that oppress them.

2. **Hope for the future** (Zephaniah 3:11–20). While the Old Testament prophets bluntly warn their listeners to expect judgment, they also reaffirm God's lasting love for his own. Sins will be punished, but God is committed to save his people in the end. As God says through his prophet . . .

ZEPHANIAH 3:17

The LORD your God in your midst,
The Mighty One, will save;
He will rejoice over you with gladness,
He will quiet you with His love,
He will rejoice over you with singing. (NKJV)

Habakkuk

. . . living by faith

Who	Habakkuk dialogues with God
What	about how God's justice can be understood
Where	in Jerusalem
When	during the reign of Josiah
Why	in view of the coming Babylonian invasion

Why, God, Why?

the big picture

Habakkuk

The prophet raises vital questions about God's justice. How can God permit the terrible sins that mar every human society? Is God really silent and withdrawn? The book of Habakkuk explores this issue through the prophet's questions and God's surprising answers. The book can be outlined as follows:

- Habakkuk's first complaint (Habakkuk 1:1–11)
- Habakkuk's second complaint (Habakkuk 1:12–17)
- Principles of present judgment (Habakkuk 2:1–20)
- Habakkuk's prayer (Habakkuk 3:1–19)

Habakkuk was troubled. Despite Josiah's best efforts to stimulate revival, Judah's society is marked by violence and injustice. When Habakkuk asks God how he can permit this, the Lord reveals that he is about to send the Babylonians to punish his sinning people. But Habakkuk objects. The Babylonians are more wicked than the people of Judah! God reassures his prophet that the Babylonians aren't getting away with anything. Then God shares hidden principles of divine judgment with Habakkuk, making it clear that even when most successful, the wicked are still being punished. Satisfied, the prophet urges God to judge and purify his people quickly, even though he himself will suffer from the invasion.

What's Special in Habakkuk?

1. **Judah's sinful society** (Habakkuk 1:1–11). Despite the outward appearance of a religious revival, Judah's society is marked by violence, conflict, and injustice. Habakkuk cannot believe a holy God can permit this to go on unpunished. When he prays, God tells him of the coming Babylonian invasion. God will punish sin.

2. **God's use of the "more wicked"** (Habakkuk 1:12–17). God's answer troubles Habakkuk. "Why do You look on those who deal treacherously, and hold Your tongue when the wicked devours a person more righteous than he?" (Habakkuk 1:13 NKJV). The people of Judah are bad, but the godless Babylonians are worse! The success of the wicked makes it seem like God is uninvolved in human affairs.

3. **God is not silent** (Habakkuk 2:1–20). God reveals to Habakkuk that while the wicked devour those more righteous, God is not silent. In fact, God is judging even while the wicked seem to enjoy their greatest success! Here's how:

Habakkuk 2:2–4	Their success never brings the wicked satisfaction or peace.
Habakkuk 2:5–8	Their treatment of others creates enemies who will turn on them. They struggle for security.
Habakkuk 2:12–14	Their future is empty, for God will rule on earth.

Habakkuk 2:15–17	Their disgrace is certain: violence leads to violence.
Habakkuk 2:18–20	They have no God to deliver them when their turn comes.

Don't envy the wicked. They may appear successful. But even while they appear successful outwardly, inwardly they are unsatisfied and insecure.

envy the wicked
Psalm 73

Protestant Reformation
a movement emphasizing salvation by faith that led to the founding of Protestant churches

Luther
Martin Luther; a German monk whose teaching launched the Protestant Reformation

John Wesley
a British preacher who founded the Methodist Church

4. In troubled times the believer will live by faith (Habakkuk 3:1–19). God gives Habakkuk a series of visions of divine judgment in earlier times. Habakkuk realizes that when God judges his society he too will suffer. But then Habakkuk struggles through to faith.

HABAKKUK 3:18–19

Yet I will rejoice in the LORD,
I will joy in the God of my salvation.
The LORD God is my strength;
He will make my feet like deer's feet,
And He will make me walk on my high hills. *(NKJV)*

what others say

Norman L. Geisler

Although often neglected, Habakkuk's prophecy is one of the most influential in the Bible. Habakkuk 2:4 is quoted three times in the New Testament (Romans 1:17; Galatians 3:11; Hebrews 10:38), more than almost any other verse. It served as the basis for the **Protestant Reformation** and, through **Luther**'s Commentary on Galatians, the conversion of **John Wesley**. Habakkuk is a book of faith.[1]

Jeremiah

. . . the weeping prophet

Who	Jeremiah
What	wrote this book
Where	urging Judah
When	during the last forty years of its existence
Why	to submit to Babylon

Standing Alone

oracles
messages from God delivered by a prophet

the big picture

Jeremiah

The book contains a number of **oracles**. These messages are organized by theme, though they were preached at different times during Jeremiah's forty-year ministry. An outline of the book reflects these themes.

- Jeremiah's mission explained (Jeremiah 1–10)
- The broken covenant (Jeremiah 11–20)
- Judgment draws near (Jeremiah 21–29)
- New Covenant promises (Jeremiah 30–39)
- Jerusalem the fallen (Jeremiah 40–51)
- History appendix (Jeremiah 52)

Jeremiah was a patriot who was commissioned by God to urge the people of Judah to submit to the Babylonians. This he faithfully did through the reigns of Judah's last five kings. But his unpopular message was rejected by his fellow countrymen, and Jeremiah himself was persecuted as a traitor. For forty long years Jeremiah faithfully warned the nation that God was determined to punish his people's sins. He urged surrender as the only way to avoid national extinction. Jeremiah lived to see his prophecies fulfilled, to witness the destruction of Jerusalem and Solomon's temple, and to see the people of Judah taken captive to Babylon.

What's Special in Jeremiah?

Jeremiah's book is both long and powerful, filled with deep emotion and vivid images. Here are some of the many special features of this great Old Testament book.

1. **Jeremiah's personal anguish** (Jeremiah 15:12–18; 20:7–18). It is almost impossible to imagine how isolated Jeremiah felt as a lone spokesman for God. He was a sensitive person, who was hurt deeply by the ridicule and hostility he constantly faced. Jeremiah's only recourse was to share his feelings with the Lord, which he records in several passages.

Historical Context of Jeremiah's Oracles

Josiah's Reign

Jeremiah 2, 3	Judah's sinful heart
Jeremiah 3–6	Jerusalem to be destroyed
Jeremiah 7–10	Ruin and exile
Jeremiah 11–13	The broken covenant
Jeremiah 18–20	The potter

Zedekiah's Reign

Jeremiah 21	Advice for the king
Jeremiah 24	Zedekiah abandoned
Jeremiah 27	Judah must submit
Jeremiah 28	**God's iron yoke**
Jeremiah 29	To the exiles
Jeremiah 30–33	The New Covenant
Jeremiah 34	Judah's broken covenant
Jeremiah 37–39	Jerusalem's fall
Jeremiah 49	The nation warned

Jehoiakim's Reign

Jeremiah 14, 15	Prayers are fruitless
Jeremiah 16, 17	Jeremiah's celebacy
Jeremiah 22	The king rejected
Jeremiah 23	False prophets charged
Jeremiah 25	Nebuchadnezzar
Jeremiah 26	Jeremiah threatened
Jeremiah 35	The Rechabites' example
Jeremiah 36	The burned scroll
Jeremiah 45	Promises to Baruch
Jeremiah 46–48	Against foreign nations

Under Governor Gedaliah

Jeremiah 40–43	The flight to Egypt
Jeremiah 44	In Egypt

Later

Jeremiah 50, 51	Judgment on Babylon
Jeremiah 52	Jerusalem

God's iron yoke
his unchangeable purpose

indignation
frustration and anger

apologists
people who defend an idea, faith, cause, or institution

JEREMIAH 15:15, 17–18

O LORD, You know;
Remember me and visit me. . . .
I did not sit in the assembly of the mockers,
Nor did I rejoice;
I sat alone because of Your hand,
For You have filled me with ***indignation****.*
Why is my pain perpetual
And my wound incurable,
Which refuses to be healed? (NKJV)

2. **The sins of Judah** (Jeremiah 5:7–25; 10:1–16). Jeremiah boldly confronted the people of his day about the sins that demanded judgment. But like men and women today who consider immorality a private matter, the people of Judah refused to repent. Compare what we read from a prophet like Jeremiah with stories featured in our newspapers and on television . . . and with the reaction of the guilty and their **apologists**.

Moses had warned
Deuteronomy 28:49–68

New Covenant
Hebrews 8:6–13; 2 Corinthians 3:7–18

Sins Described . . .	Man's Reaction . . .
"I had fed them to the full, Then they committed adultery And assembled themselves by troops in the harlots' houses. They were like well-fed lusty stallions; Every one neighed after his neighbor's wife. Shall I not punish them for these things?" says the Lord. (Jeremiah 5:7–9 NKJV)	They have lied about the LORD, And said, "It is not He. Neither will evil come upon us, Nor shall we see sword or famine. And the prophets become wind, For the word is not in them. Thus shall it be done to them." (Jeremiah 5:12–13 NKJV)

But God saw, and he sees today. God will not leave the guilty unpunished.

3. **The punishment decreed** (Jeremiah 25:1–14). Moses had warned God's people of what must happen if they refused to honor and obey God. Now Jeremiah reminds them that again and again the prophets have urged, "Repent now everyone of his evil way and his evil doings" (Jeremiah 25:5 NKJV). But Judah would not listen or pay attention. Through Jeremiah, God says, "I will send and take all the families of the north . . . and Nebuchadnezzar the king of Babylon, My servant, and will bring them against this land. . . . This whole land shall be a desolation and an astonishment, and these nations shall serve the king of Babylon seventy years" (Jeremiah 25:9, 11 NKJV).

4. **The promise of a New Covenant** (Jeremiah 30–31). Genesis 12 records covenant promises God made to Abraham. These promises stated what God would do for and through Abraham's descendants. The key promise was that the whole world would be blessed through Abraham. Later God added a covenant promise to David—the One who would fulfill God's promise to Abraham would be from David's family line. Now Jeremiah reveals even more of God's plan for blessing humanity.

Jeremiah, whose mission was to announce the coming fall of his nation, was given the privilege of communicating the promise that one day God would make a New Covenant with his people. The following scripture describes this New Covenant:

JEREMIAH 31:31–34 *Behold, the days are coming, says the LORD, when I will make a new covenant with the house of Israel and with the house of Judah—not according to the covenant that I made with their fathers in the day that I took them by the hand to lead them out of the land of Egypt, My covenant which they broke, though I was a husband to them, says the LORD. But this is the covenant that I will make with the house of Israel after those days, says the LORD: I will put My law in their minds, and write it on their hearts; and I will be their God, and they shall be My people. No more shall every man teach his neighbor, and every man his brother, saying, "Know the LORD," for they all shall know Me, from the least of them to the greatest of them, says the LORD. For I will forgive their iniquity, and their sin I will remember no more.* (NKJV)

Keys to Understanding the New Covenant

1.	2.	3.	4.
It replaces the Law Covenant	It operates in the human heart	It provides complete forgiveness	The New Covenant was instituted when Jesus died on the cross

We'll learn more about the New Covenant when we reach the New Testament. In fact, New Testament means "New Covenant." But the important thing to note here is that in the darkest of times, through Jeremiah God gave his people what is surely the brightest, most wonderful promise in God's Word.

what others say

Kay Arthur

You may relate to faithless Israel because you have not loved God as you should, or because you have not lived for him as you should have lived. My friend, know that God is still standing there in mercy, waiting for you to cry in faith, Heal me, "O Lord, and I will be healed; save me and I will be saved" (Jeremiah 17:14).[2]

queen of heaven a goddess worshiped by pagan peoples

5. **The flight to Egypt** (Jeremiah 40–44). After Jerusalem was destroyed, most of the Jewish population was deported to Babylon. A few Jews remained under a governor appointed by Nebuchadnezzar. When that governor was assassinated, the remaining Jews were terrified and planned to flee to Egypt, but first they asked Jeremiah to ask the Lord what they should do. Jeremiah prayed and reported God's Word. The remaining Jews should stay in their homeland. God would keep them safe. But if they refused to listen and went to Egypt, Nebuchadnezzar would attack Egypt and they would be wiped out.

Instead of listening to Jeremiah, the people angrily rejected God's guidance. They told Jeremiah, "As for the word that you have spoken to us in the name of the LORD, we will not listen to you! But we will certainly do whatever has gone out of our mouth, to burn incense to the **queen of heaven** and pour out drink offerings to her, as we have done, we and our fathers, our kings and our princes, in the cities of Judah and in the streets of Jerusalem" (Jeremiah 44:16–17 NKJV).

The last remaining Jews of Judah then left for Egypt . . . and disappeared from history.

Ezekiel

. . . prophet to the exiles

Who	Ezekiel
What	warned the captives
Where	in Babylon
When	six years before the fall of Jerusalem
Why	to prepare God's people for a lengthy captivity

Not Wet, but Dry Bones

the big picture

Ezekiel

The book contains a series of messages acted out and preached by the prophet. The bulk of the book dates from before the fall of Jerusalem and is about its coming doom. After Jerusalem was destroyed, Ezekiel spoke of a restored Jerusalem and of a new temple to be built on the same site as the one that had been destroyed.

- Prophecies against Judah (Ezekiel 1–24)
- Prophecy against foreign nations (Ezekiel 25–32)
- Prophecies of restoration (Ezekiel 33–39)
- Prophecy of the rebuilt temple (Ezekiel 40–48)

personal responsibility
Ezekiel 18

The Babylonians invaded Judah three times and on each occasion took a number of captives. In 597 BC Ezekiel was taken to Babylon after the second invasion. In 592 BC, as a thirty-year-old, he was called to be a prophet. His messages to the exiles in Babylon parallel the warning of certain defeat that Jeremiah was uttering at the same time in Judah. Through a series of visions, Ezekiel was able to describe events for the captives that were taking place in Judah long before word from the homeland could reach them.

soul
here, the person himself or herself

What's Special in Ezekiel?

1. **The emptied temple** (Ezekiel 8–11). The people of Jerusalem based their belief that the city would not fall on the existence of God's temple. Surely God would not permit his dwelling-place to be destroyed by pagans. But in a vision, Ezekiel saw God withdraw his presence from the temple and the Holy City. Afterward, the temple was an empty shell. God would not remain with a people whose sins showed him total disrespect.

2. **Personal responsibility** (Ezekiel 18). Many in Jerusalem shrugged off the warnings of Ezekiel and Jeremiah. If their forefathers had displeased God, and he was intent on punishing them, there was nothing they could do about it. Ezekiel confronted this fatalistic attitude, announcing the **soul** who sins is the one who will die (Ezekiel 18:4).

Ezekiel's announcement is one of personal responsibility. In the coming invasion God would distinguish between the righteous and the wicked. The wicked would be killed while the righteous would survive to go into captivity. In Ezekiel 18, the prophet gives four examples to show that God deals with human beings individually.

What will happen . . .

1. If a righteous man has a violent son	the son will die.	Ezekiel 18:5–13
2. If the violent son has a righteous son	the righteous son will live.	Ezekiel 18:14–18

breath of life
Genesis 2:7

What will happen . . . (cont'd)

3. If a wicked man turns from his ways	he will live.	Ezekiel 18:19–23
4. If a righteous man turns to evil	he will die.	Ezekiel 18:24–29

EZEKIEL 18:30–32 *"Therefore I will judge you, O house of Israel, every one according to his ways," says the Lord GOD. "Repent, and turn from all your transgressions, . . . and get yourselves a new heart and a new spirit. For why should you die, O house of Israel? For I have no pleasure in the death of one who dies," says the Lord GOD. "Therefore turn and live!" (NKJV)*

3. **The restoration of Israel described** (Ezekiel 37). Ezekiel is shown a valley filled with scattered and dried bones. He is told to prophesy, and the bones reassemble and are covered with flesh. But they do not live until they are given the breath of life (Ezekiel 37:1–10).

God explains the vision. The bones represented the Jewish people scattered throughout the nations. Their reassembling symbolized the Jews regathering to the Promised Land. But only when the people are filled with God's Spirit will they have life (Ezekiel 37:11–14).

Many believe this prophecy is being fulfilled in our time. For thousands of years the Jewish people were scattered throughout the world, with no homeland. Then, in 1948, Israel became a nation, but a secular state without spiritual life and vitality. When Jesus, the Messiah of the Old Testament, returns to rule, God's Old Testament people will recognize him and be saved (Ezekiel 37:15–28).

4. **The rebuilt temple** (Ezekiel 40–48). Like the other prophets, Ezekiel's message concluded on a strong note of hope. The prophet looks forward to a time of blessing at history's end, when God's people will live in their land and worship the Lord at a temple that will be constructed at that time.

Chapter Wrap-Up

- Godly King Hezekiah's reliance on God saved Judah from the Assyrian forces that destroyed Israel (2 Kings 18–19).
- The prophet Nahum described the coming fall of Nineveh as divine judgment on the Assyrians (Nahum).
- The prophet Zephaniah warned the people of Judah that God would judge them too (Zephaniah 1:1–2:3).
- The prophet Habakkuk predicted the Babylonian invasion as a punishment for Judah's sins (Habakkuk 1).
- The prophet Jeremiah struggled for forty years to reach the people of Judah. His message was rejected, and he lived to see his predictions of disaster come true (Jeremiah 37–39).
- The prophet Ezekiel had visions in which he witnessed the sins of the people in his homeland and the withdrawal of God's presence from the Jerusalem temple (Ezekiel 8–11).
- Despite the sins of Judah that called for judgment, God would deliver the righteous (Ezekiel 18) and would keep his promises to Abraham. He would save his people at history's end (Jeremiah 30–31).

Study Questions

1. Revival under what godly king saved Judah when the Assyrians destroyed Israel?
2. What sins of Judah did the prophets point to as the cause of the Babylonian victory?
3. Name three of the four prophets who preached in Judah, the surviving kingdom.
4. Name the prophet who preached to the exiles in Babylon before the destruction of Jerusalem.

Lamentations • Daniel • Esther • Ezra • Nehemiah Haggai • Zechariah • Malachi

Let's Get Started

In a series of three devastating invasions, the Babylonians under King Nebuchadnezzar stripped Judah of her wealth and population. In 586 BC the remaining Jews of Judah were resettled in Babylon, many in the capital city itself. Some seventy years later the Babylonian Empire fell to the Medes and Persians. The new ruler, Cyrus, reversed the Babylonian policy of resettlement, and permitted captive peoples to return to their homeland. But at first the captivity forced God's people to review their sins and ask a terrifying question: Has God totally rejected his people?

Three answers to that question are provided in the three books that reflect conditions during the captivity.

While the Jews were captives in Babylon, in . . .

Greece	Solon the lawgiver introduced a code of laws in Athens, and Aesop first told his fables.
Persia	Zoroaster founded a new religion.
Assyria	Water clocks were developed.
Lydia	Coins made of gold and silver were introduced.
Africa	Africa was circumnavigated by Phoenician mariners.

Lamentations

. . . the agony of defeat

Who	Tradition says Jeremiah
What	wrote these dirge poems
Where	in Babylon
When	after Jerusalem fell
Why	to express the anguish felt by the Jewish captives

Oh, Woe Is Me

acrostic
a poem in which each successive line begins with the next letter of the twenty-two-letter Hebrew alphabet

Zion
a poetic name for Jerusalem

the big picture

Lamentations

Dirge poems that express anguish and sorrow were a common literary form in the ancient Near East. The poems of Lamentations express the sense of loss experienced by the captives in Babylon, who at last realize how foolish they were to have turned away from God. The five poems depict:

- Jerusalem in mourning (Lamentations 1:1–22)
- Jerusalem in ruins (Lamentations 2:1–22)
- A call for renewal (Lamentations 3:1–66)
- Restitution to come (Lamentations 3:1–22)
- A cry for relief (Lamentations 4:1–22)

The people of Judah who had scorned the warnings of Jeremiah finally experienced the consequences of abandoning God. Their despair and anguish are captured in five **acrostic** poems that make up Lamentations.

What's Special About Lamentations?

1. **Lamentations gives insight into the Jews' doubt and despair.** These poems express the suffering and regret felt by the exiles. It is their belated recognition that their own sins led to their present, pitiful state. Yet, even in darkest despair there was a glimmer of hope.

what others say

Samuel Schultz

The author vividly pictures the plight of God's people as exiles in foreign lands. Can the Lord have forgotten his people? **Zion** is in ruins and Israel seems to be abandoned. Out of a broken heart, crushed and overwhelmed with sorrow, the author makes his plaintive appeal to God who reigns forever, imploring him to restore his own. In confession of sin and an implicit faith in God rests the final appeal for restoration.[1]

Three Sentiments of Lamentations

Suffering	Confession	Hope
Is it nothing to you, all you who pass by? Behold and see If there is any sorrow like my sorrow, Which has been brought on me, Which the LORD has inflicted In the day of His fierce anger. (Lamentations 1:12 NKJV)	Let us search out and examine our ways, And turn back to the LORD; Let us lift our hearts and hands To God in heaven. We have transgressed and rebelled; You have not pardoned. (Lamentations 3:40–42 NKJV)	You, O LORD, remain forever; Your throne from generation to generation. . . . Turn us back to You, O LORD, and we will be restored; Renew our days as of old, Unless You have utterly rejected us, And are very angry with us! (Lamentations 5:19, 21–22 NKJV)

synagogue
the local meeting place and assembly of the Jewish people during New Testament times

2. **Lamentations reminds us to remain confident.** To the exiles, the Babylonian captivity seemed to be a tragedy. Yet God's people benefited from the captivity in many ways. After being sent to Babylon the Israelites were never again tempted by idolatry. There the **synagogue** was invented, as small groups of Jews began to gather to worship and study the Old Testament. In the end, the captivity proved to be a blessing, purifying God's people from many of the sins that had called for divine punishment.

Only God is able to turn what we experience as a tragedy into a blessing in disguise.

Daniel

. . . the influential captive

Who	Daniel, a young captive,
What	delivers prophecies
Where	as a student in the king's school in Babylon
When	around 605 BC
Why	to tell people about the future history of the world

Dare to Be a Daniel

settled
Jeremiah 29:4–7

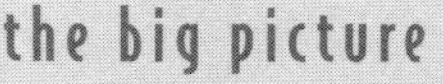

Daniel

The book of Daniel is divided into two parts. The first half of the book relates stories of Daniel and his relationships with world rulers. The second half of the book contains visions that God gave Daniel to reassure his people that, although gentile powers would rule the Holy Land for centuries, God was still in complete control of human history.

- Daniel's life and work (Daniel 1–6)
- Daniel's visions and prophecies (Daniel 7–12)

Most of the captives taken to Babylon settled in suburbs of the capital city, where they owned their own homes and raised garden crops. Records recovered by archaeologists indicate many Jews went into business and prospered. Daniel, taken captive in the invasion of 605 BC, was enrolled in a school that trained administrators for the Babylonian Empire. Daniel rose to become a high official in both the Babylonian and Persian Empires, showing God's continuing care of the faithful even in foreign lands. But Daniel was also a prophet, whose visions of the future told the captives that God remained in control of history, and that one day he would bring his people back to their land.

What's Special in Daniel?

1. **Daniel's personal experiences** (Daniel 1–6). Daniel developed a close relationship with Nebuchadnezzar and subsequent world rulers. Many believe that through Daniel's influence the Babylonian ruler became a believer. Several adventures of Daniel and his friends are recorded for us.

Adventures of Daniel

Adventure	Reference
Daniel's determination to follow God's Laws	Daniel 1:1–21
Daniel interprets Nebuchadnezzar's dream	Daniel 2:1–49
Daniel's companions in the fiery furnace	Daniel 3:1–30
Daniel and Nebuchadnezzar's conversion	Daniel 4:1–37
Daniel and the handwriting on the wall	Daniel 5:1–31
Daniel in the lions' den	Daniel 6:1–28

goat
in prophecy, symbolic of political power

week
seven years

2. **Daniel's visions of future history** (Daniel 7–12). The book of Daniel reports visions of the future. The visions showed that for centuries to come the Promised Land would be ruled by gentile world powers. Yet the visions were reassuring. A God who could predict the future was clearly in control of history! One day the promises given to Abraham and repeated by the prophets would surely be kept. The captivity definitely did not mean God had abandoned his people. He was still caring for his own!

The Visions of Daniel

Gentile Kingdom	God's Statue (Daniel 2)	Four Beasts (Daniel 7)	Two Beasts (Daniel 8)
Babylonian	Head of gold	Lion	—
Medo-Persian	Chest/arms of silver	Bear	Ram with two horns
Greek	Belly/thighs of bronze	Leopard	**Goat** with one horn
Roman	Legs of iron/feet of iron and clay	Strong Beast	—

These visions so accurately depict history that some have argued Daniel must have been written around 100 BC, after the events, rather than in the 540s BC, Daniel's actual date. Just as Daniel described beforehand, the Persian Empire was overcome by Alexander the Great (the goat with one horn), and on Alexander's death his empire was divided into four parts by his four generals (the four horns that replace the one)!

3. **The prophecy of the seventy weeks** (Daniel 9:20–27). These verses contain the most spectacular prophecy in Daniel. The prophecy gives a specific date for the appearance of Israel's Messiah in Jerusalem, counting from a future decree to rebuild Jerusalem. In a book called *The Coming Prince*, Sir Robert Anderson calculated that the Messiah, Christ, would enter Jerusalem and be acclaimed as king at the end of the sixty-ninth **week** on April 6, AD 32. But according to Daniel, the Messiah would then be cut off (killed)! And this is exactly what happened. Jesus made a triumphal entry into Jerusalem, but then that same weekend he was crucified!

Daniel's predictions shed light on the debate over whether Old Testament prophecy should be taken as images intended simply to convey spiritual truths, or should be understood to describe actual future events. No one doubts that Daniel accurately describes the succession of kingdoms in the Mediterranean world. Similarly the prediction that the Messiah would suffer and die, and that a time gap would exist between Jesus' first and second comings, has been literally fulfilled. We may not be able to tell exactly what a prophecy involves before the predicted event takes place. But looking back, fulfilled prophecy teaches us that we can expect Bible predictions to be literally fulfilled in the real world.

Esther

. . . born to be queen

Who	An unnamed author
What	wrote this book
Where	in Persia
When	between 460 BC and 350 BC
Why	to demonstrate through a series of unusual circumstances that God was taking care of his captive people

God Watches over All

the big picture

Esther

When King Ahasuerus divorced his queen he chose a young girl, Esther, as her successor. About the same time a high official in Ahasuerus court, Haman, felt he had been insulted by a lower official, a man named Mordecai who happened to be a Jew. Haman determined to wipe out the whole Jewish race as revenge, and was given permission to do so by Ahasuerus! But then through a series of amazing "coincidences," Ahasuerus decided to honor Mordecai, Esther revealed that she herself was a Jew, Haman angered the king and was executed, and the Jews were saved.

Esther is one of the most unusual books in the Bible. It tells the story of a young Jewish woman who became queen of Persia just in time to save God's people from extermination. While God is never mentioned in the book, coincidence after coincidence makes it clear that God is at work in what appears to be normal cause and effect to guarantee the security of his people. Even when exiled from their homeland, God has not forsaken his people. He guards and protects them.

providence
God's shaping of events to accomplish his own purposes

What's Special About Esther?

1. **The book illustrates the doctrine of divine providence.** God does not need to work miracles to protect his people. He is able to shape what appears to be the normal course of cause and effect so that his will is accomplished.

2. **The book delights readers of all ages.** Esther is best read through in one sitting, as a short story. Adults and children find the story fascinating, and are attracted to the brave young queen who risks her own life for her people.

The story of Esther reminds us that God's control of circumstances is hidden from the doubter, but obvious to the person of faith. God is always at work behind the scenes on our behalf. Even those events that we experience as tragedy can be transformed into good by our loving Father.

The Return Home

In 538 BC (see page 142) a pioneering group of 42,360 Jews set out for Judah, intent on reestablishing a temple in Jerusalem. A second group, led by Ezra, returned eighty years later in 458 BC, and a third group led by Nehemiah in 444 BC. Once again there was a Jewish presence in the Promised Land. Yet throughout the last five hundred years of the Old Testament era, far more Jews lived scattered throughout Persia and subsequent Eastern empires than lived in the land God had promised to Abraham.

Ezra

. . . the exiles return

Who	Ezra
What	wrote much of this book
Where	in Judah
When	around 430 BC
Why	to recount the Jews' return to Jerusalem

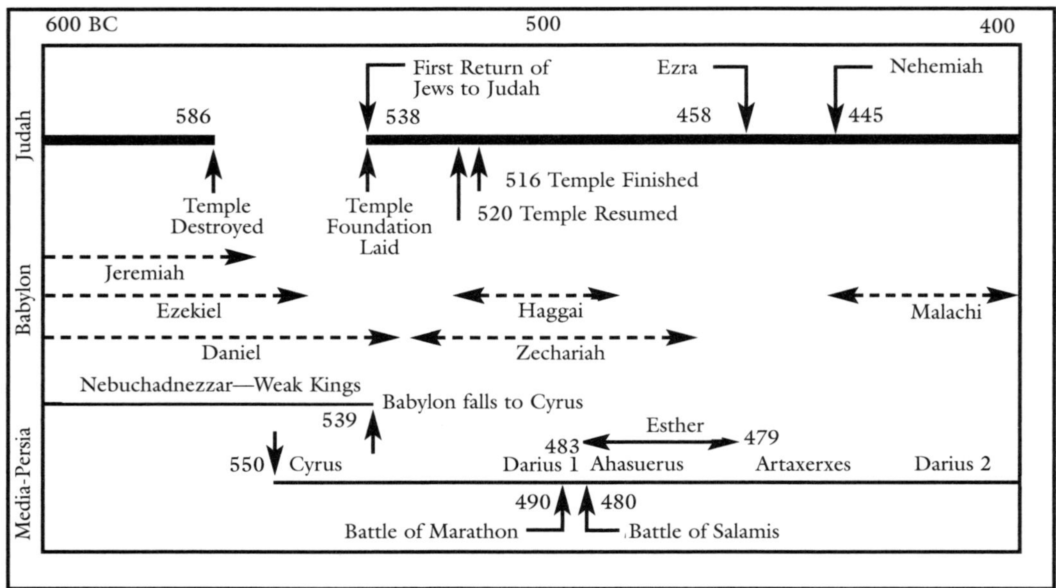

Time Line #7
The Captivity and Return of the Jews

EZRA: Ezra was a scribe, a highly trained person who was well educated in the Scriptures. His commission from the Persian ruler was to administer God's Law in Judah. He led a second group of pilgrims from Babylon to Judah eighty years after the first group had returned.

magistrates
government officials with administrative and judicial responsibilities

the big picture

Ezra

The first Jewish return took place shortly after Cyrus the Persian conquered Babylon. Some forty-three thousand Jews returned, intent on rebuilding the Jerusalem temple. While the temple foundation was laid immediately, opposition from the semi-pagan peoples then in the land delayed its completion for eighteen years. Then, stimulated by the prophets Haggai and Zechariah, the temple was completed in four years. Ezra himself led another group back to Judah, with authority to appoint **magistrates** and administer both Persian and God's Law. The book is organized by the two returns it describes.

- The first return (Ezra 1–6)
- The second return (Ezra 7–10)

What's Special in Ezra?

1. **Cyrus's decree allowing the return** (Ezra 1). About 150 years before the Persians overcame Babylon, God through the prophet Isaiah identified Cyrus by name as the ruler he would raise up to bring the Jewish exiles home. In the very first year of his reign, Cyrus the Persian fulfilled this prophecy. He issued a decree that permitted the Jews to return to the Holy Land, and to take with them the temple treasures! At the same time, Cyrus permitted other displaced persons to return to their homelands also. Many believe that Daniel influenced this reversal of policy.

Cyrus
Isaiah 44:24–45:7;
Ezra 1

2. **Local opposition** (Ezra 4–6). When the Assyrians deported the people of Israel in 722 BC, they had resettled the land with pagan peoples. The descendants of these people now offered to help rebuild God's temple so they could worship there. The Jews refused. The locals were not members of the covenant community; they were pagans.

Angry, the locals began a campaign of lies, rumors, and false accusations that halted work on the temple for eighteen years. The issue was finally settled when King Darius had his officials locate Cyrus's original decree in the archives. The victory of the Jews was complete, for Darius even diverted their opponents' taxes to pay for the temple's construction!

3. **Ezra's reforms in Judah** (Ezra 7–10). Ezra arrived in Judah fifty-eight years after the temple was completed. He was shocked to discover that priests and people had married pagan wives in direct violation of God's Law. His prayer, confessing this sin, moved the people of Judah to repent. The foreign wives were divorced, and the people promised to faithfully observe God's Law.

Nehemiah

. . . Jerusalem's walls restored

Who	Nehemiah
What	wrote much of this book
Where	in Judah
When	around 430 BC
Why	to recount the rebuilding of the city walls, which reestablished Jerusalem as a city worthy of respect

Rebuild Those Walls

the big picture

Nehemiah

Nehemiah gave up his position in the Persian court to become governor of Judah in 444 BC. He rallied the Jews to rebuild the walls of Jerusalem and to repopulate the city. Nehemiah was also deeply concerned about the spiritual state of the Jews. He worked closely with Ezra to teach and enforce God's Law, always setting a personal example as a godly leader. The book can be divided into three parts.

- The walls are rebuilt (Nehemiah 1–6)
- The covenant is renewed (Neheniah 7–12)
- Judah's sins are purged (Nehemiah 13)

Ezra and Nehemiah recount the difficulties and challenges faced by the few Jews who chose to leave comfortable Babylon to return to the Jewish homeland. Those who did return were moved by religious fervor, first to rebuild the temple, then to teach God's Law, and finally to restore Jerusalem's status as an important city by rebuilding the city's walls.

NEHEMIAH: Nehemiah was a high official in the court of the Persian ruler Artaxerxes in 444 BC. When Nehemiah learned that Jerusalem's walls lay in ruins, he asked for and received a commission to be governor of Judah. There, despite opposition from neighboring peoples, Nehemiah succeeded in rebuilding the city walls and thus restoring Jerusalem's status as a significant city.

What's Special About Nehemiah?

1. **Nehemiah's moral courage** (Nehemiah 5, 6). Nehemiah himself was the key to the successful rebuilding of the city walls. He set an example in his selfless service, and with the courage he displayed when his own life was threatened by the enemies of the Jews. How important it is to have leaders we can admire, who set an example for society.

2. **Leaders influence the whole society** (Nehemiah 10). Nehemiah's example and Ezra's teaching moved the people of Judah to make a fresh commitment of themselves to the Lord.

How important it is to have leaders we can admire, who set an example for society.

3. **Nehemiah's final reforms** (Nehemiah 13). After a successful term as Judah's governor, Nehemiah returned to the Persian court for a time. When Nehemiah returned to Judah in 431 BC, he found that the people had slipped back into their old sinful ways. Once again Nehemiah was successful in introducing reforms. But it was clear that without strong, godly leaders, the people would simply not remain faithful to the Lord.

what others say

William Sanford La Sor

Through the work of Ezra and Nehemiah, Israel's new identity became centered around the Law and [the] Temple. At this critical juncture, through the providence of God's redemptive acts, the identity of the people of God was created by the very religious forms and content that, prior to the Exile, never successfully became the center of their life.[2]

Prophetic Voices

Three prophets ministered to the little group of Jews who had come back to their homeland. Two of them were influential in moving the people to complete the temple, which had been left unfinished for eighteen years. The third prophet ministered after the time of Nehemiah, and provides a gloomy picture of a people who have again lost any interest in worshiping and obeying God.

Haggai

. . . rebuild the temple!

Who	The prophet Haggai
What	preached four sermons
Where	to the people in Judah
When	in 520 BC
Why	urging them to complete the rebuilding of the temple

God Has a New House

wrest
take in spite of great difficulties

the big picture

Haggai

Through a series of four dated messages, the prophet moved the little Jewish community to complete rebuilding the Jerusalem temple. The messages and their themes are

• Put God first. Finish the temple.	August 29, 520 BC
• God will provide needed finances.	October 17, 520 BC
• From this day I will bless you.	December 18, 520 BC
• David's throne will be established.	December 18, 520 BC

The temple foundations had been laid, but no work had been done on it for years. In part, this was because the Jews were struggling to **wrest** a living from a land that had been untended for decades. Then, on the twenty-ninth of August, 520 BC, the prophet Haggai announced that material blessings had been withheld because God's people had failed to put him first. The little Jewish community took Haggai's words to heart, and, encouraged by additional messages from Haggai, set out to finish building the temple.

What's Special About Haggai?

1. **The glory of the new temple** (Haggai 2:1–15). The little Jewish community was almost destitute. How could they rebuild the temple or beautify it? Through Haggai God reminded the Jews, "The silver is Mine, and the gold is Mine" (Haggai 2:8 NKJV). So the Jews set out in faith to rebuild the temple. Ezra tells us how God provided. The Persian ruler ordered the Jews' enemies to divert their tax money to pay for building the temple!

By the time of Christ, the temple constructed in the year 520 BC had been expanded and beautified to become one of the wonders of the ancient world.

what others say

Martin Luther

Faith is a living, daring confidence in God's grace. It is so sure and certain that a man could stake his life on it a thousand times.[3]

Zechariah

. . . the future of Israel

Who	Zechariah
What	prophesied
Where	to the settlers in Judah
When	at the same time as Haggai
Why	to encourage them to rebuild the temple and expect the appearance of the promised Messiah

fasting
not eating; in Bible times people fasted to show sorrow for sin or fervor in prayer

Riding on a Donkey

the big picture

Zechariah

This book is divided into two main parts. The first part of the book contains a series of visions about the future of the Jewish people and a response to questions about **fasting** by the returned exiles. The second part of the book describes God's intervention at history's end.

- Part I

Eight visions	Zechariah 1:1–6:15
Questions on fasting	Zechariah 7:1–8:23

- Part II

God's shepherd rejected	Zechariah 9:1–11:17
God's final intervention	Zechariah 12:1–14

The prophet Zechariah preached his first sermon on the same day that Haggai preached his second message, October 17, 520 BC. While Zechariah added his voice to Haggai's in urging the Jews to complete the temple, the bulk of Zechariah is filled with visions. His visions incorporate powerful images that focus on history's end. Many of Zechariah's images are incorporated in the final book of the Bible, Revelation.

While Zechariah encouraged his own generation to rebuild the temple, he wanted every generation of God's people to know that God will fulfill the visions of the future that were given to earlier prophets. God's Messiah will come, and his rule will be established on the earth.

What's Special in Zechariah?

1. The eight visions (Zechariah 1:1–8:19). On February 15, 519 BC, Zechariah was given a series of visions. Each vision has to do with the future of the Jewish people. Although gentile world powers would control the Holy Land, God would keep his ancient promises. Below is a list of what Zechariah's visions meant and where the visions can be found:

1. God is watching over Jerusalem. (Zechariah 1:7–17)
2. The nations that dominate Jerusalem will fall. (Zechariah 1:18–21)
3. God will protect and prosper Jerusalem. (Zechariah 2:1–13)
4. The Messiah will come and take away sins. (Zechariah 3:1–10)
5. God will provide the needed resources. (Zechariah 4:1–14)
6. God will punish evildoers. (Zechariah 5:1–4)
7. God will purify the land of wickedness. (Zechariah 5:5–11)
8. God's Messiah will be both priest and king. (Zechariah 6:1–15)

Compare just two of these prophecies and their fulfillments.

Zechariah's Prophecy	New Testament Fulfillment
Behold, your King is coming to you; He is just and having salvation, Lowly and riding on a donkey, A colt, the foal of a donkey. (Zechariah 9:9 NKJV)	They brought the donkey and the colt, laid their clothes on them, and set Him on them. . . . Then the multitudes who went before and those who followed cried out, saying: "Hosanna to the Son of David! Blessed is He who comes in the name of the LORD! Hosanna in the highest!" (Matthew 21:7–9 NKJV)
And the LORD said to me, "Throw it to the potter"—that princely price they set on me. So I took the thirty pieces of silver and threw them into the house of the LORD for the potter. (Zechariah 11:13 NKJV)	Then Judas, His betrayer, seeing that He had been condemned, was remorseful and brought back the thirty pieces of silver to the chief priests and elders. . . . Then he threw down the pieces of silver in the temple and departed, and went and hanged himself. . . . And they consulted together and bought with them the potter's field, to bury strangers in. (Matthew 27:3, 5, 7 NKJV)

2. Questions about <u>fasting</u> (Zechariah 7–8). During the captivity the Jews had observed two solemn holidays commemorating the fall of the city and the destruction of the temple. Zechariah is asked whether, now that the temple is almost completed, the people should continue to observe these holidays, during which they fasted. God's answer?

fasting
Matthew 9:14–15; Acts 13:3

ZECHARIAH 7:9–10
Thus says the LORD of hosts:
"Execute true justice,
Show mercy and compassion
Everyone to his brother.
Do not oppress the widow or the fatherless,
The alien or the poor.
Let none of you plan evil in his heart
Against his brother." (NKJV)

3. God's intervention at history's end (Zechariah 9:1–14:20). These chapters are remarkable because they contain a number of clear prophecies about the Messiah, which were fulfilled by Jesus Christ.

Once again history reveals how accurately Old Testament prophecies are fulfilled in the real world. A number of prophecies in Zechariah correspond to events that took place near the end of Jesus' life. On the first "Palm Sunday," Jesus entered Jerusalem riding on the animal predicted in Zechariah 9:9 (compare Matthew 21:4–5; John 12:12–16). Zechariah predicted his arrest (13:7, compare Matthew 26:31) and that he would be sold for the price of a slave (Zechariah 11:12, compare Matthew 27:3–10). Even his wounding in the "house of [his] friends" (Zechariah 13:6 NKJV) and the piercing of his body on the cross (Zechariah 12:10) were foretold. And they happened just as predicted nearly five hundred years earlier!

Malachi

. . . darkness falls

Who	The prophet Malachi
What	wrote this last Old Testament book
Where	telling the people of Jerusalem
When	around 400 BC
Why	to examine their actions and respond to God's continuing love

We Haven't Done Anything Wrong

God chose the descendants
Romans 9:10–13

Esau
Genesis 36:1–9

the big picture

Malachi

The prophet challenges God's people to honor the Lord, but they insist that they are already on good terms with God. Malachi strips away their self-deceit, giving God's answers to objections they raised denying God's charges. Malachi makes it clear that God's chosen people:

- Neglect God (Malachi 1:6–2:9)
- Break commitments (Malachi 2:10–16)
- Deny God's significance (Malachi 3:4–4:2)

Nehemiah 13 gives details about the repeated sins of those who had resettled Jerusalem. Writing about thirty years later, the prophet Malachi makes it clear that within a few decades God's people were again indifferent to him. This last book of the Old Testament serves as a reminder that throughout history God had been gracious to his people, but again and again they had strayed from him. Surely God must do something dramatically different if he would keep his ancient promises, and redeem humankind.

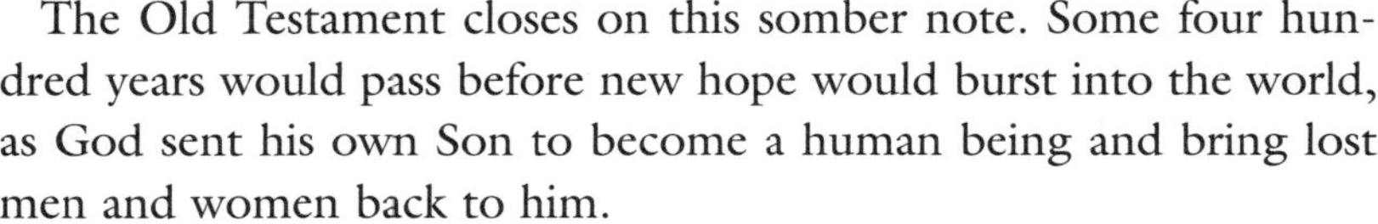

The Old Testament closes on this somber note. Some four hundred years would pass before new hope would burst into the world, as God sent his own Son to become a human being and bring lost men and women back to him.

The book concludes with a promise and a challenge. God will send his people an Elijah to turn their hearts back to him . . . "Lest I come and strike the earth with a curse" (Malachi 4:6 NKJV).

What's Special About Malachi?

1. **God affirms his continuing love for his people** (Malachi 1:2–5). In ancient times God chose the descendants of Abraham, Isaac, and Jacob, to be his own people, while rejecting any claim of the descendants of Esau to a special relationship with him. God has never wavered from that choice, and never will.

2. **God's people have become indifferent and unresponsive** (Malachi 1:6–2:16). Malachi points to actions that support God's charge. The people offer God broken-down animals as sacrifices,

the priests view serving in the temple as a burden, and the people are unfaithful to their spouses. If the people of Judah truly honored God in their hearts, their attitudes and actions would be very different indeed.

People who care deeply about pleasing God are recognized by the lives they live, not by the words they speak.

3. **God marks and remembers individuals who love him** (Malachi 3:14–18). However corrupt the society we live in, people who love God are to meet together and honor him. Malachi contains these special words of promise concerning true believers.

Malachi 3:16–18

Then those who feared the Lord spoke to one another,
And the Lord listened and heard them;
So a book of remembrance was written before Him
For those who fear the Lord
And who meditate on His name.
"They shall be Mine," says the Lord of hosts,
"On the day that I make them My jewels.
And I will spare them
As a man spares his own son who serves him."
Then you shall again discern
Between the righteous and the wicked,
Between one who serves God
And one who does not serve Him. *(NKJV)*

Chapter Wrap-up

- The experiences of Daniel and Esther showed that God continued to care for his people even though they had been expelled from the Promised Land.
- Cyrus the Persian fulfilled Isaiah's prediction by permitting the Jews to return to their homeland and rebuild the Jerusalem temple.
- The prophets Haggai and Zechariah moved the Jews to finish the temple after construction had been halted for eighteen years.
- Ezra was appointed by the Persian king to oversee the administration of Persian law and God's Law in Judah.

- Nehemiah served as governor of Judah. He rebuilt the walls of Jerusalem and kept the people of Judah focused on keeping God's Laws.
- The last book of the Old Testament, Malachi, shows how difficult it was for God's Old Testament people to maintain their zeal for the Lord. To effectively deal with sin, God would have to do something truly new.

Study Questions

1. What Old Testament book expresses the despair of the Jews who were taken captive to Babylon?
2. What book contains a specific prediction about the date on which the promised Messiah would enter Jerusalem as God's promised King?
3. Who were the two leaders whose books tell of the exiles' return to Judah?
4. What book of the Bible teaches by example that God is in control of the details of our lives?
5. What is the name of the ruler whom Isaiah predicted would permit the Jews to return to Jerusalem?
6. What two prophets encouraged the people who returned to finish building God's temple?
7. Approximately when was the last book of the Old Testament written?

The New Testament • Part Two

What Is the New Testament?

The New Testament is a collection of twenty-seven books, all written in the first century **AD**. They tell the story of Jesus of Nazareth, the Savior promised in the Old Testament.

AD
"in the year of our Lord," as opposed to BC, before Christ

Why Is It Called the "New" Testament?

This collection of twenty-seven books is "New" in contrast to the "Old" Testament. It is also called the New Testament because when Jesus died on the cross and rose from the dead, he made possible a new relationship with God for everyone who believes in him.

Get to Know God Personally—by Reading the New Testament

The Old Testament helps us understand what God is like. The New Testament shows us how we can have a personal relationship with God right now. When we have a personal relationship with Jesus we can find fulfillment by loving God and loving other people.

What Is in the New Testament?

The books of the New Testament are divided into four different kinds of writings. All of these books tell about Jesus Christ and what it means to be a follower of Jesus. The most important questions any person can raise are asked and answered in these New Testament writings.

Questions the Bible Raises and Answers

The Gospels

Mattthew, Mark, Luke, John	Who is Jesus? What did Jesus' miracles prove? What did Jesus teach about God? Why did Jesus have to die? Did Jesus really rise from the dead?

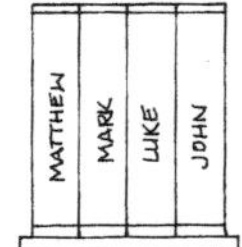

Acts

Acts	What happened to Jesus' followers after he rose from the dead? How did the Christian movement spread? Who did early Christians believe Jesus was?

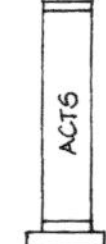

Letters Written by the Apostle Paul

Romans, 1 and 2 Corinthians, Galatians, Ephesians, Philippians, Colossians, 1 and 2 Thessalonians, 1 and 2 Timothy, Titus, Philemon	What does it means to be "saved"? What special powers has God given to Christians? What will happen when Jesus comes back?

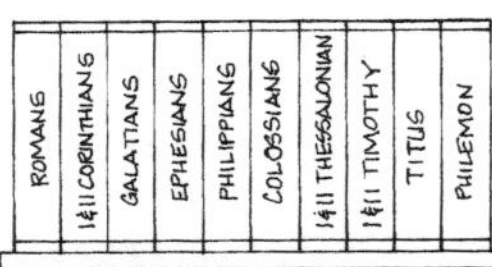

Letters Written by Other Apostles

Hebrews, James, 1 and 2 Peter, 1, 2, and 3 John, Jude	How are followers of Jesus different? Does God talk to believers today? Where is Jesus, and what is he doing right now?

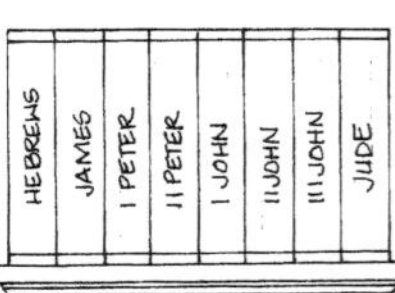

Revelation

Revelation	How will the world end? What will happen to people who have not trusted Jesus as Savior? What will heaven be like?

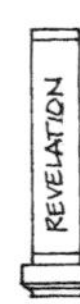

Jesus, the Promised Savior

Let's Get Started

Everyone knows that the central figure of the New Testament is Jesus Christ. Most people have heard the story of his birth in Bethlehem and know that we celebrate Christmas as his birthday. In fact, every time we look at a calendar or write the date, we acknowledge the fact that Jesus is the most important person who ever lived. The way we count time itself is by the days, months, and years before and after Jesus' birth! It makes sense, then, to find out just who this Jesus was as we begin to explore the second half of the Bible, the New Testament. The New Testament is about Jesus. But why? Who is Jesus, anyway?

really lived
Acts 2:22–24

actually God
Hebrews 1:1–4

Apostles' Creed
an early Christian statement of what Jesus' followers believed and taught

creed
from the Latin credo "I believe"

Holy Spirit
God; the third person of the Trinity of this notion about Jesus is found in the Apostles' Creed—a statement that sums up the beliefs of early Christians.

Who Is This Jesus, Anyway?

Everyone admits that Jesus was a real person. He wasn't just a myth or a fictional hero. He really lived. But people do have different ideas about him. Some say he was an ordinary but an especially good person. Some say he was an extraordinary person who was close to God, much like other great religious leaders. Some people even argue that Jesus was a little bit mad, and pictured himself as some sort of Divine Messenger until he got himself killed by going too far.

Christians, though, have a very different idea about Jesus. For almost two thousand years, Christians have been sure that Jesus is actually God. Christians believe that God chose to become a human being and live among us. One of the earliest expressions of this notion about Jesus is found in the Apostles' Creed—a statement that sums up the beliefs of early Christians.

The **Apostles' Creed:**

> I believe in God the Father Almighty, and in Jesus Christ his only Son our Lord, who was born of the **Holy Spirit** and the Virgin Mary; crucified under Pontius Pilate, and buried; the third day he rose from the dead; he ascended

> into heaven and sits at the right hand of the Father, from thence he shall come to judge the quick and the dead. And in the Holy Spirit; the holy Church; the forgiveness of sins; the resurrection of the body; the life everlasting.

So it's clear that to Christians, Jesus, who was a real person, is far from an "ordinary" or even an "extraordinary" man. Christians claim that Jesus was unique. Only Jesus can be called the Son of God, because Jesus was God the Son. Only Jesus rose from the dead and is in heaven today. Only Jesus will come back to judge the living and the dead at history's end.

But why do Christians look at Jesus in this way? The answer is that the whole Bible, not just the New Testament, teaches that Jesus is God.

He Is in the Old Testament

There are hundreds of prophecies in the Old Testament that speak of an Anointed One whom God will send to deliver his people. In Hebrew, "Anointed One" is *Messiah.* In Greek, "Anointed One" is *Christ.* So the name Jesus Christ really means "Jesus the Anointed One," or "Jesus the Messiah."

Many of the Old Testament prophecies describe what the coming Messiah will do. But some of the Old Testament prophecies state very clearly who the Anointed One will be. When we look at these prophecies, we find out that the Old Testament really does teach that the Christ is to be God himself! Here are some of these prophecies.

Psalm 2:7

> ***I will declare the decree:***
> ***The Lord has said to Me,***
> ***"You are My Son,***
> ***Today I have begotten You."*** *(NKJV)*

1. **Psalm 2 pictures the revolt of men against God** (Psalm 2:1–3). It describes God's response to the revolt (Psalm 2:4–6), and tells of the future reign of Christ the Messiah (Psalm 2:7–9). These last verses express God's intention to install his Messiah as the ruler of the whole world. In Psalm 2:7 God calls the Messiah "My Son." The phrase "today I have begotten You" refers to a day when the

Messiah is proved to be God's Son, not to the day he was born. So we have to ask, what day was the Messiah proved to be God the Son?

oracle
2 Samuel 7:12

The New Testament says that when Jesus Christ was raised from the dead he was declared to be the Son of God with power (Romans 1:3). In Acts 13:32–33 the apostle Paul applies Psalm 2:7 to the Resurrection, and so does Hebrews 1:5, where the writer quotes Psalm 2:7 to show that as God, Jesus is greater than angels. The prediction in Psalm 2 was right! God did provide proof that Jesus Christ is the Son of God.

PSALM 45:6–7
Your throne, O God, is forever and ever;
A scepter of righteousness is the scepter of Your kingdom.
You love righteousness and hate wickedness;
Therefore God, Your God, has anointed You
With the oil of gladness more than Your companions.
(NKJV)

2. **This psalm celebrates the final reunion of God with human beings, using the metaphor of a marriage.** In this psalm the bridegroom is the Messiah, who is not only addressed as God, but who because he is God, will reign forever and ever.

what others say

James Smith

Obviously, the only throne which could legitimately be called everlasting would have to be occupied by deity. Nathan's oracle which promised to David an everlasting throne finds fulfillment in this Ruler. He shall reign over the house of Jacob forever, and of his kingdom there shall be no end (Luke 1:33). For this reason Peter speaks of the everlasting kingdom of our Lord and Savior Jesus Christ (2 Peter 1:11).[1]

ISAIAH 7:14 ***Therefore the Lord Himself will give you a sign: Behold, the virgin shall conceive and bear a Son, and shall call His name Immanuel. (NKJV)***

3. **Three things are striking about this prophecy.** The first is that it speaks of the child of a virgin, born without a human father. The second is that the child is to be named Immanuel. The name in Hebrew means God with us. And the third is that Isaiah made this prophecy seven hundred years before Jesus was born!

What God promised through Isaiah was that God would come to be with us by being born as a baby to a virgin. And this is exactly what we celebrate at Christmas: the birth of the baby Jesus to the Virgin Mary!

what others say

John F. MacArthur Jr.

The virgin birth is an underlying assumption of everything the Bible says about Jesus. To throw out the virgin birth is to reject Christ's deity, the accuracy and authority of Scripture, and a host of other related doctrines that are the heart of the Christian faith. No issue is more important than the virgin birth to our understanding of who Jesus is. If we deny that Jesus is God, we have denied the very essence of Christianity.[2]

Isaiah 9:6–7

For unto us a Child is born,
Unto us a Son is given;
And the government will be upon His shoulder.
And His name will be called
Wonderful, Counselor, Mighty God,
Everlasting Father, Prince of Peace.
Of the increase of His government and peace
There will be no end,
Upon the throne of David and over His kingdom,
To order it and establish it with judgment and justice
From that time forward, even forever.
The zeal of the LORD of hosts will perform this. (NKJV)

4. **This prophecy of Isaiah makes it very clear that the Messiah is God as well as man.** Isaiah says that the child who is born is already a Son when he is given. It was God the Son, not God the Father, who was born in Bethlehem. As far as his human family was concerned, he was a descendant of David, for his mother and stepfather, Joseph, were both descendants of King David. But what does Isaiah say about him as the Son? Look at the names Isaiah assigns to him.

- He is Mighty God.
- He is Everlasting Father, a phrase that in Hebrew means the father, or source, of Eternity!
- As the Messiah, he will reign on David's throne forever.

Clearly the Old Testament teaches that the child who is to be born is to be God himself!

what others say

Edward J. Young

With this revealed truth may our hearts delight, for he who is born the mighty God is therefore able to save all those who put their trust in him.[3]

ruler
Luke 1:34–35; Matthew 1:20–21

everlasting
before time began or anything was created

Jews
not the Jewish people, but the religious leaders

Sabbath
Saturday, the seventh day of the week

MICAH 5:2

But you, Bethlehem Ephrathah,
Though you are little among the thousands of Judah,
Yet out of you shall come forth to Me
The One to be Ruler in Israel,
Whose goings forth are from of old,
*From **everlasting**.* (NKJV)

5. **This famous prophecy identifies Bethlehem** (see Illustration #13) **as the birthplace of the Messiah**. Some seven hundred years after Micah made this prediction, Jesus was born—in Bethlehem. As the promised Messiah, he is to be ruler over Israel. But this prophecy adds that although born as a baby, his origins are from of old, from everlasting (eternity). And who has existed from eternity? Only God.

Once again we see that the Old Testament indicates that the promised Messiah or Christ is to be God as well as a human being.

what others say

C. F. Keil

The announcement of the origin of this Ruler as being before all worlds unquestionably presupposes his divine nature; but this thought was not strange to the prophetic mind in Micah's time; it is expressed without ambiguity by Isaiah, when he gives the Messiah the name of the Mighty God.[4]

It's clear that the Old Testament did teach that the promised Christ was to be God as well as man. Some, though, have said that Jesus never claimed to be God. But when we read the Gospels, which describe Jesus' life on earth, we find that he really did say that he was God—and that his listeners understood his claims!

JOHN 5:17–18 *Jesus answered them, "My Father has been working until now, and I have been working." Therefore the **Jews** sought all the more to kill Him, because He not only broke the **Sabbath**, but also said that God was His Father, making Himself equal with God.* (NKJV)

I AM
Exodus 3:14

JOHN 8:58–59 ***Jesus said to them, "Most assuredly, I say to you, before Abraham was, I AM." Then they took up stones to throw at Him; but Jesus hid Himself and went out of the temple, going through the midst of them, and so passed by.*** *(NKJV)*

MALACHI 3:1
Behold, I send My messenger,
And he will prepare the way before Me.
And the Lord, whom you seek,
Will suddenly come to His temple. *(NKJV)*

6. **The people in Malachi's day were asking "Where is the God of justice?"** God through the prophet warned them that "the Lord, whom you seek, will suddenly come to His temple." In this prophecy about the Messiah he is identified in the Hebrew as the Lord—God himself—who comes to his own temple.

How Could He Claim That?

1. **Jesus' listeners understood what we might miss.** In comparing what he was doing to God's working in this world, and in calling God his Father, Jesus was actually claiming equality with God! The religious leaders either had to accept Jesus' claim and worship him as God, or reject Jesus' claim. They refused to believe that Jesus was God's Son, and instead tried to kill him!
2. **When God revealed his personal name to Moses, he identified himself as I AM.** John 8 records a debate Jesus had with some of the Jewish religious leaders. Christ not only claimed God as his Father but told them, "Your father Abraham rejoiced to see My day, and he saw it and was glad" (John 8:56 NKJV). The leaders objected that Jesus, not even fifty years old, should claim to have known what Abraham had thought. Jesus' response was to claim that he existed long before Abraham was born—because Jesus was himself the I AM, the Jehovah, of the Old Testament!

Again Christ's contemporaries understood his claim of deity. They reacted by trying to stone him to death, because they did not believe he was who he said.

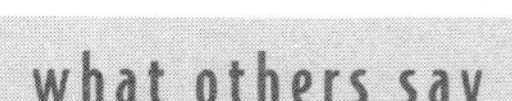

Craig S. Keener

I AM was a title for God. Jesus is claiming more than that he merely existed before Abraham.[5]

MATTHEW 16:16–17 ***Simon Peter answered and said, "You are the Christ, the Son of the living God." Jesus answered and said to him, "Blessed are you, Simon Bar-Jonah, for flesh and blood has not revealed this to you, but My Father who is in heaven."*** *(NKJV)*

raised from the dead
1 Corinthians 15:3–8

Sanhedrin
the Jewish supreme court

3. **Jesus had sent his disciples to circulate among the crowds and listen to what they were saying about him.** The disciples reported that everyone knew he was someone special, as great as the prophets of old. Jesus then asked the disciples who they said he was. Peter answered for them. Jesus was not merely a prophet but the Messiah, the Son of God.

Jesus' response to Peter makes it very clear that he confirmed the disciples' impression. Jesus was far greater than any prophet of old, for as the promised Christ, Jesus was God the Son.

MATTHEW 26:63–64 ***The high priest answered and said to Him, "I put You under oath by the living God: Tell us if You are the Christ, the Son of God!" Jesus said to him, "It is as you said."*** *(NKJV)*

4. **Jesus had been arrested and dragged before the Sanhedrin. Finally the high priest ordered Jesus to tell them whether he was the Christ.** Note that the high priest added "the Son of God." The high priest, who knew the Old Testament, was well aware that the Christ was to be God himself!

Jesus told them yes, he was the Christ, and he was God the Son. Jesus knew who he was. The religious leaders simply refused to believe him.

what others say

C. S. Lewis

Christians believe that Jesus Christ is the Son of God because he said so. The other evidence about him has convinced them that he was neither a lunatic nor a quack.[6]

Proof Positive

After Jesus was crucified and raised from the dead, the apostle Peter preached a powerful sermon in Jerusalem. That sermon is recorded in chapter 2 of the New Testament book of Acts. Peter talked about Jesus, whose miracles his listeners had witnessed, and whose crucifixion, which had taken place just two months prior, they were well aware of.

prophecies
Psalm 16:9–10;
Isaiah 53:9, 11

Peter quoted Old Testament prophecies that foretold that the Messiah would die and be raised to life again, and that such proved the Messiah was God himself. Pointing to the resurrection of Jesus as the final proof, Peter announced,

ACTS 2:36 ***Therefore let all the house of Israel know assuredly that God has made this Jesus, whom you crucified, both Lord and Christ.*** *(NKJV)*

The resurrection of Jesus was proof positive. Jesus was both Lord (God) and Christ (the promised Messiah). With the resurrection of Jesus all doubt about who Jesus is was put to rest.

He's in the New Testament Too?

After the resurrection of Jesus, there was no room for doubt about who Jesus was and is. The New Testament makes a number of absolutely clear statements about him.

JOHN 1:1–3, 10, 14 ***In the beginning was the Word, and the Word was with God, and the Word was God. He was in the beginning with God. All things were made through Him, and without Him nothing was made that was made. . . . He was in the world, and the world was made through Him, and the world did not know Him. . . . And the Word became flesh and dwelt among us, and we beheld His glory, the glory as of the only begotten of the Father, full of grace and truth.*** *(NKJV)*

1. **John the Apostle was one of Jesus' followers.** He wrote his Gospel some fifty years after Jesus was crucified and raised from the dead. John's special name here for God the Son is "the Word." What John is saying is that God the Son has always been associated with communicating God to human beings. As the Word he spoke to Abraham and to Moses. As the Word he spoke through the prophets. And now God the Son, the eternal Word, became flesh. He was born as a human being, and lived for a while among us. Jesus Christ is God and has always been God.

ROMANS 1:1–4 ***The gospel of God which He promised before through His prophets in the Holy Scriptures, concerning His Son Jesus Christ our Lord, who was born of the seed of David***

according to the flesh, and declared to be the Son of God with power according to the Spirit of holiness, by the resurrection from the dead. *(NKJV)*

2. The apostle Paul reminds us that there were no real secrets about the coming Messiah. God had told his people about the Christ beforehand. All a person had to do was to read the Old Testament prophets to know that the Christ would be a descendant of David, and to know that the Christ would also be God! The resurrection of Jesus was the final proof that Jesus was the One about whom the prophets spoke.

Jesus was and is the Son of God. In Philippians the apostle Paul urges Christians to follow Jesus' example of thinking of others. He then describes how much God the Son sacrificed in order to come to earth as a human being.

PHILIPPIANS 2:5–11 ***Let this mind be in you which was also in Christ Jesus, who, being in the form of God, did not consider it robbery to be equal with God, but made Himself of no reputation, taking the form of a bondservant, and coming in the likeness of men. And being found in appearance as a man, He humbled Himself and became obedient to the point of death, even the death of the cross. Therefore God also has highly exalted Him and given Him the name which is above every name, that at the name of Jesus every knee should bow, of those in heaven, and of those on earth, and of those under the earth, and that every tongue should confess that Jesus Christ is Lord, to the glory of God the Father.*** *(NKJV)*

3. While on earth Christ never stopped being God, but he gave up the prerogatives of deity. Jesus allowed himself to be treated as a slave and even put to death by creatures he himself had created!

Even though the Old Testament prophets said that the Christ would be God, some in the first century were confused. Was Jesus an angel rather than God himself? To make very clear just who Jesus was and is, the apostle Paul wrote these words in a letter to the Colossians:

COLOSSIANS 1:15–17 ***He is the image of the invisible God, the firstborn over all creation. For by Him all things were created that are in heaven and that are on earth, visible and invisible, whether thrones or dominions or principalities or powers. All***

things were created through Him and for Him. And He is before all things, and in Him all things consist. (NKJV)

4. **Several phrases in this paragraph are important.** . . . the image of the invisible God . . .Jesus is the visible expression of the invisible God. . . . the first born over all creation . . . In Bible times "firstborn" was a legal term that identified a person as the heir with the right to inherit an estate. Paul is not implying that the Son of God was created. Paul is saying that as God the Son, Jesus is the rightful heir to the universe . . . for by Him all things were created. . . . To make sure that his reference to firstborn is not misunderstood, Paul goes on to declare that Jesus is the Creator of everything that exists. In the Bible, powers or rulers or authorities are angels. Jesus can't be an angel, because he created every being that exists in the invisible as well as the visible realm.

Who is Jesus? He is the very One the Old Testament said the Christ would be: the promised Messiah, God himself! As God, Christ not only created the universe, but even now his power is all that holds the universe together.

HEBREWS 1:1–3 ***God, who at various times and in various ways spoke in time past to the fathers by the prophets, has in these last days spoken to us by His Son, whom He has appointed heir of all things, through whom also He made the worlds; who being the brightness of His glory and the express image of His person, and upholding all things by the word of His power . . .*** (NKJV)

5. **The writer of Hebrews begins by reviewing how God has communicated with human beings in the past.** Those older ways of speaking to us have now been superseded. These verses make a number of important points.

- God spoke to us by his Son.
- Jesus is the Son of God.
- The Son is the One who made the worlds.
- The Son is the brightness of God's glory.
- The Son is the express image of his being.
- The Son even now upholds all things.

manifest
revealed, clearly seen

what others say

F. F. Bruce

He is the very image of the essence of God—the impress of his being. Just as the image and superscription on a coin exactly correspond to the device on the die, so the Son of God bears the very stamp of his nature. . . . What God essentially is, is made **manifest** in Christ. To see Christ is to see what the Father is like.[7]

So Why Did He Come?

When we look at the evidence, it's clear that the Old and New Testaments agree on who Jesus is. Jesus is God the Son. The Old Testament Messiah promised by the prophets was to be God himself. Jesus himself claimed to be the Son of God, and the resurrection of Jesus is proof that he was telling the truth. The New Testament writers unequivocally identify Jesus as the very God who created the universe. So the testimony of the Bible is consistent and clear.

But why would God choose to come into our world and live here as a human being? Why would God let his Son be crucified, and why would Jesus willingly go to the cross?

That's something we'll find out as we look further into the New Testament, and see how it explains Jesus' death and resurrection. For now, though, we can contemplate something that Jesus said:

> **JOHN 3:16** ***For God so loved the world that He gave His only begotten Son, that whoever believes in Him should not perish but have everlasting life.*** *(NKJV)*

Jesus came because God loves us. And because Jesus came, everyone who believes in him can have everlasting life.

Chapter Wrap-Up

- The Apostles' Creed is an early statement of the Christian's belief that Jesus is God.
- The prophet Isaiah predicted that a virgin would have a child, and that her child would be God with us. (Isaiah 7:14)
- The prophet Micah predicted that the Christ would be born in Bethlehem but that his origins would be from everlasting. (Micah 5:2)
- Jesus claimed to be the I AM—the God—of the Old Testament. (John 8:58)
- The resurrection of Jesus proved that he really was the Son of God. (Romans 1:3)
- Hebrews says that Jesus is the express image of God's being. (Hebrews 1:3)
- Jesus said that love motivated God to send his Son into the world, to give everlasting life to those who believe in Jesus. (John 3:16)

Study Questions

1. Who is the central figure in the New Testament?
2. Identify two of the four Old Testament passages that indicate the Messiah is to be God himself.
3. Identify two of the four passages that report Jesus' own claim to be God.
4. What New Testament passage teaches specifically that even though Jesus was God, he became a real human being?
5. What event proved that Jesus really was and is God?

Jesus' Birth and Preparation

Let's Get Started

The New Testament begins with four Gospels. Each **Gospel** is an account of Jesus' life on earth. The first three Gospels are called **synoptic** Gospels, because they are each organized chronologically. In this chapter we'll look briefly at each of the four Gospels, and begin to trace the story of Jesus' life on earth.

gospel
"good news"

synoptic
a summary, telling the story of Jesus' life in chronological order

Roman Empire
in the first century, Europe, England, Egypt, Asia Minor, and the whole Middle East were part of Rome's empire

Holy Land
modern-day Israel and Palestine

All About Jesus

Each Gospel tells the same story, often describing the same events in almost the same words. Why, then, are their four accounts of Jesus' life in the New Testament? The reason is that each of the Gospel writers shapes his account of Christ's life for a different group of people in the first-century **Roman Empire**. Matthew shaped his account for the Jewish reader, emphasizing how Jesus fulfilled the Old Testament's prophecies about the Messiah. Mark shaped his account for the Romans, to show that Jesus was a man of action. Luke shaped his account for the Greeks, to show that Christ was the ideal human being. John's Gospel emphasizes Christ's deity, and was written to stimulate saving faith in Jesus, the Son of God.

Matthew

. . . good news for the Jews

Who	The disciple Matthew
What	wrote this account of Jesus' life
Where	in the **Holy Land**
When	around AD 60
Why	to prove to the Jews that Jesus is the promised Messiah of the Old Testament

pragmatic
practical

MATTHEW: Matthew was a tax collector—a collaborator with the Romans in exploiting his own people. When Jesus called him to become a disciple, Matthew immediately left his despised occupation and committed himself to follow Christ.

What's Special About Matthew's Gospel?

Over and over again Matthew quotes or refers to the Old Testament to show how Jesus fulfilled its prophecies concerning the Messiah. Highlights in Matthew's Gospel, which are emphasized more than in the other Gospels, are

- Jesus' Sermon on the Mount (Matthew 5–7)
- Jesus' parables of the kingdom (Matthew 11–13)
- Jesus' teaching about the future (Matthew 24, 25)

Mark

. . . good news for the Romans

Who	John Mark
What	wrote this account of Jesus' life
Where	in Rome
When	around AD 55
Why	to present Jesus to the Romans as a man of authority and action

MARK: Mark was a young person when Jesus died. After Jesus' resurrection, Mark became one of the apostles on Peter's missionary team. His Gospel records Peter's eyewitness stories of Jesus' life and ministry.

What's Special About Mark's Gospel?

Mark is the shortest of the Gospels. It focuses on Jesus' actions, rather than on his teachings, in order to demonstrate his authority, which appealed to the **pragmatic** Roman. About a third of the book is about Jesus' last week on earth, ending with Christ's death and resurrection.

Luke

. . . good news for the Greek

Who	The physician Luke
What	wrote this account of Jesus' life
Where	in Caesarea
When	around AD 58, while Paul was in prison
Why	to present Jesus as an ideal human being who came to seek and to save the lost

LUKE: Luke was a medical doctor who was converted on the apostle Paul's first missionary journey, and who became a member of Paul's missionary team. His writing style shows him to have been a highly educated man. Luke traveled with Paul until the apostle was executed. He also wrote the book of Acts, an account of the spread of the gospel after Jesus' resurrection.

What's Special About Luke's Gospel?

Luke is the longest of the Gospels, written after he carefully investigated everything from the beginning (Luke 1:3) by interviewing eyewitnesses to the events of Jesus' life. Luke was particularly interested in showing Jesus' concern for women, the poor, and the oppressed. While Luke follows the same chronological plan as Matthew and Mark, Luke includes six miracles and nineteen parables that are not found in the other Gospels.

John

. . . good news for all!

Who	The apostle John
What	wrote this theological account of Jesus' acts and teachings
Where	in Ephesus of Asia Minor
When	from AD 80 to AD 90
Why	to inspire saving faith in Jesus Christ

JOHN: John was a partner in a successful fishing business with his brothers James and Peter when all three were invited by Jesus to follow him. John lived well into his nineties. He also wrote three of the New Testament Epistles and the book of Revelation.

What's Special About the Gospel of John?

John's Gospel is not organized chronologically. Instead, John selects miracles and teachings of Jesus that emphasize key theological themes, such as New Birth (John 3), Everlasting Life (John 5), Truth (John 8), Life (John 11), and Belief and Unbelief (John 4, 7, 12). Also, all of the events reported by John take place in Judea and Jerusalem. John does not report events that took place in Galilee (see Illustration #13).

Highlights in John's Gospel, which are not found in any of the others, include:

- Jesus' raising of Lazarus (John 11)
- Jesus' last teachings to his disciples (John 13–16)
- Jesus' prayer for believers (John 17)

They All Flow in Harmony

One way to review the life of Christ is to study each Gospel separately. Another way is to follow the chronological order set in the first three Gospels, and to draw from each Gospel. We'll follow the second approach. Here's an outline.

Overview of the Life of Jesus Christ

Chapter 13	Jesus' miraculous birth
	John the Baptist
	Jesus' baptism
	Jesus' temptation
Chapter 14	Jesus demonstrates his authority
	Jesus' teachings about God
	Jesus' involvement in controversies
Chapter 15	Jesus' instructions to his disciples
	Jesus faces opposition
Chapter 16	Jesus' presentation as Israel's king
	Jesus' rejection and death
	Jesus' resurrection

Away in a Manger

Jesus was born
Matthew 1–2;
Luke 1–3

God the Son
John 1:1–3

the big picture

Jesus' Birth

When Jesus was born, the Roman Empire (under the emperor Augustus) dominated the Mediterranean world. The Holy Land was governed by King Herod the Great, who ruled for Rome. The first hint that the long-awaited age of the Messiah was about to dawn was a series of angelic visitations to a couple of surprisingly ordinary people. But both met one vital criteria: They were both descendants of King David, from whose line the prophets said the Messiah would come.

MARY: At the time Jesus was born Mary was a teenage girl of modest means, engaged to a carpenter named Joseph. Mary's simple and complete faith in God was displayed when she accepted the role of being Christ's mother, even though she was a virgin and her pregnancy would be misunderstood.

JOSEPH: Joseph the carpenter was engaged to Mary. When he heard she was pregnant he planned to break the engagement, but was visited by an angel who told him that Mary had not been unfaithful to her engagement commitments.

HEROD THE GREAT: The powerful king of the Jews was aged and dying when Jesus was born. Yet when he heard that a King of the Jews had been born, Herod tried desperately to murder the young child.

What's Special About the Story of Jesus' Birth?

1. **Christ was God the Son before Jesus was born** (John 1:1–14). John 12 shows that the Old Testament, Jesus himself, and the New Testament all teach that Jesus Christ is God the Son, who existed from eternity. Christ's life did not begin when Jesus was born!
2. **Jesus' two genealogies prove he descended from David** (Matthew 1:2–17; Luke 3:23–37). The Old Testament stated that the promised Messiah would be a descendant of David. Both Matthew and Luke trace Jesus' ancestry, naming only the most significant individuals. Both include David, but the two lists do not name all the same ancestors! Is the Bible wrong? The answer

is that one genealogy is that of Mary, Jesus' mother, while the other is that of Joseph, whom neighbors supposed was Jesus' father!

announced by angels
Luke 15–23; 1:26–38; 2:8–19; Matthew 1:18–25

> **what others say**
>
> **Graham Scroggie**
>
> The Davidic descent of Jesus was never questioned. The claim to be the Messiah was never contested on the ground that his descent from David was doubtful. Those who did not accept the virgin birth would know that Jesus' title was determined by Joseph's line, and those who did accept the virgin birth must have had some reason for believing that Mary was of Davidic descent.[1]

angels
spirit beings who serve God

Gabriel
an archangel

archangel
a leader or angel of the highest rank

betrothed
engaged to be married

3. Angelic visitations are associated with Jesus' birth! While every child's birth is special, they are not normally announced by **angels**. Yet the Gospels record no less than six angelic visitations linked with the birth and infancy of Jesus! Jesus was special indeed.

1. The angel **Gabriel**; an **archangel**, the most powerful of angels, foretold the birth of John the Baptist. The Old Testament predicted that God would send a messenger like Elijah to his people just before the Messiah appeared (see Malachi 4:5–6). Gabriel appeared to a priest named Zechariah and announced he would have a son named John who would fulfill this prophecy.
2. The angel Gabriel appeared to a young virgin named Mary and announced she would have a child who would be the Messiah and also the Son of the Most High.
3. The angel Gabriel appeared to Joseph, who was **betrothed** to Mary, and told him that Mary's child was the Son of God the Holy Spirit. The angel told Joseph to name the child Jesus, because he will save his people from their sins.
4. The night Jesus was born, a host of angels appeared to shepherds in fields near Bethlehem, announcing that "there is born to you this day in the city of David a Savior, who is Christ the Lord" (Luke 2:11 NKJV).
5. Later, an angel warned Joseph to leave Bethlehem and take his son to Egypt (see Matthew 2:13).

6. Still later, another angel told Joseph it was safe to return to his Jewish homeland (see Matthew 2:19–21).

4. Jesus' birth and childhood fulfilled Old Testament prophecies. Matthew, who was especially concerned with showing Jesus to be the Messiah promised in the Old Testament, notes a number of prophecies that were fulfilled by Jesus' birth:

Prophecy	Given in . . .	Fulfilled in . . .
He was born of a virgin	Isaiah 7:14	Matthew 1:20
He was born in Bethlehem	Micah 5:2	Matthew 2:3–6
Herod murdered infants in an attempt to kill Jesus	Jeremiah 31:15	Matthew 2:16–18
He was then taken to Egypt	Hosea 11:1	Matthew 2:13
He grew up in Nazareth	Isaiah 40:3	Matthew 2:21–23

what others say

J. W. Shepherd

Matthew desiring to link the person of the Messiah with ancient prophecy gave his own independent account. Luke narrates in simplicity and brevity, with consummate art the circumstances of the birth, and adds the testimony of various divinely chosen witnesses, who give the interpretation and worldwide significance of the event. Matthew adds to this testimony of universal interest, introducing the narrative of the Magi, the providential flight into Egypt and return to Nazareth in fulfillment of God's plan revealed in prophecy.[2]

5. Witnesses confirm the identity of Jesus (Matthew 2:1–12; Luke 2:12–38). Matthew and Luke report other witnesses who confirm the uniqueness of Jesus. Two of the witnesses gave their testimony publicly when Mary, following Old Testament Law, came to the temple with Jesus to offer a sacrifice for her purification. The other witnesses appeared when Jesus was about two years old. These witnesses are:

1. Simeon, a devout Jew who had been promised he would see the Messiah before he died. God led him to the temple and to the infant Jesus.
2. Anna, a prophetess who served God in the temple after her husband died. The day of her husband's death, Anna identified Jesus as the Messiah to all who were looking forward to the redemption of Jerusalem.

Magi
Persian scholars

evangelistic
calling people to respond to the message of the gospel

3. The wise men (Matthew 2:1–12). They are called **Magi** by Matthew. They saw a special star that indicated a "King of the Jews" had been born, and they traveled westward from Persia to Jerusalem. Although the story is told at Christmas, Jesus was about two years old when the wise men appeared. The gifts they brought were rich ones, and financed the family's flight to Egypt when King Herod tried to have Jesus killed.

6. Jesus lived and grew up as an ordinary child (Luke 2:40–51). The only incident from Jesus' childhood reported in the Bible tells how at age twelve he showed an understanding of God and his ways that amazed adult teachers.

what others say

Alfred Edersheim

Of the many years spent in Nazareth, during which Jesus passed from infancy to childhood, from childhood to youth, from youth to manhood, the **evangelistic** narrative has left us but briefest notice. Of his childhood: that he grew and waxed strong in spirit, filled with wisdom, and the grace of God was upon him (Luke 2:40); of his youth: besides the account of his questioning the Rabbis in the Temple, the year before he attained Jewish majority—that he was subject to his parents and that he increased in wisdom and stature, and in favour with God and man (Luke 2:52).[5]

Repent

the big picture

John the Baptist

Jesus' cousin. His birth and mission had also been announced by an angel. When Jesus was about thirty years old, John the Baptist began to preach in the Jordan River Valley. His message to Israel was "repent," because the promised Messiah was about to appear.

What's Special About John the Baptist's Mission?

1. John's ministry was predicted by Old Testament prophets (Luke 3:4–6). The Gospel writers quote Isaiah 40:3–5 to describe John's role in preparing the way for Jesus. That prophecy says:

LUKE 3:4–6 *The voice of one crying in the wilderness: "Prepare the way of the Lord; make His paths straight. Every valley shall be filled and every mountain and hill brought low; the crooked places shall be made straight and the rough ways smooth; and all flesh shall see the salvation of God."* (NKJV)

baptism, Jesus
Matthew 3:13–17;
Mark 1:9–11;
Luke 3:21–23;
John 1:19–34

baptized
symbolizing the complete renewal and change in the believer's life

2. **John's message was one of repentance** (Luke 3:7–14; Matthew 3:4–10; Mark 1:2–6). John urged those who came to hear him to repent, stop sinning, and seek forgiveness. John **baptized** those who confessed their sins and promised to change.

3. **John's promise of the coming Savior** (Matthew 3:11–12; Mark 1:7–8; Luke 3:15–18). When people asked if John might be the Messiah, John told them that Christ was coming. He baptized them with water. John told them the Messiah was far greater than he. He promised that the Messiah would baptize with the Holy Spirit and with fire.

He Has Come

the big picture

Jesus' Baptism

One day Jesus came to the riverside and asked John to baptize him. John refused at first, knowing that his cousin was not guilty of the sins against which he preached. Jesus insisted on being baptized to show his solidarity with John's message. When Jesus was baptized, John heard God speak from heaven, identifying Jesus as "my beloved Son," and the Holy Spirit settled on Christ in the form of a dove. John realized that Jesus was the Messiah he had been sent to announce, and told some of his own followers that Jesus was the One.

What's Special About Jesus' Baptism?

1. **At the baptism, Jesus was identified as the Messiah** (John 1:29–34). God had told John that the Holy Spirit would descend visibly on the Messiah. The voice from heaven and the dove marked Jesus as the promised Messiah.

John's baptism signified repentance for sins committed. But Jesus had committed no sins. Knowing this, John, who was Jesus' cousin, at first refused to baptize him. Why did Jesus want to be baptized? Because it was the right thing for Jesus to show solidarity with John's message.

2. **After the baptism John pointed Jesus out as the Messiah** (John 1:35).

John's announcement that Jesus was God's Son was Jesus' official presentation to the nation as their promised Messiah. John's work as the forerunner who would prepare the way for the promised Savior was completed when he identified Jesus as the One the Old Testament promised.

Jesus' temptation
Matthew 4:1–11; Mark 1:12–13; Luke 4:1–13

tempted
Genesis 3:1–7

I Dare You

the big picture

Jesus' Temptation

After Jesus was baptized he was led by the Holy Spirit into the wilderness. There he went without eating for forty days. When he was physically weakened, Satan appeared and tempted Jesus, three times. Jesus resisted each temptation and by so doing proved his moral right to be mankind's Savior. Only a sinless person could die for the sins of others. Only after Jesus had demonstrated his own ability to triumph over temptation did he begin to preach to others.

JESUS: Jesus, who is both fully human and truly God, faces each temptation using resources available to everyone who trusts God.

SATAN: Satan is the evil angel who tricked Eve into sinning in the Garden of Eden. Satan tries, but is unable to get Jesus to do anything that is out of the will of God.

What's Special About the Temptation of Jesus?

1. **The temptation to turn stones to bread** (Matthew 4:1–4). Physical needs and desires are one source of temptation that all human beings experience. When Jesus hungered, Satan challenged him to turn stones into bread. Jesus refused, quoting Deuteronomy 8:3, which teaches that human beings are not to live by bread alone but by every word that comes from the mouth of God. Human beings aren't animals who live by instinct. We can make choices, and our choices are to be guided by God.

2. The temptation to prove God is present (Matthew 4:5–7). Satan took Jesus to the highest point of the temple and challenged him to jump. Satan quoted Psalm 91:11–12 to show that God would intervene and not let Jesus be hurt. Jesus quoted Deuteronomy 6:16, which says people are not to test God. Human beings are to live by faith, not by trying to make God prove he is there for us.

abyss
chasm, depths

what others say

G. Campbell Morgan

To have cast himself from the wing of the Temple into the **abyss** would have been to tempt God, and in the last and final analysis would have demonstrated not trust, but lack of confidence. It is when we doubt a person that we make experiments to discover how far they are to be trusted. To make experiment of any kind with God, is to reveal the fact that one is not quite sure of him.[4]

3. The third temptation (Matthew 4:8–11). Satan then offered Jesus immediate control of all the kingdoms of the world— if only Jesus would worship him. In the end Jesus would rule over the universe, but this would happen only after he went to the cross. Jesus refused to avoid the suffering that lay ahead. He would worship and serve God alone.

4. Jesus used Scripture in meeting each temptation. In the Old Testament Scriptures Jesus found an answer to each of Satan's temptations. God's Word can help us overcome our temptations too, but we must use the Bible the same way Jesus did. Christ did not just quote a Bible verse, he acted on what that verse taught.

When we commit ourselves to do what the Bible teaches, we too will be well on our way to overcoming our temptations.

Chapter Wrap-Up

- The four Gospel accounts of Jesus' life on earth were shaped to appeal to the major groups of people in the first-century Roman Empire.
- John's Gospel is the "universal Gospel." It emphasizes the fact that Jesus came and died to save all human beings, whatever their ethnic backgrounds.
- Jesus' birth was unique in that (1) it was announced several times by angels, (2) it was a fulfillment of several Old Testament prophecies, and (3) he was born of a virgin without a human father. (Matthew 1, 2; Luke 1–3)
- John the Baptist fulfilled the prophecy of Isaiah, that a prophet would announce the Messiah's appearance. (Isaiah 40:1–3)
- God identified Jesus as the Messiah when he was baptized by John. (Matthew 3; Luke 3)
- Jesus proved his moral right to be the Savior by overcoming Satan's temptations. (Matthew 4; Luke 4)

Study Questions

1. Who wrote the Gospel directed to the Jews?
2. Who wrote the Gospel directed to the Romans?
3. Which Gospel does not tell the story of Jesus' life in chronological order?
4. Why are the two genealogies of Jesus different?
5. What marked Jesus' birth as special and unusual?
6. What was the message of John the Baptist?
7. What happened at Jesus' baptism that showed he was the promised Messiah?
8. Why was it important that Jesus not surrender to Satan's temptations?

Jesus' Early Ministry

Let's Get Started

After Jesus' baptism and triumph over temptation, he began to instruct and preach in Galilee and Judea (see Illustration #13). He was quickly labeled different from other teachers when he performed miracles that stunned those who came to hear him. He taught as if he spoke with God's own authority. The religious leaders felt threatened by this wonder-worker, so they opposed him, even though ordinary people flocked to hear him. But everyone remained at least a little uncertain about who Jesus really was.

Palestine
the Holy land

disciple
a person being trained by another

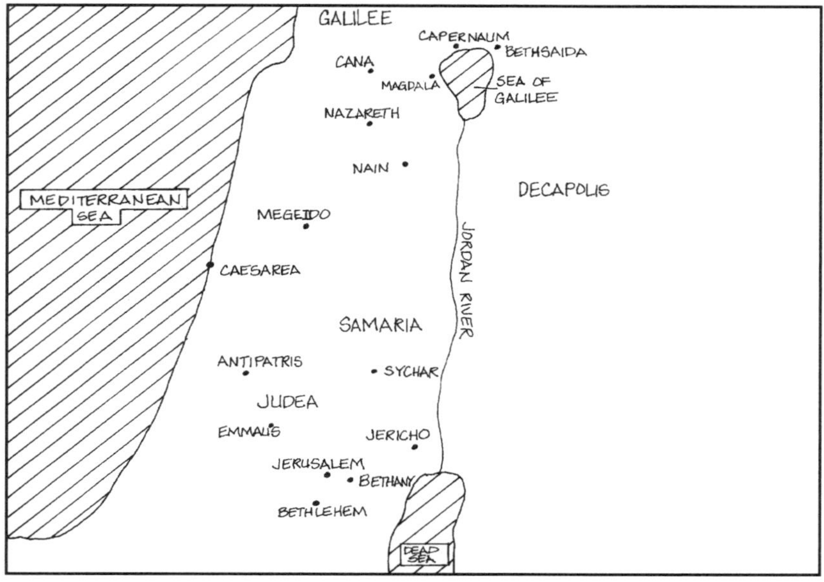

Illustration #13
First-century **Palestine**—Jesus taught and performed miracles in Galilee and in Judea for about three years.

THE DISCIPLES: Several significant groups appear in the Gospel stories about Jesus. The most important are Jesus' disciples and the religious leaders who opposed him.

Jesus chose twelve men to travel with him. He was training them to continue his work when he was gone. While the word "**disciple**" is sometimes used to describe anyone who followed Jesus, "the disciples" refers to these twelve. Of the twelve, Peter, James, and John were closest to Jesus. The twelve disciples were:

Peter	Andrew	Matthew	Thaddaeus
James	Philip	Thomas	Simon
John	Bartholomew	James (the less)	Judas

miracles that Jesus performed
Matthew 4–12;
Mark 1–3;
Luke 4–6;
John 2–5

THE PHARISEES: The Pharisees were a small but influential group of men who claimed to follow every detail of God's Law. They believed that both the Scriptures and the **rabbis'** interpretations of Scripture were equally binding. Jesus followed the Scripture but ignored the interpretations of the rabbis. The Pharisees quickly became Jesus' enemies.

rabbis
teachers of Old Testament Law

miracles
events supernaturally caused by God

THE SADDUCEES: The Sadducees were wealthy men who controlled the priesthood. They were rivals of the Pharisees, and recognized only the first five books of the Old Testament as Scripture. But they joined the Pharisees in opposing Jesus, whom they saw as a threat to their wealth and power.

Miracles from on High

the big picture

Miracles

The Gospels contain many accounts of **miracles** that Jesus performed. These miracles made it clear that Jesus was a messenger from God. As a man who had been blind from birth (until Jesus gave him sight) stated, "If this Man were not from God, He could do nothing" (John 9:33 NKJV). Even more significantly, the healing miracles that Jesus performed had never been done before, and the Old Testament identified them as miracles that would be done by the promised Messiah. The miracles of Jesus were evidence of his authority—as God's spokesman, as Messiah, and as God the Son!

what others say

Charles C. Ryrie

Some characteristics of Christ's miracles:

1. They were performed for high purposes. He did not use them for his personal convenience (remember his temptation) but to meet definite needs of others.
2. They were not confined to a single sphere of life, so they could never be considered trickery. They were done on nature, on human beings, and on demons.
3. They were done openly in front of spectators and wit-

nesses. When the gospels were written, there would have been many persons living who had seen his miracles and who would have known and objected if the gospel writers had not accurately recorded the stories.[1]

demons
evil spirits, the fallen angels who follow Satan

What's Special in the Miracle Stories of the Gospels?

1. **Jesus' first miracle produced faith** (John 2:1–11). After Jesus was baptized he returned to Galilee with five of the men who later became his disciples. They stopped off at a wedding in Cana. Wedding parties often lasted for days. When the wine ran out, Jesus turned water into wine. Jesus' companions saw him perform this miracle and his disciples put their faith in him.

2. **Jesus' miracles showed his authority over nature** (Matthew 4:18–22; Mark 1:16–20; Luke 5:1–11). Jesus told several fishermen who later became his disciples to go out in their boats and let down their nets. Fishing was done at night, so the experienced Peter thought it would do no good, but he said, "Nevertheless at Your word I will let down the net" (Luke 5:5 NKJV). Such a large school of fish swam into their nets that the nets began to break, and the boats began to sink. Jesus controlled the course of fish in the sea!

Astonished, Peter begged Jesus, "Depart from me, for I am a sinful man" (Luke 5:8 NKJV). Instead, Jesus invited Peter to follow him. Jesus' miracles amazed people, but were intended to draw others to him rather than drive them away.

Other Miracles—Authority over the Forces of Nature

Miracle	Scripture
Jesus stops a storm	Matthew 8:23–27; Mark 4:35–41; Luke 8:22–25
Jesus feeds 5,000	Matthew 14:15–21; Mark 6:31–44; Luke 9:10–17; John 6:1–13
Jesus walks on water	Matthew 14:22–33; Mark 6:45–52; John 6:14–21
Jesus feeds 4,000	Matthew 15:32–39; Mark 8:1–10
Jesus withers a fig tree	Matthew 21:18–22; Mark 11:12–26
Coin in fish's mouth	Matthew 17:24–27
Another catch of fish	John 21:1–17

3. **Jesus' miracles showed his power over demons** (Mark 1:21–28; Luke 4:31–37). The Gospels frequently mention indi-

viduals who were possessed by demons. In this situation the demon had gained a grip and tormented the victim by simulating a painful disease or handicap.

The demons who victimized people with whom Jesus came in contact recognized him as the "Holy One of God" (Luke 4:34 NKJV). Jesus invariably ordered demons to leave their victims. And the demons were forced to obey him.

Jesus' obvious authority over demons amazed those who witnessed these miracles. As Luke notes, "They were all amazed and spoke among themselves, saying, 'What a word this is! For with authority and power He commands the unclean spirits, and they come out'" (Luke 4:36 NKJV).

Authority over Demons

Incident	Scripture
Jesus and a deaf/blind man	Matthew 12:22–37; Mark 3:22, 30; Luke 11:14–23
Jesus and demoniacs of Gadara	Matthew 8:28–34; Mark 5:1–20; Luke 8:26–39
Jesus and a mute	Matthew 9:32–34
A woman's daughter	Matthew 15:21–28; Mark 7:24–30
Jesus and an epileptic boy	Matthew 17:14–21; Mark 9:14–29; Luke 9:37–43
Jesus and a bent woman	Luke 13:10–17

4. **Jesus' miracles showed his authority over sickness** (Matthew 8:14–17; Mark 1:29–34; Luke 4:42–44). A number of passages mention occasions on which Jesus healed many. These passages describe one healing that led to many others. Mark's version reads:

MARK 1:29–34 ***Now as soon as they had come out of the synagogue, they entered the house of Simon and Andrew, with James and John. But Simon's wife's mother lay sick with a fever, and they told Him about her at once. So He came and took her by the hand and lifted her up, and immediately the fever left her. And she served them. At evening, when the sun had set, they brought to Him all who were sick and those who were demon-possessed. . . . Then He healed many who were sick with various diseases. (NKJV)***

what others say

Charles C. Ryrie

Why was she [Simon's mother-in-law] miraculously cured? So she might serve the Lord. Here is the clue to why God permitted her to be sick as well as many others of his children: so that we might learn that life and health and strength are given to us that we might serve. Sickness can be used to teach us what we should do with our health.[2]

Other Healing Miracles That Jesus Performed:

Healing Miracle	Scripture
An officer's son	John 4:43–54
A leper	Matthew 8:2–4; Mark 1:40–45
A paralyzed man	John 5:1–23
A paralyzed man	Matthew 9:1–8; Mark 2:1–12; Luke 5:17–26
A withered hand	Matthew 12:9–14; Mark 3:1–5; Luke 6:6–11
A centurion's servant	Matthew 8:5–13; Luke 7:1–10
A hemorrhaging woman	Matthew 9:20–22; Mark 5:25–34; Luke 8:43–48
Two blind men	Matthew 9:27–31
A mute	Mark 7:31–37
A man born blind	John 9:1–41
A man with dropsy	Luke 14:1–6
Ten lepers	Luke 17:11–19
Blind Bartimaeus	Matthew 20:29–34; Mark 10:46–52; Luke 18:35–43
Malchus's ear	Matthew 26:51–54; Mark 14:46–47; Luke 22:49–51; John 18:10–11

5. Jesus' miracles showed his authority over biological death (Mark 5:35–43; Matthew 9:18–26; Luke 8:41–56). Jesus was called to the home of a religious leader whose daughter was ill. Before he arrived the girl died. Those who had gathered for the funeral, which in first-century Judaism took place immediately, ridiculed Jesus when he reassured the parents. But Mark reports:

MARK 5:40–42 ***But when He had put them all outside, He took the father and the mother of the child, and those who were with Him, and entered where the child was lying. Then He took the child by the hand, and said to her, "Talitha, cumi," which is translated, "Little girl, I say to you, arise." Immediately the girl arose and walked, for she was twelve years of age. And they were overcome with great amazement. (NKJV)***

The Gospels report two other persons whom Jesus raised from the dead. The most significant was Lazarus, who had been dead for three days when Jesus called him back to life. Here is where these stories can be found:

Jesus' Authority over Biological Death

Person	Scripture
Raising a widow's son	Luke 7:11–16
Raising Lazarus	John 11:1–44

6. Jesus' miracles showed his authority to forgive sin (Matthew 9:1–8; Mark 2:1–12; Luke 5:17–26). When the friends of a paralyzed man literally dug through the roof of a house in which Jesus was teaching, Christ said to the paralytic, "'Man, your sins are forgiven you.' And the scribes and the Pharisees began to reason, saying, 'Who is this who speaks blasphemies? Who can forgive sins but God alone?'" (Luke 5:20–21 NKJV).

Jesus knew what they were thinking, and challenged them. Was it easier to pronounce sins forgiven, or to tell a paralyzed man to get up and walk? It is of course easier to say, "Your sins are forgiven." If a person tells a paralytic to "get up and walk," everyone will know for sure he possesses the power to heal! So Jesus, to prove he had authority to forgive sins, told the paralyzed man to get up and walk. And he did!

what others say

Dwight Pentecost

Christ demonstrated by this miracle of healing that he was God and had the authority to forgive sin. The miracle silenced the Pharisees and the teachers of the Law, who had resisted Christ's claim that he was God and could forgive sin.[3]

The miracles of Jesus were truly unique, and they fully supported his claim to be the promised Messiah, and his authority to teach about God.

The Heart First

the big picture

Sermon on the Mount

As Jesus performed miracles he also taught the crowds that gathered to see him. Two sermons from the early ministry of

Jesus are recorded for us. Jesus spoke about the same subjects in what is called the Sermon on the Mount, recorded by Matthew, and the Sermon on the Plain, recorded by Luke. Jesus must have preached these sermons often as he traveled and spoke to crowds in Galilee and in Judea. Jesus' Sermon on the Mount highlights important truths that Christ emphasized to his first-century listeners.

Sermon on the Mount
Matthew 5:1–7:29; Luke 6:17–42

Beatitudes
declarations of blessedness in the Sermon on the Mount

Hedonistic
pleasure-seeking

What's Special in Jesus' Sermon on the Mount?

1. **Jesus taught values** (Matthew 5:3–10). The **Beatitudes** present a set of values which Jesus expects his followers to adopt, because they are important to God. These are not the values most people think of as important.

MATTHEW 5:3–10

Blessed are the poor in spirit,
For theirs is the kingdom of heaven.
Blessed are those who mourn,
For they shall be comforted.
Blessed are the meek,
For they shall inherit the earth.
Blessed are those who hunger and thirst for righteousness,
For they shall be filled.
Blessed are the merciful,
For they shall obtain mercy.
Blessed are the pure in heart,
For they shall see God.
Blessed are the peacemakers,
For they shall be called sons of God.
Blessed are those who are persecuted for righteousness' sake,
For theirs is the kingdom of heaven. (NKJV)

What God Values and What People Value

God Values	People Value
The poor in spirit	The self-confident, the competent, the self-reliant
Those who mourn	**Hedonistic**
The meek	The proud, the powerful
Those who hunger for righteousness	The satisfied, the well-adjusted
The merciful	The practical, the successful
The pure in heart	The "adult," the sophisticated, the broad-minded

Law and the Prophets
the entire Old Testament

piety
reverence for God

hypocrite
an actor putting on a show to impress others

alms
money given to the needy

What God Values and What People Value (cont'd)

God Values	People Value
The peacemakers	The assertive, the competitive
Those persecuted because of righteousness	The popular, the tolerant

2. Jesus explained the true intent of Old Testament Law (Matthew 5:17–47). Jesus told his listeners that he had not come to abolish the **Law and the Prophets** but to fulfill them. In the first century a teacher who fulfilled the Law explained its deepest and true meaning. Jesus explained what God had intended people to understand from the laws God had given to Israel.

When Jesus did this it became clear why he called for a "righteousness [that] exceeds the righteousness of the scribes and Pharisees" (Matthew 5:20 NKJV). The Pharisees focused on the behavior the Law described. But Jesus made it clear that God is concerned with the heart, not just with behavior.

In a series of illustrations, Jesus contrasted both scriptural commandments and rabbinic interpretations with the inner righteousness that God requires.

What Jesus Taught About True Righteousness

Matthew 5	Matthew 21–26	Matthew 27–30	Matthew 31–32	Matthew 33–35	Matthew 38–48
Behavior (Pharisees)	Do not murder	Do not commit adultery	Give legal divorce	Keep oaths	Hate enemies
Source	Old Testament Law	Old Testament Law	Old Testament Law	Rabbis	Rabbis
Righteousness (Jesus)	Do not even be angry	Do not even lust	Do not divorce; be faithful	Do not have need of oaths; always be truthful	Do good to your enemies; love them

3. Jesus emphasized the personal nature of a relationship with God (Matthew 6:1–8). Jesus went on to contrast those who truly love God with those whose real love is a reputation for **piety**. Key phrases in Jesus' examples are "to be seen" and "in secret." In reality, relationship with God is a secret, internal thing. Both the **hypocrite** and the true believer will give **alms** and pray, but the motive and nature of their actions will differ. Jesus taught:

MATTHEW 6:2–4 ***Therefore, when you do a charitable deed, do not sound a trumpet before you as the hypocrites do in the synagogues and in the streets, that they may have glory from men. Assuredly, I say to you, they have their reward. But when you do a charitable deed, do not let your left hand know what your right hand is doing, that your charitable deed may be in secret; and your Father who sees in secret will Himself reward you openly.*** *(NKJV)*

what others say

John Wesley

The pure in heart are they whose hearts God has purified through faith in the blood of Christ.[4]

4. Jesus taught how to approach God in prayer (Matthew 6:9–13). What we call the "Lord's Prayer" is found in Jesus' Sermon on the Mount. What is significant is not merely the words, but the attitudes that the words express. Jesus said, "In this manner, therefore, pray":

MATTHEW 6:9–13

Our Father in heaven,
Hallowed be Your name.
Your kingdom come.
Your will be done
On earth as it is in heaven.
Give us this day our daily bread.
And forgive us our debts,
As we forgive our debtors.
And do not lead us into temptation,
But deliver us from the evil one.
For Yours is the kingdom and the power and
the glory forever. Amen. *(NKJV)*

Each Phrase of the Lord's Prayer Is Significant

The Prayer	The Significance
Our Father	We need a personal relationship with God
in heaven,	We acknowledge him as Lord over all
Hallowed be Your name.	We honor God as real and powerful
Your kingdom come.	We accept God's right to rule in our lives
Your will be done . . .	We submit to God's will as our guide in life
Give us this day	We acknowledge our dependence on God
our daily bread.	We rely on him to daily supply our basic needs
And forgive us our debts,	We acknowledge our faults
As we forgive our debtors.	We commit to live as a forgiven and forgiving people

Each Phrase of the Lord's Prayer Is Significant (cont'd)

The Prayer	The Significance
And do not lead us	We express dependence on God for direction
into temptation,	We ask not to be tested
But deliver us from	
the evil one.	We express dependence on God for protection

5. **Jesus taught personal priorities** (Matthew 6:19–24). Jesus taught that a person cannot focus on what can be gained in this world and truly serve God at the same time. His warning is summed up in Matthew 6:24: "No one can serve two masters" (NKJV). The importance of this teaching is explained a few verses earlier. Human beings are destined to exist eternally, long after physical death ends our life on this earth. It is only reasonable to give priority to the eternal and lasting, rather than the fleeting and temporary. So Jesus said . . .

> MATTHEW 6:19–21 ***Do not lay up for yourselves treasures on earth, where moth and rust destroy and where thieves break in and steal; but lay up for yourselves treasures in heaven, where neither moth nor rust destroys and where thieves do not break in and steal. For where your treasure is, there your heart will be also. (NKJV)***

6. **Jesus taught trust in God as a loving Father** (Matthew 6:25–34). While the rabbis spoke of God as the Father, or source, of the Jewish people, they did not think of an individual's relationship with God as being like that between a child and his own daddy. Jesus taught that God is by nature a heavenly Father, and that he has a father's love for human beings. Anyone who has a personal relationship with God has God for a Father, and this means that God is committed to caring for him or her.

Jesus expressed this revolutionary teaching in a familiar passage that emphasizes freedom from anxiety for the person who knows God as Father:

> MATTHEW 6:25–34 ***Therefore I say to you, do not worry about your life, what you will eat or what you will drink; nor about your body, what you will put on. Is not life more than food and the body more than clothing? Look at the birds of the air, for they neither sow nor reap nor gather into barns; yet your heavenly***

Father feeds them. Are you not of more value than they? Which of you by worrying can add one cubit to his stature? So why do you worry about clothing? Consider the lilies of the field, how they grow: they neither toil nor spin; and yet I say to you that even Solomon in all his glory was not arrayed like one of these. Now if God so clothes the grass of the field, which today is, and tomorrow is thrown into the oven, will He not much more clothe you, O you of little faith? "Therefore do not worry, saying, "What shall we eat?" or "What shall we drink?" or "What shall we wear?" For after all these things the Gentiles seek. For your heavenly Father knows that you need all these things. But seek first the kingdom of God and His righteousness, and all these things shall be added to you. Therefore do not worry about tomorrow, for tomorrow will worry about its own things. Sufficient for the day is its own trouble. (NKJV)

The key to understanding this teaching is in the phrase "seek first the kingdom of God and His righteousness" (Matthew 6:33 NKJV). To trust God as Father means to put pleasing him first. Because God is our Father, he will care for us when we put him first.

7. **Jesus taught coming to God with our needs** (Matthew 7:7–11). Jesus encouraged conscious dependence on God. One way that dependence on God is expressed is in prayer. To encourage prayer, Jesus drew an analogy between the love of human fathers and the love of our heavenly Father.

MATTHEW 7:7–11 ***Ask, and it will be given to you; seek, and you will find; knock, and it will be opened to you. For everyone who asks receives, and he who seeks finds, and to him who knocks it will be opened. Or what man is there among you who, if his son asks for bread, will give him a stone? Or if he asks for a fish, will he give him a serpent? If you then, being evil, know how to give good gifts to your children, how much more will your Father who is in heaven give good things to those who ask Him! (NKJV)***

8. **Jesus taught life-building** (Matthew 7:24–27). When Jesus' sermon drew to a close, he summed up the choice each hearer would have to make. As Christ often did, he used a story to emphasize his point. In this case it was the story of two men who were building houses. The one built on a foundation of solid rock; the other built on a foundation of sand.

God's kingdom really was at hand
Matthew 12:26–29

MATTHEW 7:24–27 ***Therefore whoever hears these sayings of Mine, and does them, I will liken him to a wise man who built his house on the rock: and the rain descended, the floods came, and the winds blew and beat on that house; and it did not fall, for it was founded on the rock. But everyone who hears these sayings of Mine, and does not do them, will be like a foolish man who built his house on the sand: and the rain descended, the floods came, and the winds blew and beat on that house; and it fell. And great was its fall.*** *(NKJV)*

To be able to weather the storm of life we need to hear and to practice the teachings of Jesus Christ.

Trouble on the Way

the big picture

Controversy

Jesus' miracles and teaching brought the issue facing Israel into clear focus. Would God's people accept Christ as the Messiah and Son of God? At first it seemed they might. But the religious leaders, who could not and did not deny Christ's miracles, began to challenge Christ and to publicly oppose him. Their fierce opposition led to rising doubt and uncertainty. Both Matthew and Mark describe a critical confrontation.

MATTHEW 12:22–24 ***Then one was brought to Him who was demon-possessed, blind and mute; and He healed him, so that the blind and mute man both spoke and saw. And all the multitudes were amazed and said, "Could this be the Son of David?" Now when the Pharisees heard it they said, "This fellow does not cast out demons except by Beelzebub, the ruler of the demons."*** *(NKJV)*

Jesus pointed out the foolishness of their theory. If Jesus' powers were demonic, that would mean Satan was fighting against himself. Such a spiritual civil war would lead to the destruction of Satan's kingdom. It was far more reasonable to assume that Jesus drove out demons by the power of God, in which case Christ was greater than Satan, and God's kingdom really was at hand.

The issue was clear. But the people, used to following their leaders, were confused. As the controversy over who Jesus was grew, the story of the wise and foolish builder became more and more significant. Would God's Old Testament people build their future on the solid foundation of Jesus' words, or would they turn from him and build on sand?

Chapter Wrap-Up

- Jesus performed many miracles in Galilee and Judea.
- Jesus' miracles demonstrated his authority over nature, over demons, over sickness, over death, and his authority to forgive sin.
- Jesus taught the people as well as performed miracles. He tried to help them understand the meaning of a personal relationship with God.
- Jesus taught about God's values, the real meaning of God's Law, how to pray, and how to trust God as a loving Father.
- In all that Jesus did and said, he showed himself to have authority. But opposition to Jesus by the religious leaders led to controversy and confusion about who Jesus really was.

Study Questions

1. Who were Jesus' disciples, how many of them were there, and what made them special?
2. Who were the Pharisees and Sadducees?
3. Jesus' miracles proved he spoke with divine authority. What kinds of miracles did Jesus perform?
4. What are the Beatitudes about?
5. How did Jesus fulfill the Law and the prophets?
6. Why was Jesus' insistence that God is a Father so important?
7. Why weren't the people convinced by Jesus' miracles and teaching that he really was the Christ?

Jesus Faces Opposition

Let's Get Started

As the religious leaders' opposition became more and more overt, it became clear that the nation would not hail Jesus as Messiah and King. Therefore, he began to teach in parables, and to give private instruction to the disciples, who did believe in him.

opposition to Jesus
John 7–9;
Luke 11

Feast of Tabernacles
the greatest of Hebrew feasts; lasted seven days

We'll Get You Somehow

The Pharisees had accused Jesus of drawing on Satan's power to perform miracles. As their opposition to Jesus hardened, the religious leaders took every opportunity to challenge him and to undermine his appeal to the people.

Chapters 7 through 9 of John's Gospel describe what happened one year during the **Feast of Tabernacles**. John sets the scene for us, describing the tension as everyone waited for Jesus to appear in Jerusalem.

> JOHN 7:11–13 *Then the Jews sought Him at the feast, and said, "Where is He?" And there was much complaining among the people concerning Him. Some said, "He is good"; others said, "No, on the contrary, He deceives the people." However, no one spoke openly of Him for fear of the Jews [the religious leaders].* (NKJV)

What Happened When Jesus Arrived at the Festival?

1. **The leaders attacked Jesus' authority** (John 7:11–15).

> JOHN 7:14–17 *Now about the middle of the feast Jesus went up into the temple and taught. And the Jews marveled, saying, "How does this Man know letters, having never studied?" Jesus answered them and said, "My doctrine is not Mine, but His who sent Me. If anyone wills to do His will, he shall know concerning the doctrine, whether it is from God or whether I speak on My own authority."* (NKJV)

Bethlehem
Micah 5:2

In the first century a person had to study for years with a recognized rabbi to be accepted as a teacher of religion. How could Jesus be a teacher without having served such an apprenticeship? The implication was that Jesus had no authority to teach. Jesus answered that his teaching came directly from God. Anyone who was committed to do God's will would realize Jesus was teaching the true Word of God.

2. **The leaders attacked Jesus' person** (John 7:25–29).

JOHN 7:25–29 ***Now some of them from Jerusalem said, "Is this not He whom they seek to kill? But look! He speaks boldly, and they say nothing to Him. Do the rulers know indeed that this is truly the Christ? However, we know where this Man is from; but when the Christ comes, no one knows where He is from." Then Jesus cried out, as He taught in the temple, saying, "You both know Me, and you know where I am from; and I have not come of Myself, but He who sent Me is true, whom you do not know. But I know Him, for I am from Him, and He sent Me."*** *(NKJV)*

The leaders' opposition to Jesus, and their desire to see him dead, was common knowledge. The crowds could not understand why the leaders didn't simply arrest him. But at the same time, they had accepted their leaders' argument that Jesus couldn't be the Messiah because he was from Nazareth. If they had checked the genealogical records, they would have found he was born in Bethlehem, where Micah 5:2 said the Messiah would be born.

But Jesus focused on the central issue. He had come directly from God! And this the nation was not ready to accept.

what others say

F. F. Bruce

Jesus asserts afresh his unique relation to the Father, and his hearers cannot miss the implication of his words.[1]

3. **The leaders attempted to trap Jesus** (John 8:3–11).

JOHN 8:3–6 ***Then the scribes and Pharisees brought to Him a woman caught in adultery. And when they had set her in the midst, they said to Him, "Teacher, this woman was caught in***

adultery, in the very act. Now Moses, in the law, commanded us that such should be stoned. But what do You say?" This they said, testing Him, that they might have something of which to accuse Him. But Jesus stooped down and wrote on the ground with His finger, as though He did not hear. (NKJV)

Jesus challenged the accusers: "'He who is without sin among you, let him throw a stone at her first.' . . . Then those who heard it, being convicted by their conscience, went out one by one. . . . Jesus said to her, 'Neither do I condemn you; go and sin no more'" (John 8:7–11 NKJV). The Law was valid, but Jesus came bringing a forgiveness so transforming that those who accepted him would be able to leave their life of sin.

4. **The leaders rejected conclusive evidence of Jesus' authority** (John 9:1–41). Additional incidents depicting opposition to Jesus culminate in the story of when Jesus gave sight to a man who was born blind. When the miracle is brought to the attention of the Pharisees, at first they try to deny the miracle. But when many witnesses come forward to testify that the man really was born blind, the Pharisees desperately try to discredit Jesus.

Upon learning that Jesus had made mud and put it on the man's eyes on the Sabbath, they announced: "This Man is not from God, because He does not keep the Sabbath" (John 9:16 NKJV). But the problem with this theory was expressed by others: "How can a man who is a sinner do such signs?" (v. 16 NKJV).

Finally the Pharisees bluntly rejected the evidence before them, and railed at the man whom Jesus had healed.

JOHN 9:28–34 ***Then they reviled him and said, "You are His disciple, but we are Moses' disciples. We know that God spoke to Moses; as for this fellow, we do not know where He is from." The man answered and said to them, "Why, this is a marvelous thing, that you do not know where He is from; yet He has opened my eyes! Now we know that God does not hear sinners; but if anyone is a worshiper of God and does His will, He hears him. Since the world began it has been unheard of that anyone opened the eyes of one who was born blind. If this Man were not from God, He could do nothing." They answered and said to him, "You were completely born in sins, and are you teaching us?" And they cast him out.*** (NKJV)

parables
Matthew 13;
Mark 4

kingdom of heaven
Matthew 13:11

parables
stories teaching a lesson

what others say

F. F. Bruce

Without knowing it, the man anticipates a rabbinical maxim later expressed in the form: "Every one in whom is the fear of heaven, his words are heard." A miracle of this magnitude must be recognized as an answer to prayer; the man who received this answer must be no ordinary man.[2]

The religious leaders were now so firm in their opposition to Jesus that when argument failed, they used their power to oppress those who acknowledged Jesus as the Christ. It became increasingly clear that the religious leaders had succeeded in preventing the nation from acclaiming Jesus as Messiah and King.

You Won't Understand

As the controversy over Jesus grew, Christ began to teach in **parables**. When Jesus' disciples asked why he spoke to the crowds in parables, Jesus gave a surprising answer:

Matthew 13:11, 13 ***It has been given to you to know the mysteries of the kingdom of heaven, but to them it has not been given. . . . Therefore I speak to them in parables, because seeing they do not see, and hearing they do not hear, nor do they understand.*** *(NKJV)*

Jesus had presented his claim to be the promised Messiah in powerful and unmistakable terms. Yet the religious leaders had rejected him and tried desperately to deny the authenticating evidence of his miracles. There are some teachings of Jesus that believers need to understand, but unbelievers would only distort. The parables contain truths Jesus' followers need to understand—truths that those who reject him would only distort or deny.

What's Special About Jesus' Parables?

1. **The parables concerned the kingdom of heaven**. Jesus said that his parables concerned the secrets of the kingdom of heaven. The phrase "kingdom of heaven" means the rule of heaven, and thus how God exercises his authority in our world. What Jesus revealed in his parables were secrets, in that what he now taught had not been revealed in the Old Testament.

2. The parables contrast the expected form of God's kingdom with a "secret" form that Jesus revealed (Matthew 13:1–50). The Old Testament prophets pictured a visible kingdom of God on earth. That kingdom will exist one day, but because Israel rejected her Messiah King, God introduced an unexpected form of his kingdom. This secret form of God's kingdom will exist until the crucified and resurrected Savior returns to earth.

How important it is that we respond to Jesus, and through faith in him enter that secret kingdom of his today.

Kingdom Parables

Parable	Expected Form of God's Kingdom	Secret Form of God's Kingdom
The sower (Matthew 13:2–9, 18–23)	Messiah turns all Israel and nations to himself	Individuals respond differently to the Word of the Messiah
Wheat and tares (Matthew 13:24–30, 27–43)	The kingdom's righteous citizens rule the world with the king	The kingdom's citizens live among the men of the world, growing together until God's harvest
Mustard seed (Matthew 13:31–32)	The kingdom begins in majestic glory	The kingdom begins in insignificance, its greatness comes as a surprise
Leaven (Matthew 13:33)	Only the righteous enter the kingdom; other "raw material" is excluded	The kingdom begins with corrupt "raw material" and grows to fill the believer with righteousness
Hidden treasure (Matthew 13:44)	The kingdom is public, and for all	The kingdom is hidden, for individual "purchase"
Priceless pearl (Matthew 13:45–46)	The kingdom brings all good things to men	The kingdom demands we abandon all other values (Matthew 6:33)
Dragnet (Matthew 13:47–50)	The kingdom begins with separation of the righteous	The kingdom ends with separation of the righteous

For You Alone

MATTHEW 16:13–15 ***When Jesus came into the region of Caesarea Philippi, He asked His disciples, saying, "Who do men say that I, the Son of Man, am?" So they said, "Some say John the Baptist, some Elijah, and others Jeremiah or one of the prophets." He said to them, "But who do you say that I am?" (NKJV)***

With this event a significant change took place in Jesus' ministry. Although the people recognized Jesus as a prophet, they failed to

the rock is Christ
1 Corinthians 3:11

Hades
Greek term for place of the dead

crucifixion
form of capital punishment whereby the victim was tied or nailed to a cross

resurrection
the art of being brought from death to unending life

accept him as the Messiah. However, as Peter's answer to Christ's question "But who do you say that I am?" showed, the disciples did recognize Jesus as both the Christ and the Son of God. From this point on, Jesus focused on instructing his disciples.

There is much in each Gospel that reflects the private teaching Jesus gave to those who did believe in him. We'll sample some of that private and personal instruction now.

What's Special in Jesus' Instruction of His Disciples?

1. The instruction is for those who believe in Jesus as the Christ, the Son of God.

MATTHEW 16:15–18 *[Jesus] said to them, "But who do you say that I am?" Simon Peter answered and said, "You are the Christ, the Son of the living God." Jesus answered and said to him, "Blessed are you, Simon Bar-Jonah, for flesh and blood has not revealed this to you, but My Father who is in heaven. And I also say to you that you are Peter, and on this rock I will build My church, and the gates of* ***Hades*** *shall not prevail against it."* (NKJV)

Today we define a disciple or follower of Jesus by his or her trust in Jesus as the Christ, the Son of the living God. Jesus' private instruction in the Gospels is addressed to all who share Peter's belief.

Some have thought Christ was saying that Peter was the rock on which Jesus would build his Church. In fact, the rock is Christ himself. Jesus is the Christ, the Son of God; he is the foundation on which Christianity rests.

2. Jesus began to speak of his coming crucifixion.

MATTHEW 16:21 *From that time Jesus began to show to His disciples that He must go to Jerusalem, and suffer many things from the elders and chief priests and scribes, and be killed, and be raised the third day.* (NKJV)

Until there was clear evidence that the nation would reject Jesus as the Messiah, Christ had not mentioned the Cross. When it was clear that the people would not acknowledge him, Jesus began to tell his followers of his coming **crucifixion** (see Illustration #14, page 212) and **resurrection**.

3. Jesus taught his disciples what it would mean to follow him.

MATTHEW 16:24–26 *Then Jesus said to His disciples, "If anyone desires to come after Me, let him deny himself, and take up his cross, and follow Me. For whoever desires to save his life will lose it, but whoever loses his life for My sake will find it. For what profit is it to a man if he gains the whole world, and loses his own soul? Or what will a man give in exchange for his soul?" (NKJV)*

A Disciple of Jesus is to

1. deny himself and
2. take up his cross; in so doing he will
3. lose his life, but at the same time he will
4. find it.

What was Jesus saying? In Scripture the cross represents Jesus' crucifixion, but it also represents God's will for Jesus. A disciple's cross represents God's will for the disciple. Jesus expects disciples to do God's will, even when that means denying something they would rather do.

The life that the disciple loses is his or her old life, lived apart from God. The life that the disciple finds is the new life that Jesus gives to his followers—a life of love, joy, and fulfillment—that lasts eternally.

4. Jesus taught his disciples about God's attitude toward sinners. Luke 15 records three stories Jesus told to illustrate God's attitude toward sinners: God is like a shepherd who seeks a lost sheep, and rejoices when it is found; God is like a woman who loses a coin, and celebrates when it is found; God is like a father who rejoices at the return of a son, even though the son has sinned and abused his father's love.

5. Jesus taught his disciples about servanthood. Shortly after Jesus had again foretold his coming death and resurrection, James and John, two of the disciples, had their mother ask Christ for the two most important posts in his future kingdom. When the other disciples heard this, they were upset and angry. Jesus used the opportunity to teach them about greatness:

MATTHEW 20:25–28 *You know that the rulers of the Gentiles lord it over them, and those who are great exercise authority over them. Yet it shall not be so among you; but whoever desires to become great among you, let him be your servant. And who-*

love
1 Corinthians 13;
1 John 3:11–29

ever desires to be first among you, let him be your slave—just as the Son of Man did not come to be served, but to serve, and to give His life a ransom for many. (NKJV)

what others say

John Wesley

Do all the good you can, by all the means you can, in all the ways you can, in all the places you can, at all the time you can, to all the people you can and as long as you can.[3]

6. **Jesus taught his disciples to love one another.** One of the most intimate and private of Christ's times with his disciples is described in John 13–16, when the disciples shared a meal with Jesus the evening before he was crucified. Jesus began that evening's teaching by giving his disciples what Christ called a new commandment:

JOHN 13:34–35 ***A new commandment I give to you, that you love one another; as I have loved you, that you also love one another. By this all will know that you are My disciples, if you have love for one another.*** (NKJV)

7. **Jesus taught his disciples that he alone provides access to God:**

JOHN 14:6 ***Jesus said to him, "I am the way, the truth, and the life. No one comes to the Father except through Me."*** (NKJV)

While Jesus' claim is exclusive, and a decisive rejection of the notion that "all religions lead to God," it is also inclusive. Because Jesus is the way, the truth, and the life, anyone who wants to can come to the Father through him! The disciples needed to grasp this truth firmly, not just for themselves, but to motivate them to share Christ with others.

what others say

Thomas à Kempis

Follow thou me. I am the way and the truth and the life. Without the way there is no going; without the truth there is no knowing; without the life there is no living. I am the way which thou must follow; the truth which thou must believe; the life for which thou must hope. I am the inviolable way; the infallible truth; the never-ending life. I am the straightest way; the sovereign truth; life true, life blessed, life uncreated.[4]

8. Jesus taught his disciples that only love can motivate true obedience. The rabbis of Christ's day taught that a person gained merit by obeying God's Law, and could thus earn a place in the world to come. Jesus offered eternal life to sinners as a free gift. Obedience is a product of salvation, not a means to it. People are not saved because they obey, but obey because they love the One who has saved them.

love
Leviticus 19:18; Matthew 5:43–48

JOHN 14:23–24 ***Jesus answered and said to him, "If anyone loves Me, he will keep My word; and My Father will love him, and We will come to him and make Our home with him. He who does not love Me does not keep My words."*** *(NKJV)*

Johannine writings
writings of John

what others say

F. F. Bruce

The vital link between their love for him and their obedience to him is a recurring theme in the **Johannine writings**.This is the love of God, that we keep his commandments (1 John 5:3), and chief among these is the commandment that the followers of Jesus should love one another; indeed, we know that we love the children of God when we love God and obey his commandments (1 John 5:2). To love the Father is to love his children; to love the Son is to love his followers; for them to love one another is to love the Father and the Son.[5]

9. Jesus taught his disciples that to be fruitful they must stay close to him. One of the New Testament letters describes the fruit that God produces in the believer's life as "love, joy, peace, longsuffering, kindness, goodness, faithfulness, gentleness, self-control" (Galatians 5:22–23 NKJV). But Jesus warned his followers that these gifts would be theirs only if they stayed close to him. In the private instruction he gave his disciples the night before he was crucified, Jesus used the image of a vine and its branches to convey this important message.

JOHN 15:1, 4–5, 9–11 ***I am the true vine, and My Father is the vinedresser. . . . Abide in Me, and I in you. As the branch cannot bear fruit of itself, unless it abides in the vine, neither can you, unless you abide in Me. I am the vine, you are the branches. He who abides in Me, and I in him, bears much fruit; for without Me you can do nothing. . . . As the Father loved Me, I also have loved you; abide in My love. If you keep My commandments, you will abide in My love, just as I have kept My Father's***

bear witness
to testify to what they saw and heard

commandments and abide in His love. These things I have spoken to you, that My joy may remain in you, and that your joy may be full. (NKJV)

what others say

J. Dwight Pentecost

Christ used the illustration of the branch and the vine to show what it meant to remain in him. The branch has no life in itself; it draws its life from the vine. The branch is nourished and sustained by the life of the vine. As long as there is an uninterrupted flow of life from the vine into the branch, the branch is capable of bearing fruit. The moment the branch is severed from the life of the vine, it is rendered incapable of bearing fruit. What was true in the natural realm was most certainly true of these men in their forthcoming ministry.[6]

10. Jesus commissioned his disciples to **bear witness** about him.

JOHN 15:27 ***You also will bear witness, because you have been with Me from the beginning.*** (NKJV)

The private instruction that Jesus gave his disciples is recorded in Scripture to guide Jesus' followers today. Christians today are defined by the conviction stated by Peter, that Jesus is the Christ, the Son of the living God. For following Jesus means submitting to God's will, having a concern for the sinners God loves and yearns to save, and seeking to serve others.

Christians committed to Jesus will love each other as he commanded, be moved by love to obey God, maintain that intimate relationship with Jesus which is required for fruitfulness, and tell others about the love and grace of God expressed in Jesus Christ.

Chapter Wrap-Up

- The Pharisees and other religious leaders openly attacked and tried to undermine Jesus.
- The Pharisees and other religious leaders used their powers of excommunication to punish those who supported Jesus.
- When it became clear that the nation would not accept Jesus as the Messiah and Son of God, he began to teach in parables.
- Jesus' parables were about a form of God's rule on earth that had not been predicted in the Old Testament.
- Jesus gave private instruction to the disciples, who did believe in him as Christ, the Son of God.
- Jesus taught his disciples to choose God's will, to love each other, and to serve others.
- Jesus taught that love for him would produce obedience, and that disciples who obey him will live fruitful, productive lives.

Study Questions

1. Who brought the charge that Satan was behind the miracles Jesus performed?
2. Why was the charge that Jesus had not "studied" important?
3. What argument of the blind man did the Pharisees reject in order to condemn Jesus?
4. Why did Jesus begin to use parables in speaking to the crowds?
5. What was the subject of the parables of Jesus?
6. What belief marks a person as a true disciple of Jesus?
7. What is the key to greatness for a disciple of Jesus?
8. What was Jesus' new commandment to his disciples?

Jesus' Death and Resurrection

Let's Get Started

During the last week of his life, Jesus again went to Jerusalem for the Passover Festival. When he entered the city he was loudly acclaimed the Messiah. But within a few days he was arrested, tried before religious and Roman courts, condemned to death, and executed. The hopes of his followers were dashed. But within three days, Jesus rose from the grave!

A King on a Donkey?

the big picture

Final Week

The week began when Jesus entered Jerusalem riding on a donkey. He was praised as the Son of David by the crowds who had come for the festival. The leaders reacted by unsuccessfully trying to trap him. Jesus finally openly condemned them. But Jesus privately instructed his disciples about what to expect in the future.

What Was Special About Jesus' Last Week on Earth?

1. **The triumphal entry** (Matthew 21:1–17; Mark 11:1–11; Luke 19:28–44). Some four hundred years earlier, the prophet Zechariah had announced that Israel's king would enter Jerusalem "lowly and riding on a donkey, a colt, the foal of a donkey" (Zechariah 9:9 NKJV). Matthew describes the scene in Jerusalem on what we call "Palm Sunday":

MATTHEW 21:7–11 ***[The disciples] brought the donkey and the colt, laid their clothes on them, and set [Jesus] on them. And a very great multitude spread their clothes on the road; others cut down branches from the trees and spread them on the road. Then the multitudes who went before and those who followed cried out, saying:***

Hosanna
a Hebrew expression meaning "Save!"

> *"**Hosanna** to the Son of David!*
> *'Blessed is He who comes in the name of the LORD!'*
> *Hosanna in the highest!"*

And when He had come into Jerusalem, all the city was moved, saying, "Who is this?" So the multitudes said, "This is Jesus, the prophet from Nazareth of Galilee." (NKJV)

2. **Jesus drove merchants out of the temple** (Matthew 21:12–17; Mark 11:12–17). Jewish pilgrims who came to worship God at the temple were forced by the chief priests to use only "temple money" to pay a tax that Old Testament Law required. "Money changers" had set up tables in the temple where the correct coins, Tyran Duodrachma, could be purchased at an exorbitant price. Other merchants sold sacrificial animals that had been certified by the priests as being without blemish, again charging high rates. The chief priests received a percentage of the income. After coming into the city . . .

MATTHEW 21:12–13 *Jesus went into the temple of God and drove out all those who bought and sold in the temple, and overturned the tables of the money changers and the seats of those who sold doves. And He said to them, "It is written, 'My house shall be called a house of prayer,' but you have made it a 'den of thieves.'"* (NKJV)

3. **Jesus exposed the motives of the religious leaders when they challenged his authority** (Matthew 21:22–27; 33–45; Mark 11:27–12:12). In driving the merchants from the temple, Jesus had directly challenged the chief priests. A delegation of priests, with teachers of the Law and elders, demanded that Jesus tell them who gave him the authority to do what he had done. Jesus refused, and told a story about tenants who were left to tend their owner's vineyard. When the owner sent servants to collect his share, the tenants beat some and killed others. Finally the owner sent his son.

Jesus Concluded . . .

MARK 12:7–9 *But those vinedressers said among themselves, "This is the heir. Come, let us kill him, and the inheritance will be ours." So they took him and killed him and cast him out of the vineyard. Therefore what will the owner of the vineyard do? He will come and destroy the vinedressers, and give the vineyard to others.* (NKJV)

The religious leaders realized that Jesus was speaking about them. They were the tenants, left in charge of God's vineyards. The servants were the prophets God had sent their forefathers; Jesus was the son. They wanted desperately to arrest Jesus, but they feared the reaction of the crowd.

Later at midnight they would seize Jesus . . . and by dawn they would condemn him to death.

Herodians
a political party that supported the royal family of King Herod

Caesar
emperor of Rome; here, it is a symbol for civil authority

4. **The leaders tried desperately to turn the people against Jesus** (Matthew 22:15–22; Mark 12:13–17; Luke 20:20–26). The most dangerous trap was set by a group of Pharisees and **Herodians**. They asked Jesus the question, "Is it lawful to pay taxes to **Caesar**, or not?" (Matthew 22:17 NKJV).

Alfred Edersheim explains why the Pharisees were convinced that this question would bring Jesus down.

what others say

Alfred Edersheim

There was a strong party in the land, with which, not only politically but religiously, many of the noblest spirits would sympathize, which maintained, that to pay the tribute-money to Caesar was virtually to own his royal authority, and so to disown that of Jehovah, who alone was Israel's king. They would argue, that all the miseries of the land and people were due to this national unfaithfulness. Indeed, this was the fudamental principle of the Nationalist movement.

To have said No, would have been to command rebellion; to have said simply Yes, would have been to give a painful shock to deep feeling, and, in a sense, in the eyes of the people, the lie to his own claim of being Israel's Messiah King.[1]

Jesus stunned his opponents by asking them for a coin, and then asking whose portrait was on it. When the Pharisees answered, Caesar's, Jesus said, "Render therefore to Caesar the things that are Caesar's, and to God the things that are God's" (Mark 12:17 NKJV). This, with other attempts to trap Jesus on that last week, failed utterly.

5. **Jesus successfully exposed the hypocrisy of the religious leaders** (Matthew 22:41–46; Mark 12:35–37; Luke 20:41–44). Jesus exposed the hypocrisy of the leaders when he asked the Pharisees a question about Old Testament teaching on the Christ.

Matthew 22:41–45 ***Jesus asked them, saying, "What do you think about the Christ? Whose Son is He?" They said to Him, "The Son of David." He said to them, "How then does David in the Spirit call Him 'Lord,' saying:***
'The Lord said to my Lord,
"Sit at My right hand,
Till I make Your enemies Your footstool"'?
If David then calls Him 'Lord,' how is He his Son?" (NKJV)

what others say

J. Dwight Pentecost

Psalm [110] was universally recognized as messianic. The one invited to sit at the Lord's right hand was the Messiah. The "Lord" who invited him to sit at his right hand was the God of Abraham. The Messiah was referred to as "my Lord." With this interpretation the Pharisees would have been in agreement. Christ addressed this question to them: If the Messiah was the "son," or descendant, of David, "How is it then that David, speaking by the Spirit, calls him 'Lord'?" It was not natural for one to call his own son "my Lord." The fact that Messiah was David's son testified to Messiah's true humanity, but the fact that David called him "my Lord" testified to his true and undiminished deity, for "Lord" was a title for Deity. . . . It was just such a claim as the psalmist foretold of Messiah that Jesus made for himself. If the Pharisees answered that David called him his Lord because he is God, then they could not object to Christ, David's son according to the flesh, claiming to be the Son of God. If they agreed that Messiah was to be truly human and truly God, they must cease their objections to Christ's claim concerning his person. The Pharisees realized the dilemma that faced them and refused to answer.[2]

The incident proved that the Pharisees knew the rightness of Jesus' claims—and hated him anyway. The religious leaders who claimed the right to interpret God's Word were rebellious tenants who, rather than submit to the authority of God's Son, would seek any excuse to kill him.

With this established, Jesus openly and forcefully condemned the teachers of the Law and Pharisees as hypocrites.

6. **Jesus then taught his disciples about the future** (Matthew 24, 25; Mark 13; Luke 21:5–36). Jesus was well aware that the religious leaders were determined to kill him. That last week he took the time to speak with his disciples privately about what would

happen after his death and resurrection. Included in Jesus' teaching were three key points.

First, Jesus himself would return to earth in power and glory.

MATTHEW 24:30–31 ***They will see the Son of Man coming on the clouds of heaven with power and great glory. And He will send His angels with a great sound of a trumpet, and they will gather together His elect from the four winds, from one end of heaven to the other.*** *(NKJV)*

Second, no one would be able to predict when he would return.

MATTHEW 24:36 ***Of that day and hour no one knows, not even the angels of heaven, but My Father only.*** *(NKJV)*

Third, until he does come, Jesus' followers are to watch for him and serve him faithfully.

MATTHEW 24:42, 44 ***Watch therefore, for you do not know what hour your Lord is coming. . . . Therefore you also be ready, for the Son of Man is coming at an hour you do not expect.*** *(NKJV)*

7. **Even while Jesus was speaking to his disciples, the leaders were plotting to kill him** (Matthew 26:3–5).

MATTHEW 26:3–5 ***Then the chief priests, the scribes, and the elders of the people assembled at the palace of the high priest, who was called Caiaphas, and plotted to take Jesus by trickery and kill Him. But they said, "Not during the feast, lest there be an uproar among the people."*** *(NKJV)*

Tomorrow Doesn't Look Good

Each of the Gospels gives a detailed account of Jesus' last day on earth, which, according to Jewish reckoning, began at sundown. But not each Gospel account includes every feature of that final, fateful day. As evening approached, several disciples made arrangements to share a meal with Jesus (the Last Supper), even as Judas arranged with the high priest to betray Jesus for thirty pieces of silver. John's Gospel describes the meal and the conversation there, and records a prayer that Jesus offered for all believers. Other events followed, in this order:

a prayer that Jesus offered for all believers
John 17

Caiaphas
high priest at the time of Jesus' crucifixion

Abba
"daddy" in Aramaic, the language Jesus spoke!

Jesus' Last Day on Earth

Event	Matthew	Mark	Luke	John
Jesus prays in Gethsemane	26:36–46	14:32–42	22:39–46	18:1
Jesus is arrested there	26:47–56	14:43–52	22:47–53	18:2–12
Jesus is tried before Annas	—	—	—	18:12–23
Jesus is tried before Caiaphas	26:57–68	14:53–65	22:54–65	18:24
Peter denies Jesus	26:69–75	14:66–72	22:54–62	18:15–27
Jesus is condemned by Sanhedrin	27:1	15:1	22:66–71	—
Judas commits suicide	27:3–10	—	—	—
Jesus is tried by Pilate	27:11–14	15:2–5	23:1–5	18:28–38
Jesus is tried by Herod	—	—	23:6–12	—
Jesus is condemned by Pilate	27:15–26	15:6–15	23:13–25	18:39–19:16
Jesus is mocked and scourged	27:27–30	15:16–19	—	19:2–3
Jesus is led to Calvary	27:31–34	15:20–23	23:26–33	19:16–17

What's Special in Jesus' Last Day?

1. **Jesus' prayer in Gethsemane** (Matthew 26:36–46; Mark 14:32–42; Luke 22:39–42). Gethsemane was an olive grove on a hill across the Kedron Valley from Jerusalem.

MARK 14:32–36 ***They came to a place which was named Gethsemane; and He said to His disciples, "Sit here while I pray." And He took Peter, James, and John with Him, and He began to be troubled and deeply distressed. Then He said to them, "My soul is exceedingly sorrowful, even to death. Stay here and watch." He went a little farther, and fell on the ground, and prayed that if it were possible, the hour might pass from Him. And He said, "Abba, Father, all things are possible for You. Take this cup away from Me; nevertheless, not what I will, but what You will."*** *(NKJV)*

The prayer of Jesus has puzzled many. Did Jesus really beg to avoid the Crucifixion? He had said earlier that he had come to earth not "to be served, but to serve, and to give His life a ransom for many" (Matthew 20:28 NKJV). Pentecost gives the best explanation of Christ's prayer:

legions
military units usually comprising 4,000 to 6,000 soldiers

tribunals
courts of justice

blasphemy
to speak of God in an irreverent way

> **what others say**
>
> **J. Dwight Pentecost**
>
> Christ prayed that God might accept his death as full payment of the sin of sinners and bring him out of death and restore him to life again. Thus the prayer should be understood as a prayer for restoration to physical life by resurrection, and a restoration to full fellowship with his Father out of the spiritual death into which he would enter. The evidence that God answered Jesus' prayer is seen, first, in the fact that Christ was raised from the dead on the third day and given a glorified body. Second, it is seen in the fact that on the fortieth day he ascended to the Father to be seated at his right hand in glory.[3]

2. **Jesus' arrest** (Matthew 26:47–56; Mark 14:43–52; Luke 22:47–53; John 18:2–12). Judas led a mob sent by the high priest to seize Jesus. When one of the disciples tried to resist, Jesus said something that showed he remained in full control of the situation.

MATTHEW 26:53–54 *Do you think that I cannot now pray to My Father, and He will provide Me with more than twelve* ***legions*** *of angels? How then could the Scriptures be fulfilled, that it must happen thus? (NKJV)*

3. **Jesus was examined at night by three religious tribunals** (Matthew 27:57–68; Mark 14:53–65; Luke 2:54–71; John 18:12–27). The critical point was reached near dawn when the high priest asked Jesus a question to which he knew Christ's answer.

MATTHEW 26:63–66 *But Jesus kept silent. And the high priest answered and said to Him, "I put You under oath by the living God: Tell us if You are the Christ, the Son of God!" Jesus said to him, "It is as you said. Nevertheless, I say to you, hereafter you will see the Son of Man sitting at the right hand of the Power, and coming on the clouds of heaven." Then the high priest tore his clothes, saying, "He has spoken* ***blasphemy****! What further need do we have of witnesses? Look, now you have heard His blasphemy. What do you think?" They answered and said, "He is deserving of death." (NKJV)*

Jesus was hung on a cross
Matthew 27:32–66; Mark 15:21–47; Luke 23:26–56; John 19:16–42

The problem was that no first-century Jewish court had the authority to impose a death sentence. That right was reserved to Roman courts alone. While the charge of blasphemy might call for the death penalty in Judaism, it was not a capital crime to the Romans. They would have to charge Jesus with a crime other than the one they had convicted him of!

4. **Jesus was then accused of political crimes** (Matthew 27:11–26; Mark 15:2–19; John 18:28–19:16). John's Gospel describes in detail Jesus' trial before the Roman governor Pilate. The charge was political: in presenting himself as the Christ, Jesus had laid claim to being the King of the Jews, for the Messiah was to be a king.

subterfuge
deceptive ploy

Praetorian Guard
the bodyguard of the Roman emperor

Pilate saw through the **subterfuge** but finally gave in and ordered Christ be crucified. The pressure to which Pilate finally submitted is expressed in John 19:12:

> ***From then on Pilate sought to release Him, but the Jews cried out, saying, "If you let this Man go, you are not Caesar's friend. Whoever makes himself a king speaks against Caesar."*** (NKJV)

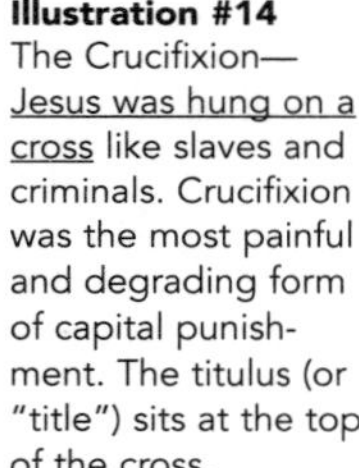

Illustration #14
The Crucifixion—Jesus was hung on a cross like slaves and criminals. Crucifixion was the most painful and degrading form of capital punishment. The titulus (or "title") sits at the top of the cross.

In Rome the man who had sponsored Pilate, a commander of the emperor's **Praetorian Guard**, a man named Sejanus, had recently been executed by the emperor Tiberius. Many of Sejanus's government appointees had been executed or exiled as well. Pilate knew he was vulnerable, and was terrified that the Jewish leaders might accuse him to the emperor. In the end Pilate, knowing that Jesus was innocent, decided to have Jesus crucified rather than run any personal risk!

Later in a sermon the apostle Peter would say, "Those things which God foretold by the mouth of all His prophets, that the Christ would suffer, He has thus fulfilled" (Acts 3:18 NKJV). God providentially arranged distant events to bring about what he had foretold through the prophets.

titulus
Latin for "title"; here, a sign

scourging
to punish by whip or lash

Preparation Day
the day before the Sabbath (people prepared for the Sabbath because they could not work on the Sabbath)

centurion
Roman commander of a "century" (100 troops)

Nailed to a Cross

The Nelson Illustrated Bible Handbook describes crucifixion this way: "Crucifixion [see Illustration #14] was practiced as a method of torture and execution by the Persians before it was adopted by the Romans. Roman law allowed only slaves and criminals to be crucified. Roman citizens were not crucified. The victim's arms are stretched out above him, fastened to a cross bar fixed near the top of a stake slightly taller than a man. Suspended this way, blood is forced to the lower body. The pulse rate increases, and after days of agony the victim dies from lack of blood circulating to the brain and heart. The Romans often placed a **titulus** above the sufferer naming his crime. **Scourging** before crucifixion hastened death, as did breaking a victim's legs."

Mark Describes the End of That Fateful Day

> MARK 15:42–46 *Now when evening had come, because it was the **Preparation Day**, that is, the day before the Sabbath, Joseph of Arimathea, a prominent council member, who was himself waiting for the kingdom of God, coming and taking courage, went in to Pilate and asked for the body of Jesus. Pilate marveled that He was already dead; and summoning the **centurion**, he asked him if He had been dead for some time. So when he found out from the centurion, he granted the body to Joseph. Then he bought fine linen, took Him down, and wrapped Him in the linen. And he laid Him in a tomb which had been hewn out of the rock, and rolled a stone against the door of the tomb. (NKJV)*

By examining the account of Jesus' crucifixion given in the four Gospels, the details of what happened and Jesus' words from the cross can be reconstructed.

Crucifixion Events at Calvary

Event	Matthew	Mark	Luke	John
Jesus refuses drugs	27:3	—	—	—
Jesus is crucified	27:35	—	—	—
"Father, forgive them"	—	—	23:34	—
Soldiers gamble for clothing	27:35	—	—	—
Jesus is mocked by observers	27:39–44	15:29	—	—
Jesus is ridiculed by thieves	27:44	—	—	—
One thief believes	—	—	23:39—43	—
"Today you will be with me"	—	—	23:43	—
To Mary: "Behold your son"	—	—	—	19:26–27
Darkness falls	27:45	15:33	23:44	—
"My God, my God . . ."	27:46–47	15:34–36	—	—
"I thirst"	—	—	—	19:28
"It is finished"	—	—	—	19:30
"Father, into your hands"	—	—	23:46	—
Jesus releases his spirit	27:50	15:37	—	—

Matthew adds that the next day the chief priests and Pharisees asked Pilate for permission to secure the tomb.

MATTHEW 27:65–66 ***Pilate said to them, "You have a guard; go your way, make it as secure as you know how." So they went and made the tomb secure, sealing the stone and setting the guard.*** *(NKJV)*

What Is the Significance of Jesus' Death on the Cross?

The Bible makes it clear that Jesus' death on the cross was always an essential element in God's plan. The Crucifixion was prophesied in the Old Testament. Jesus informed his disciples beforehand of what would happen, and rather than call on the Father for angelic armies, Jesus chose to let himself be executed.

Here are some of the passages from the Old and New Testaments that explain the significance of Jesus' death:

transgressions
violations of the law; sin

iniquities
wicked acts

justified
pronounced not guilty

1. **Writing seven hundred years before Jesus was born, God announced through the prophet Isaiah:**

Isaiah 53:4–6
Surely He has borne our griefs
And carried our sorrows;
Yet we esteemed Him stricken,
Smitten by God, and afflicted.
But He was wounded for our transgressions,
He was bruised for our iniquities;
The chastisement for our peace was upon Him,
And by His stripes we are healed.
All we like sheep have gone astray;
We have turned, every one, to his own way;
And the Lord has laid on Him the iniquity of us all.
(NKJV)

2. **Christ died for us** (Romans 5:8–9). Writing to the Romans, the apostle Paul explained the reason for Jesus' death in these words:

Romans 5:8–9 ***God demonstrates His own love toward us, in that while we were still sinners, Christ died for us. Much more then, having now been justified by His blood, we shall be saved from wrath through Him.*** *(NKJV)*

what others say

John Stott

What is written is that while we were sinners Christ died for us (Romans 5:8), and whenever sin and death are coupled in Scripture, death is the penalty or wage of sin. This being so, the statement that Christ died for sinners, that though the sins were ours, the death was his, can mean only that he died as a sin offering, bearing in our place the penalty that our sins deserved.[4]

Max Lucado

The cross did what sacrificed lambs could not do. It erased our sins not for a year, but for eternity. The cross did what man cannot do. It granted us the right to talk with, love, and even live with God.[5]

3. The apostle Paul explained further when writing a second letter to the Corinthians. At the cross an amazing transaction took place. Jesus took our sins on himself; his death took the penalty that our sins deserved. And, wonder of wonders, God then credited the righteousness of Jesus to us! With sin paid for, there was no longer a barrier between human beings and God. With Jesus' own righteousness credited to our account, we are welcome to enter God's presence. As Paul wrote,

> **2 Corinthians 5:21** ***He made Him who knew no sin to be sin for us, that we might become the righteousness of God in Him.*** *(NKJV)*

In these and many other similar words, the New Testament shares its good news. Jesus' death was a payment for our sins—a promise of forgiveness to all who will trust God and take him at his word.

As Jesus had told one of the Pharisees at the beginning of his ministry,

> **John 3:16, 18** ***For God so loved the world that He gave His only begotten Son, that whoever believes in Him should not perish but have everlasting life. . . . He who believes in Him is not condemned; but he who does not believe is condemned already, because he has not believed in the name of the only begotten Son of God.*** *(NKJV)*

Resurrection Morning Appearances by Jesus

Event	Matthew	Mark	Luke	John
Three women set out for the tomb	—	—	3:55; 24:1	—
The stone has been rolled away	—	—	24:2–9	—
Mary Magdalene leaves to tell Jesus' disciples	—	—	—	20:1–2
The women see angels	—	—	—	20:1–2
Peter and John come and look in tomb	—	—	—	20:3–10
The women return with spices	—	—	24:1–4	—
These women see angels	—	16:5	24:5	—
The angel says Jesus is risen	28:6–8	—	—	—
Departing, they meet Jesus	28:9–10	—	—	—

Additional Appearances of Jesus

Event	Matthew	Mark	Luke	John	Other
To Peter the same day	—	—	24:35	—	
To disciple on Emmaus road	—	—	24:13–31	—	
To the apostles (but not Thomas)	—	—	24:36–45	20:19–24	
To the apostles (with Thomas)	—	—	—	20:24–29	
To seven at Lake Tiberius	—	—	—	21:1–23	
To some 500 in Galilee	—	—	—	—	1 Corinthians 15:6
To James in Jerusalem	—	—	—	—	1 Corinthians 15:7
To many at Jesus' ascension	—	—	—	—	Acts 1:3–12
To Stephen when he was stoned	—	—	—	—	Acts 7:55
To Paul near Damascus	—	—	—	—	Acts 9:3–6
To Paul in the Temple	—	—	—	—	Acts 22:17–19
To John on Patmos	—	—	—	—	Revelation 1:10–19

Up from the Grave He Rose

Jesus was buried late Friday afternoon in the garden tomb of Joseph of Arimathea, and his body remained there all of Saturday. Early Sunday—by normal Jewish reckoning, the third day—Jesus rose from the dead.

Son of God
Romans 1:3

The four Gospels each give an account of the events of that day. Working from all four, we can reconstruct the events.

Looking back on the resurrection of Jesus from the dead, the apostle Paul sees it as God's powerful and ultimate declaration that he truly was and is the Son of God.

And what significance does the resurrection of Jesus have for you and me? The Resurrection is both proof and promise that death is not the end . . . for anyone.

Chapter Wrap-Up

- When Jesus entered Jerusalem on Palm Sunday, he was acclaimed as the Messiah.
- Jesus exposed the hypocrisy of the leaders and openly condemned them.
- The religious leaders determined to kill Jesus in order to maintain their own power and position.
- Jesus told his disciples that he would be crucified, but that afterward he would come to earth again to rule.
- Jesus was seized at night, tried, and condemned by the Jewish Sanhedrin for claiming to be the Son of God.
- Jesus was crucified by the Romans as King of the Jews.
- Jesus died and was buried, but on the third day he rose from the grave and was seen by many witnesses.

Study Questions

1. What event began Jesus' last week on earth?
2. What did Jesus do in the temple that offended the chief priests?
3. Why was the Pharisees' question about paying taxes a trap, and how did Jesus answer them?
4. According to Matthew 23, what did Jesus say that the Pharisees and teachers of the Law were?
5. How did God answer the prayer Jesus made in Gethsemane?
6. What was Jesus charged with in the Jewish courts? What was Jesus charged with in Pilate's court?
7. What happened to Jesus' body after he was crucified?
8. How does the Bible explain the significance of Jesus' death?
9. What does the fact of Jesus' resurrection mean for us today?

Acts

Let's Get Started

The raising of Jesus marked the beginning of Christianity. The disciples began to proclaim Christ as resurrected Lord. Many in Jerusalem believed their message, and a vital community of believers was formed. Acts traces the early expansion of Christianity from its Jewish roots to a faith spread throughout the Roman Empire (see Illustration #15).

gospel
"good news" about Jesus as Savior

Holy Spirit
God, the third person of the Trinity

Acts

. . . the spread of the gospel

Who	Luke, a physician and companion of Paul on his missionary journeys,
What	wrote this book of history about the early Church
Where	in Rome
When	about AD 63
Why	to record the spread of the **gospel** throughout the Roman world between AD 33 and AD 63

Up, Up, and Away

The first chapter of Acts is a prelude to the New Testament. It presents three keys to understanding Christianity in the first century—and today!

Key #1

ACTS 1:8 ***But you shall receive power when the Holy Spirit has come upon you.*** *(NKJV)*

The first key to understanding Acts and the New Testament is that when Jesus returned to heaven, he sent the Holy Spirit to provide power for Christian living and Christian witness. The book of Acts is the story of the works of the Holy Spirit in and through believers in Jesus.

Illustration #15
The Roman Empire—Within thirty years of Jesus' resurrection, the gospel had spread throughout the Roman Empire. There were Christian groups in most of its major cities. The rapid spread was made possible because Rome maintained good roads, and had wiped out the pirates who had made sea travel unsafe. Everyone in the Roman Empire spoke a common tongue, Greek, which made it possible to share the gospel in different countries. And the New Testament **Epistles**, written in Greek, could be read by all.

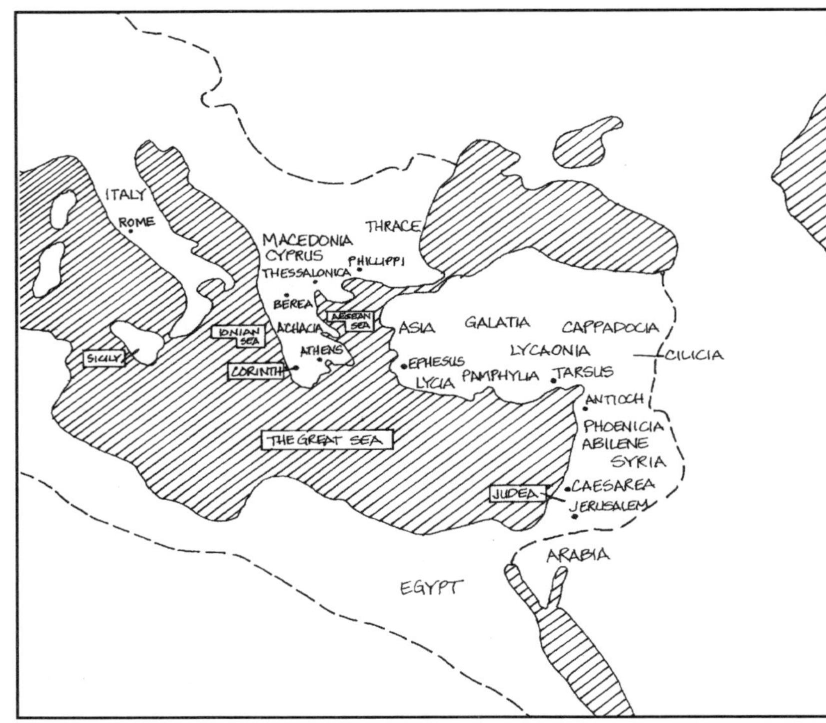

are one
Matthew 28:19; John 15:26

a person distinct
Ephesians 1:3–14

power in ministry
Matthew 12:28; Luke 4:18; John 3:34

empowered spiritually
John 14:16–17; John 16:5–15; Acts 1:8

Christian experience
Romans 8:1–4; Galatians 5:22–25

The Holy Spirit is the active power behind the events related in Acts. It's important to remember that the Spirit is a person, not an impersonal force or an "influence." While he and God the Father and God the Spirit are one, each is at the same time a person distinct from the others. As we read the New Testament we realize how important the Spirit's ministry was—and is. The Gospels picture the Holy Spirit as the one who oversaw the birth of Jesus and who was the source of Jesus' power in ministry. Jesus promised to give the Holy Spirit as a gift to his followers, that we too might be empowered spiritually. The **Epistles** contain much detailed teaching about the role of the Holy Spirit in the lives of Christians and the Christian community. There is no doubt that the vitality of our Christian experience depends on our reliance on the Holy Spirit, whom God has given to those who trust in Jesus.

Epistles
New Testament letters written by apostles

Key #2

Acts 1:9–11 ***Now when He had spoken these things, while they watched, [Jesus] was taken up, and a cloud received Him out of their sight. And while they looked steadfastly toward heaven as***

He went up, behold, two men stood by them in white apparel, who also said, "Men of Galilee, why do you stand gazing up into heaven? This same Jesus, who was taken up from you into heaven, will so come in like manner as you saw Him go into heaven." (NKJV)

advocate
a person who pleads the cause of another

witnesses
those who testify to what they have experienced

Forty days after the Resurrection, Jesus was taken up into heaven. He will remain there until, as the angels promised, he comes back again. But what is Jesus doing now?

The New Testament Tells Us . . .

What Jesus Is Doing Now	Scripture
Jesus is preparing a place for us	John 14:2
Jesus is interceding (praying) for us	Romans 8:34; Hebrews 7:25
Jesus is our **Advocate** when we sin	1 John 2:1
Jesus is guiding and directing us	Ephesians 1:22

Ephesians adds that all things have been placed under his feet (Ephesians 1:22). Today Jesus is the ultimate authority in the universe, and is actively working out God's plan for individuals and the world. While not physically present on earth, Jesus is at work within and for those who trust him.

Key #3

ACTS 1:8 *You shall receive power when the Holy Spirit has come upon you; and you shall be* ***witnesses*** *. . . to the end of the earth.* (NKJV)

The men identified as Jesus' disciples in the Gospels become his apostles in Acts, and testify to the reality of Jesus' resurrection. Although Acts emphasizes the ministry of two apostles, the privilege of being Jesus' witness is given to every believer.

Rushing Wind and Tongues of Fire

the big picture

The Church Grows

The promised coming of the Holy Spirit did empower the apostles. This section of Acts records two powerful sermons of Peter, and describes the response. Although the leaders who had conspired to have Jesus crucified threatened the apostles, and through disputes threatened the unity of the young Christian community, the church in Jerusalem multiplied rapidly.

deacon
a church officer; a servant

remission
release from guilt or penalty of sin

PETER: Peter was the leading disciple and apostle who preached the first gospel sermons.

STEPHEN: Stephen was the **deacon** and vibrant Christian witness who was stoned to death for his witness to Christ in Jerusalem.

What's Special in Acts 2–7?

1. **The Holy Spirit filled and empowered Jesus' followers** (Acts 2:1–21). Fifty days after the Resurrection, during a Jewish festival called Pentecost, the Holy Spirit filled Jesus' followers, who had been gathered for prayer. This initial coming of the Spirit was marked by visible signs: the sound of rushing wind, tongues of fire above the believers' heads, and the miraculous translation of what the believers said, so that each foreign visitor to Jerusalem "heard them speak in his own language" (Acts 2:6 NKJV).

Peter explained the phenomenon by referring to an Old Testament prophecy in which God promised, "I will pour out of My Spirit on all flesh" (Acts 2:17 NKJV).

2. **History's first two gospel sermons** (Acts 2:22–3:26). Acts records two of Peter's sermons preached to crowds gathered in Jerusalem (Acts 2:22–39; 3:12–26). The truths of these sermons remain the central truths on which Christianity rests. As Acts 2 and 3 report, the early preaching of the apostles was accompanied by miracles, authenticating their message of Jesus and his continuing power as Lord.

The Truths Preached About Jesus

Truth	First Sermon in Acts	Second Sermon in Acts
The historic person	2:22	—
Was crucified and raised from the dead	2:23–24	3:15–15
As prophecy foretold	2:25–35	3:18
He is God's Messiah	2:36	3:20
All who believe in him will receive **remission** of sins, and be given the Holy Spirit	2:37–38	3:19, 21–26

3. The overwhelming response to the gospel message (Acts 2:41; 6:7). After Peter's first sermon, some three thousand people responded to the gospel and trusted Jesus as Savior.

fellowship of believers
Acts 2:42–47; 4:32–35

ACTS 6:7 ***Then the word of God spread, and the number of the disciples multiplied greatly in Jerusalem, and a great many of the priests were obedient to the faith. (NKJV)***

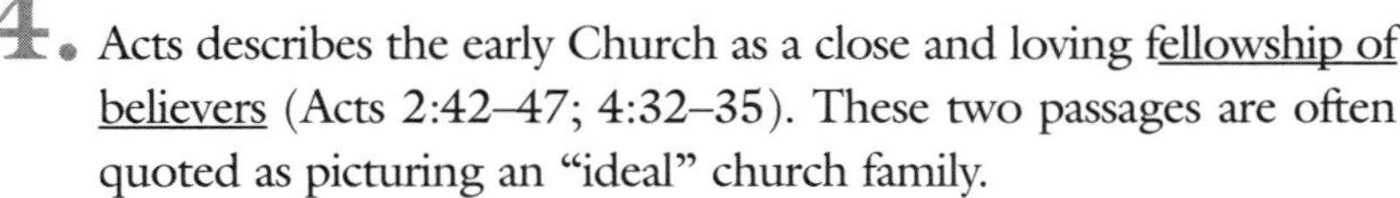

4. Acts describes the early Church as a close and loving <u>fellowship of believers</u> (Acts 2:42–47; 4:32–35). These two passages are often quoted as picturing an "ideal" church family.

When looking for a church today, it is wise to seek one devoted to the apostles' teaching, to caring fellowship, and to prayer.

5. Even the "ideal" Jerusalem church faced external and internal challenges (Acts 4–7). These chapters describe two external and two internal challenges that the Jerusalem church faced. Check out one of each of the following:

New Church Challenges

External	Challenge	Response
Acts 4:1–31`	Peter and John are threatened	The church gathers to pray
Acts 6:8–7:60	Stephen is stoned by a mob	Stephen prays for his killers
Internal	**Challenge**	**Response**
Acts 5:1–11	Two people lie to God	God publicly judges them and the apostles
Acts 6:1–7	There are complaints of unfair treatment	Deacons are appointed to oversee

<u>Go Tell It on the Mountain</u>

the big picture

Expansion

After the stoning of Stephen, the Christians in Jerusalem were persecuted, and most were forced to leave the city. But as the new believers traveled, they shared the gospel with others. Soon the message spread to Judea and even to Samaria, where Samaritans also accepted Christ as Savior. The great surprise for the early Jewish Christians took place when a retired Roman centurion named Cornelius was converted, and it dawned on all that the message of salvation was for all people, not just for God's covenant people, the Jews.

eunuch
by the first century the title of a high official in some lands

conversion
a person's turning to God

Gentile
any non-Jew

PHILIP: One of the first deacons, who launches a revival in Samaria.

SAUL: A young Pharisee who after his conversion will gain fame as the apostle Paul.

BARNABAS: An early convert who became a leader in the first gentile church, and Paul's companion on his first missionary journey.

CORNELIUS: A Roman centurion who believes in Israel's God, and becomes the first gentile convert to Christianity.

What's Special in Acts 8–12?

1. **When Philip begins to preach Christ in Samaria, many are converted** (Acts 8:1–25). The Samaritans were a foreign people who had been settled in Israel by the Assyrians after the Jews were deported in 722 BC. While they worshiped Israel's God, the Jews considered their religion corrupt and would have nothing to do with them. But Philip's preaching and the miracles he performed in Jesus' name convinced many to trust Christ.

In this case God delayed giving the Holy Spirit to believing Samaritans until the apostles Peter and John came from Jerusalem. This established the authority of the apostles and the fact that the church is one.

2. **Philip is called away from Samaria to share the gospel with one individual** (Acts 8:26–40). The Holy Spirit took Philip from a ministry of thousands to share the gospel with one individual, an Ethiopian **eunuch**. God is as concerned with the salvation of a single individual as he is with thousands.

3. **The conversion of Saul** (Acts 9). In the Roman Empire noncitizens were governed by the law of their homeland. This gave the Sanhedrin in Jerusalem authority over Jews anywhere in the empire. Saul was authorized by the Sanhedrin to arrest Christian Jews in Damascus, another country in the empire. On the way Christ spoke to Saul, and the encounter led to Saul's **conversion**.

Immediately this persecutor of the church began to promote the faith he had tried to stamp out!

4. **Peter's vision** (Acts 10:9–22). The Jews considered **Gentiles** unclean. This meant that contact with a Gentile could disqualify a

Jew from participating in worship at God's temple. God gave Peter a vision, and a voice from heaven told Peter to kill and eat unclean animals. Shocked, Peter refused. Peter was then told not to regard as impure anything that God had made clean. Immediately afterward messengers came from Cornelius, a retired Roman officer, inviting Peter to his house. Peter realized that God intended him to go, despite the fact that the Jews regarded Gentiles as unclean.

kill and eat unclean animals
Leviticus 11

5. **The conversion of Cornelius** (Acts 10–11). When Peter shared the gospel at the house of Cornelius, all who gathered there believed and began to speak in tongues. Peter saw this as a sign that God had accepted Gentiles into the church. When he reported what happened, the Jerusalem Christians praised God, saying, "Then God has also granted to the Gentiles repentance to life" (Acts 11:18 NKJV).

what others say

Craig S. Keener

Until now no one had believed that Gentiles could be saved on the same terms as Jewish people, who had been chosen for salvation by God's sovereign grace.[1]

6. **The first predominantly gentile church is established in Antioch** (Acts 11:1–30). News reached Jerusalem that a church made up of Gentiles existed in Antioch (see Illustration #15). Soon thereafter, the apostles sent Barnabas to Antioch, who became a leader there. He also brought Saul of Tarsus into the leadership team.

7. **Peter is freed from prison by an angel** (Acts 12). King Herod Antipas, a grandson of Herod the Great, executed the apostle James. When he saw that this pleased the Jewish leaders, he arrested Peter. But an angel freed Peter from prison and later struck Herod with a fatal sickness. God was protecting his Church.

In Acts this is the last we hear of Peter. Church history tells us that Peter ministered primarily to Jewish Christians throughout the Roman Empire, and that he was crucified in Rome under the emperor Nero around AD 66.

Off We Go (AD 46–57)

missionary
a person sent by a church to carry on religious work

the big picture

Paul's Journey

These chapters in Acts briefly summarize the apostle Paul's three missionary journeys (see Appendix A) to major cities of the Roman Empire. Paul and his companions established churches in these population centers. The new Christians then spread the gospel to the surrounding villages and countryside. Later, Paul revisited these churches to give them additional teaching. Paul also wrote letters of instruction to the young churches. His letters were collected and distributed to churches everywhere. Thirteen of Paul's letters are in the New Testament.

What's Special in Acts 13–20?

1. **Paul's missions strategy** (Acts 13, 14). On entering a city Paul went first to the Jewish synagogue to teach about Jesus. Many God-fearers responded to the gospel and with Jewish converts formed the core of Christian churches.

The Cities Paul and His Team Visited

City	Scripture
Psidian Antioch	Acts 13:13–52
Iconium	Acts 14:1–60
Lystra and Derbe	Acts 14:8–20
Thessalonica	Acts 17:1–9
Berea	Acts 17:10–18
Corinth	Acts 18:1–28

2. **The Jerusalem Council in AD 49** (Acts 15). Paul's success in establishing churches led to a theological dispute. Some Jewish Christians were convinced that the gentile believers should keep the Law of Moses and be circumcised.

To the apostle Paul this was a corruption of the gospel, which offers salvation to sinners solely on the basis of faith in Jesus, who died for mankind's sins. Peter agreed, and James, the brother of Jesus, summarized the council's conclusion.

Although the Jerusalem Council agreed that salvation was not linked to keeping the Law of Moses, the early Church continued to be troubled by Jewish Christians who visited gentile churches and taught that salvation came from faith plus keeping God's Law.

3. **The challenges of missionary life** (2 Corinthians 11:23–28). Reading in Acts 16 and 19, it is clear that Paul and his team faced many challenges and difficulties spreading the gospel throughout the Roman Empire. Paul sums up twenty years of missionary experience in 2 Corinthians 11:

2 Corinthians 11:23–29 ***Are they ministers of Christ?—I speak as a fool—I am more: in labors more abundant, in stripes above measure, in prisons more frequently, in deaths often. From the Jews five times I received forty stripes minus one. Three times I was beaten with rods; once I was stoned; three times I was shipwrecked; a night and a day I have been in the deep; in journeys often, in perils of waters, in perils of robbers, in perils of my own countrymen, in perils of the Gentiles, in perils in the city, in perils in the wilderness, in perils in the sea, in perils among false brethren; in weariness and toil, in sleeplessness often, in hunger and thirst, in fastings often, in cold and nakedness—besides the other things, what comes upon me daily: my deep concern for all the churches. Who is weak, and I am not weak? Who is made to stumble, and I do not burn with indignation? (NKJV)***

What drove Paul and other early Christians was not any profit they might make from the gospel, but the conviction that people everywhere needed to hear of the forgiveness of sins God offers to all who simply trust in his Son.

Cornered (AD 57–63)

the big picture

Paul's Trial

In AD 57, Paul felt led to return to Jerusalem. When a riot broke out there, Roman soldiers rescued him, and he claimed protection as a Roman citizen. The Jews claimed Paul was a political agitator and a religious renegade. The Roman governor kept Paul in Caesarea (see Illustration #15) for two years, hoping for a bribe. Then when a new governor was appointed, Paul exercised his right as a Roman citizen. He appealed to Caesar to have his case decided in Rome. Acts tells the story of Paul's journey to Rome (see Appendix A) and even includes information about a shipwreck along the way, but the book concludes before Paul goes to trial.

acquitted
declared not guilty

What's Special in Acts 21–28?

1. **The Jerusalem riot and Paul's arrest** (Acts 21:17–22:29). The riot broke out when Jews who recognized Paul falsely accused him of bringing Gentiles into the temple.

After being rescued, Paul asked to speak to the crowd. When he reported that the Lord told him to go to the Gentiles, the crowd rioted again.

2. **The trial before Felix** (Acts 24:1–27). Paul's bold witness frightened but also fascinated Felix, who kept Paul under house arrest for two years in hopes of getting a bribe.
3. **The trial before Festus** (Acts 25, 26). Paul exercised his right as a Roman citizen to appeal to Caesar, to be tried in Rome by an imperial court.

For the third time recorded in Acts, Paul tells the story of his conversion, this time to a room filled with high officials.

Paul's position seemed like madness to the Roman, but King Agrippa, who believed the prophets, understood the message. There is no historical record of his becoming a believer.

4. **The voyage to Rome** (Acts 27, 28). Acts concludes with Luke's account of a terrible storm that wrecked the ship on which Paul and other prisoners were being taken to Rome. Paul lived there under guard for two years, freely sharing the gospel with visitors and with the soldiers who guarded him.

What Happened to Paul?

Acts ends before Paul goes to trial. Tradition tells us that he was **acquitted** and continued his missionary work by going to Spain. Later, during the reign of Nero, again Paul was arrested. This time the faithful apostle, like Peter, was put to death in Rome.

Chapter Wrap-Up

- Acts is a history of the expansion of Christianity during the thirty years following Jesus' resurrection.
- Jesus ascended to heaven, where today he intercedes for believers and guides his Church.
- Jesus sent the Holy Spirit to empower his disciples to be witnesses of him throughout the world.
- Peter was the first to preach the gospel message to the Jews. He was also the first to preach to any Gentile.
- After his conversion Saul of Tarsus became Paul the Apostle, who spearheaded bringing the gospel to the gentile world.
- In three missionary journeys over a span of eleven years, the apostle Paul established churches in many of the major cities of the Roman Empire.
- Paul's arrest and trial gave him opportunities to present the gospel to important government officials in Palestine and in Rome itself.

Study Questions

1. What kind of literature is Acts?
2. With what event does Acts begin?
3. What did the coming of the Holy Spirit provide the disciples?
4. What were two of the five basic truths emphasized in Peter's first two gospel sermons?
5. What two persons are the dominant figures in Acts?
6. What was important about the conversion of Cornelius?
7. How many missionary journeys of Paul are reported in Acts?
8. Why was the Jerusalem Council significant?
9. When Acts ends, where is the apostle Paul?

Romans • Galatians

Let's Get Started

The last five chapters have covered Matthew through Acts, books of the Bible that consist of stories, or historical narrative, about Jesus and about Jesus' followers. This chapter will cover the first two books of a different kind of writing—epistles. The Epistles are letters of correspondence that were written by Jesus' apostles, sometimes to churches and sometimes to individuals. There are twenty-one of them in the New Testament, and each is designed to instruct believers through the ages. Eventually the letters were copied and circulated to all the churches. Collections of the Epistles were valued in the first century and recognized as Scripture—the authoritative Word of God, transmitted through men, but **inspired** by the Holy Spirit.

inspired
God-guided

There are two major collections of letters: the Pauline Epistles, and the General Epistles. The Pauline Epistles were written by Paul, and the General Epistles were written by Peter, John, Jude, James, and the unknown author of Hebrews.

We don't have enough space here to address each epistle from start to finish, but an outline of each will be provided, so that if you want to "dig deeper" into Scripture, you will have a guide along the way. We will, however, look at a sampling of each epistle, and then we'll discuss the key thought that sums up each book's main focus.

There are several kinds of literature in the Bible. There's narrative—books like Ruth that tell a story. There's history—books like Exodus and 1 Kings and Acts that record events. There's poetry—like Psalms—and prophecy—like Isaiah and Jeremiah. Each kind of Bible literature is God's message to us, but we find that message expressed in different ways. For instance, in Bible history the writers carefully select and describe, and we find God's message in watching the events unfold and listening carefully to the writers' descriptions.

The epistles are yet a different kind of literature. The epistles are letters written to churches or individuals by Jesus' apostles. They contain specific teaching that applies to all Christians everywhere. In their teaching the New Testament epistle writers explain, argue, illustrate, and exhort, carefully developing important truths about Christian faith. When we read the epistles we need to carefully trace the flow of thought—called the "argument" of each writer. When we understand the overall flow of thought we can more accurately grasp the meaning of individual words, phrases, and verses.

In the following introductions to each New Testament epistle you'll find an outline that will help you trace the writer's argument, his flow of thought.

We will group the epistles according to common themes as charted below.

Common Themes Found in the Epistles

The Epistles	Common Theme
Romans, Galatians	Paul's letters that explain the gospel
1 and 2 Corinthians and 1 and 2 Thessalonians	Paul's letters written to clear up misunderstandings
Ephesians, Colossians, Philippians	Paul's letters written from prison in Rome
1 and 2 Timothy, Titus, Philemon	Paul's letters written to individuals
Hebrews	Christ's superiority to Judaism
James, 1 and 2 Peter, 1, 2, and 3 John, Jude	Letters written by other apostles on various themes

In these chapters we'll find out what each letter is about, and look at particular sections in depth.

Romans

. . . God's gift of righteousness

Who	The apostle Paul
What	carefully explained the Christian gospel
Where	to Christians in Rome
When	about AD 57
Why	so that they would understand the relationship between grace and righteousness

The Old Testament reveals God as a moral Being, whose Law laid out standards of righteousness that God expected his people to maintain. Then the Christian gospel burst on the scene, and Jesus' apostles announced that because Christ died for our sins, God would forgive the sins of all who simply trust in him. To some the gospel message seemed scandalous! What about righteousness? Isn't a salvation won by faith inconsistent with the very nature of a God who is righteous and who, as the Old Testament reveals, expects righteousness from his people?

In Romans Paul answers the very real questions about the gospel that were asked in the first century, and that are often asked today.

Tracing Paul's Argument—His Flow of Thought

The argument of a New Testament epistle is its flow of thought. When we trace the argument of Romans, we not only have a summary of its content, we have an outline of the book. Here's how Paul answers the questions about righteousness.

Paul's Flow of Thought

Introduction	Romans 1:1–17
No one is righteous in God's sight	1:18–3:20
• not the Gentiles	1:18–32
• not the Jews,	2:1–3:8
• and Scripture proves this.	3:9–20
So God provided righteousness as a gift	3:21–5:21
• through the death of Christ.	3:21–31
• In fact, God has always accepted faith in place of righteousness,	4:1–25
• as the experience of Abraham and David illustrates,	4:1–17
◦ and as we can experience faith in Jesus today.	4:18–25
• So sinners today can have peace with God through Christ,	5:1–11
• who has reversed the curse that Adam's sin imposed on humankind.	5:12–21
What's more, faith in Christ makes it possible for saved sinners to live righteous lives,	6:1–39
• because faith unites us with Jesus.	6:1–23

alienation
separation

wrath
God's firm intent to punish sin and sinner

ungodliness
failure to show reverence for God

Paul's Flow of Thought (cont'd)

• We can't live up to the Law's demands in our own strength, so we do not look to the Law to help us. Instead,	7:1–25
• we rely on the Holy Spirit who gives the power to please God here and now,	8:1–17
• and who will totally transform us in bringing us to glory in eternity.	8:18–39
God is not being unrighteous in making this gift available now to Gentiles, because	9:1–11:36
• setting Israel aside is just, and	9:1–10:21
• God will yet keep the prophets' promises to Israel in the future.	11:1–36
So Christians today are called to live righteous lives,	12:1–15:13
• as members together of a community of believers,	12:1–21
• as citizens in a secular society,	13:1–14
• and as brothers and sisters who accept one another and glorify God together.	14:1–15:13
Personal greetings (closing)	15:14–16:27

A Little Sample

To get a feel for the book of Romans, let's look together at verses from Section 1 of Paul's argument above. Paul speaks directly to the issue of human righteousness by pointing out that no one is righteous in God's sight. If salvation depends on our efforts to please God by doing what he requires, we are in trouble indeed! And our trouble all begins with our **alienation** from God! It is this alienation that has brought all human beings under the wrath of God.

God's Wrath for the Unrighteous

Romans 1:18 *For the **wrath** of God is revealed from heaven against all **ungodliness** and unrighteousness of men, who suppress the truth in unrighteousness, . . . (NKJV)*

God is not indifferent to unrighteousness. People who sin are objects of God's wrath, subject to eternal punishment. That truth is being revealed even now, in the corruption of morals and in the wickedness of those who suppress the truth.

I Don't Want to Hear It

ROMANS 1:19–20 ***Because what may be known of God is manifest in them, for God has shown it to them. For since the creation of the world His invisible attributes are clearly seen, being understood by the things that are made, even His eternal power and Godhead, so that they are without excuse.*** *(NKJV)*

suppress
purposefully ignore

glorify
to give God credit and praise for what he has done

The truth that human beings **suppress** is simply the fact that a Creator God exists. Paul's point is that the Creation is like a great radio transmitter, broadcasting the message of his existence. The Greek uses a different phrase in the clause, God has made it plain to them. What the Greek says is that God has made it plain "in them." God not only shaped the universe to send the message that he formed all that exists; God also shaped human nature with a built-in receiver, tuned to God's station. Human beings who suppress the truth of God's existence are without excuse, because to reject or ignore God they must have willfully "turned down" their inner receiver. Human beings have willfully refused to accept the message God is broadcasting.

Bow Down—No Way

ROMANS 1:21 ***Because, although they knew God, they did not glorify Him as God, nor were thankful.*** *(NKJV)*

The appropriate response to God's revelation of himself in creation is to give God credit for his works and to thank him. Rather than do this, humans have suppressed the truth that God exists and deserves our worship.

Gods That Can't Talk Back

ROMANS 1:21–23 ***But became futile in their thoughts, and their foolish hearts were darkened. Professing to be wise, they became fools, and changed the glory of the incorruptible God into an image made like corruptible man—and birds and four-footed animals and creeping things.*** *(NKJV)*

Okay, Have It Your Way

Romans 1:24–25 ***Therefore God also gave them up to uncleanness, in the lusts of their hearts, to dishonor their bodies among themselves, who exchanged the truth of God for the lie, and worshiped and served the creature rather than the Creator, who is blessed forever. Amen.*** *(NKJV)*

The phrase "gave them up" is repeated in Romans 1:26, and "gave them over" appears in 1:28. Paul has said that God's wrath is being revealed from heaven (Romans 1:18). The sexual impurity and the other sins he describes in this chapter are clear evidence that God's wrath is directed against those who have rejected him. For the more morally corrupt a person or society becomes, the less peace, joy, and inner satisfaction human beings will experience. Sin may look attractive, but when indulged in, sins make us miserable! The misery that results from our sins is evidence of God's anger!

> what others say
>
> **Max Lucado**
>
> God's highest dream is not to make us rich, not to make us successful or popular or famous. God's dream is to make us right with him.[1]

Men with Men, Women with Women

Romans 1:26–27 ***For this reason God gave them up to vile passions. For even their women exchanged the natural use for what is against nature. Likewise also the men, leaving the natural use of the woman, burned in their lust for one another, men with men committing what is shameful, and receiving in themselves the penalty of their error which was due.*** *(NKJV)*

> what others say
>
> **Wolfheart Pannenberg**
>
> The New Testament contains not a single passage that might indicate a more positive assessment of homosexuality than these Pauline statements. Thus, the entire biblical witness includes practicing homosexuality without exception among the kinds of behavior that give particularly striking expression to humanity's turning away from God.[2]

Wake Up, I'm Here

ROMANS 1:28–31 *And even as they did not like to retain God in their knowledge, God gave them over to a debased mind, to do those things which are not fitting; being filled with all unrighteousness, sexual immorality, wickedness, covetousness, maliciousness; full of envy, murder, strife, deceit, evil-mindedness; they are whisperers, backbiters, haters of God, violent, proud, boasters, inventors of evil things, disobedient to parents, undiscerning, untrustworthy, unloving, unforgiving, unmerciful . . . (NKJV)*

righteous judgment
God's requirement that humans do what is right

Genesis reveals the source of all that is good in human beings. God created humankind in his own image, with the capacity to love, to respond to love, to enjoy beauty and make beautiful things. Romans traces the origin of that which we all agree is evil. In abandoning God and suppressing the truth about him, human beings open themselves up to all that is evil. The very existence of such evils in society is evidence of man's abandonment of God, for where God is known and loved such behavior is unthinkable.

That's Okay with Me

ROMANS 1:32 *Who, knowing the **righteous judgment** of God, that those who practice such things are deserving of death, not only do the same but also approve of those who practice them. (NKJV)*

To understand what Paul is saying here we need only observe those who defend what everyone knows is immoral behavior, arguing for privacy rights and the freedom to do what we wish without being subject to the morality of "religious bigots." Rather than taking a stand for what is right, such persons insist that others have the "right" to do what is wrong.

In this first chapter, then, Paul argues that the sins in which individuals and societies find themselves entangled, are in fact evidence of God's wrath, directed against those who have rejected a personal relationship with him. To argue that human beings must act in righteous ways to please God is to put the cart in place of the horse. What human beings need is to reestablish a relationship with God that will free them from their sins!

In Romans 2, Paul goes on to make it clear that all who have sinned will be judged by God.

God's Principles of Divine Judgment

divine standards
Romans 2:1–38

ROMANS 2:12 ***For as many as have sinned without law will also perish without law, and as many as have sinned in the law will be judged by the law.*** *(NKJV)*

Because not everyone knows the divine standards as revealed in Moses' Law, it would hardly be fair to use the Ten Commandments to measure everyone's behavior. That is, the Jew, to whom the Law was given, can be judged by the Law, which he knows and accepts. But Gentiles, whose moral viewpoint has not been shaped by a knowledge of the divine Law, can hardly be judged by it. However, this does not acquit the person who is ignorant of God's standards: they too will perish.

Everyone Knows "Right" and "Wrong"

ROMANS 2:14–15 ***For when Gentiles, who do not have the law, by nature do the things in the law, these, although not having the law, are a law to themselves, who show the work of the law written in their hearts, their conscience also bearing witness, and between themselves their thoughts accusing or else excusing them) . . .*** *(NKJV)*

Paul's point is that everyone, even those ignorant of God's revealed standards, still recognizes that some things are morally right, and others morally wrong. For example, some cultures consider it moral to have as many as four wives. But in every culture some kinds of sexual behavior are labeled "wrong" and others "right." This points to the fact that human beings were created with a moral sense, so that all are evaluating actions as "right" or "wrong." Societies without access to God's standards create their own standards. Even more to the point, every person's conscience bears witness to the fact that he or she has violated her own standards, if not God's!

Because God is totally just and fair, God will not judge those who do not know his Law by that Law. Instead, he will judge them by their own moral standards! And when that happens every person will be judged "guilty"! for each of us is aware that we have not always done that which we ourselves believe is right.

what others say

Everett F. Harrison

Despite the great differences in laws and customs among people around the world, what unites them in a common humanity is the recognition that some things are right and others are wrong.[3]

That Old Conscience Again

The apostle Paul quotes the Old Testament as proof that all have sinned:

ROMANS 3:9–11 ***We have previously charged both Jews and Greeks that they are all under sin. As it is written:***
"There is none righteous, no, not one;
There is none who understands;
There is none who seeks after God." *(NKJV)*

Paul has argued that God's wrath is being expressed in the sins we see all around us. God's future judgment of sinners will be fair, for God will judge those who live under the Law by the Law, and judge others by their own standards of right and wrong. But whatever standard is used, our own consciences convict us.

Now Paul offers proof. God's Word says that there is no one righteous, not even one. When a human being stands before God to be judged by him, not one will be judged righteous.

The Law Won't Get You to Heaven

ROMANS 3:19–20 ***Now we know that whatever the law says, it says to those who are under the law, that every mouth may be stopped, and all the world may become guilty before God. Therefore by the deeds of the law no flesh will be justified in His sight, for by the law is the knowledge of sin.*** *(NKJV)*

The Law was never intended as a guide to show human beings how they might please God, or as a standard we are to live up to. The Law was intended to be a mirror, to show us how far short we fall of being what we ought to be! The Law cannot save us, but through it we can become aware of our sin.

No one will be declared righteous in God's sight by observing the Law. Through the Law we become conscious of sin.

But There's Hope!

all have sinned
Romans 3:23

Romans was written for those who were scandalized by a gospel that offers salvation to sinners as a free gift. It was written for those who assumed that in promising to forgive sins, God was acting against his own nature as a righteous God.

Paul's response is profound. Those who assume such must first face a simple fact. No human being is or can become righteous. All have sinned. If salvation depends on human effort to do what is right, all are lost indeed!

Man's Problem:

The roots of sin are anchored in mankind's rejection of God.

God's Solution:

Jesus Christ died to pay the penalty for man's sin that through faith in him those who believe might not only be forgiven but reestablish a personal relationship with God! And just as man's rejection of God produced sins in individuals and society, the restoration of a personal relationship with God will produce righteousness in those who are joined to Jesus Christ!

Romans teaches us that the gospel is about righteousness! God declares those who believe in Jesus to be righteous in his sight. And then God works in the believer's life to produce a righteousness that we could never demonstrate apart from him.

what others say

Max Lucado

Simply put: The cost of your sins is more than you can pay. The gift of your God is more than you can imagine. A person is made right with God through faith, Paul explains, not through obeying the Law (Romans 3:28).[4]

John Wesley

You are called to show by the whole tenor of your life and conversation that you are renewed in the spirit of your mind.[5]

Galatians

. . . the Law, or the Spirit?

Who	The apostle Paul
What	wrote this letter
Where	to Christians in the province of Galatia
When	about AD 49
Why	to explain how freedom from the demands of Old Testament Law promotes righteous living and true goodness

Judaizers
men who taught that Christians must keep Jewish laws

Rely on the Grace of God, Not the Law

Acts reports that after Paul and Barnabas completed their first missionary journey, men came down from Judea to Antioch (see Appendix A), and were teaching the brothers, "Unless you are circumcised according to the custom of Moses, you cannot be saved" (Acts 15:1 NKJV). These **Judaizers** insisted that gentile Christians be required to obey the Law of Moses (Acts 15:5). Many new Christians were confused. After all, the Old Testament was God's Word. Shouldn't Christians be responsible to keep its laws as well as to trust in Christ?

Paul saw this teaching as a critical distortion of the gospel. He sent this letter to the Galatian churches to help them understand the limitations of the Law and the secrets of living in reliance on God's Holy Spirit.

what others say

James Montgomery Boice

Galatians has been called the "Magna Carta of Christian liberty," and this is quite correct. For it rightly maintains that only through the grace of God in Jesus Christ is a person enabled to escape from the curse of his sin and of the Law and to a new life, not in bondage or license, but in genuine freedom of mind and spirit through the power of God.[6]

Tracing Paul's Argument

The Judaizers attacked Paul on three grounds. They claimed that (1) Paul is not really an apostle, (2) God authored the Law, and Paul shouldn't teach that it is set aside, and (3) Paul's teaching is a license to sin. Paul's letter to the Galatians responds to each of these charges. The outline below traces Paul's argument.

Paul's Argument

Greetings	Galatians 1:1–5
Paul's apostleship rests on the fact that	Galatians 1:11–2:21
• Jesus himself revealed the gospel to Paul,	Galatians 1:11, 12
• God himself called Paul to his ministry,	Galatians 1:13–24
• Jesus' apostles confirmed Paul's calling.	Galatians 2:1–21
Paul's teaching distinguishes between Law and Faith.	Galatians 3:1–4:31
• Law is unrelated to	Galatians 3:1–18
◦ how we receive spiritual life,	Galatians 3:1–5
◦ how Old Testament saints were made righteous	Galatians 3:6–9
◦ how God fulfills his promises, and	Galatians 3:10–14
◦ how those promises function in our relationship with God.	Galatians 3:15–18
• The Law's role has always been limited	Galatians 3:19–4:7
◦ by the fact that it was temporary,	Galatians 3:19–20
◦ by the fact that it cannot give life,	Galatians 3:21–22
◦ by the fact that Law points to faith, and	Galatians 3:23–24
◦ by the fact that believers now have full rights as God's sons.	Galatians 3:25–4:7
• The Law is an inferior way, that leads to	Galatians 4:8–5:12
◦ loss of joy,	Galatians 4:8–19
◦ loss of freedom, and	Galatians 4:20–5:1
◦ loss of power.	Galatians 5:2–12
Paul's emphasis on freedom produces godliness that affirms love	Galatians 5:13–25
• affirms love,	Galatians 5:13–15
• relies on the Holy Spirit,	Galatians 5:16–18
• releases one from the sinful nature	Galatians 5:19–21
• produces spiritual fruit.	Galatians 5:22–26
Closing exhortations and greetings	Galatians 6:1–18

A Little Sample

Paul has argued that those who look to the Law as a means of producing righteousness fall into a trap. People who look to the Law and attempt to keep it in their own strength are sure to fail. Instead, Paul encourages believers to seek to love and serve others in the power of the Holy Spirit. What no human being can do on his own, God can and will do in those who know Jesus.

what others say

James Montgomery Boice

> Some have maintained that there is no conflict within the Christian because of the supposition that the sinful nature has been eradicated. But this is not true according to this and other passages. Naturally, the sinful nature is to become increasingly subdued as the Christian learns by grace to walk in the Spirit. But it is never eliminated. So the Christian is never released from the necessity of consciously choosing to go in God's way. There is no escape from the need to depend on God's grace.[7]

Be Led by the Spirit of God

GALATIANS 5:18 ***But if you are led by the Spirit, you are not under the law.*** *(NKJV)*

Life by the Spirit is neither legalism nor license. It is instead an openness to God's inner leading and a ready willingness to reach out to others in love.

We Know and Can See the Difference

GALATIANS 5:19–23 ***Now the works of the flesh are evident, which are: adultery, fornication, uncleanness, lewdness, idolatry, sorcery, hatred, contentions, jealousies, outbursts of wrath, selfish ambitions, dissensions, heresies, envy, murders, drunkenness, revelries, and the like; of which I tell you beforehand, just as I also told you in time past, that those who practice such things will not inherit the kingdom of God. But the fruit of the Spirit is love, joy, peace, longsuffering, kindness, goodness, faithfulness, gentleness, self-control. Against such there is no law.*** *(NKJV)*

Laws are passed against wrong behavior. They do not produce good behavior. When we understand the Christians' freedom from the Law as a freedom to follow the way of the Holy Spirit who has taken up residence in our lives, freedom is no longer frightening. When we respond to the Spirit's promptings, he produces only positive things in us.

Romans and Galatians thus find the key to both man's despair and man's hope in relationship with God. It is because of man's lost relationship with God that sin has gained its grip on individuals and society. And it is through the restored relationship with God offered to us in Jesus Christ that we have hope for living a truly good life.

Chapter Wrap-Up

- Many books in the New Testament were originally letters written by apostles to instruct Christians.
- The book of Romans was written to show how the gospel relates to righteousness.
- Romans teaches that no human being is righteous, but that when God declares as righteous a sinner who believes in Jesus, God the Holy Spirit will enable that believer to lead a righteous life.
- Romans traces the root of human sin to mankind's alienation from God.
- Galatians emphasizes that both salvation and Christian living are experienced by reliance on the grace of God, not reliance on God's Law.

Study Questions

1. What kind of literature are the New Testament Epistles?
2. What does it mean to "trace the argument" of an epistle?
3. What is the theme of Paul's letter to the Romans?
4. What are three things Romans teaches about righteousness?
5. What is the root cause of sin in individuals and society?
6. How can God judge people who have never heard of his Law?
7. What is the true role of God's Law?
8. What is the theme of Paul's letter to the Galatians?
9. What are the two contrary principles operating in a Christian's life?
10. What is the difference between trying to relate to God through the Law, and being led by the Spirit?

1 and 2 Corinthians
1 and 2 Thessalonians

Let's Get Started

Paul's missionary team traveled from city to city spreading the gospel. In each city a young church was established. Paul and his companions would spend a few months or even a year with most congregations, teaching the basic truths of the gospel. The missionaries would then move on to another city and repeat the process.

Even though Paul and his team revisited the newly established churches whenever possible, the young believers often had unanswered questions. So when Paul heard about questions or problems in one of the churches he founded, he often sat down to write them. Some letters instructed a congregation on how to deal with a problem. Others clarified his earlier teaching. In this chapter we'll look at four letters of Paul that are clearly problem-solving epistles.

Aphrodite
the Greek goddess of love and beauty

1 Corinthians

. . . getting back on track

Who	The apostle Paul wrote this letter
What	in response to messengers who reported disputes that were tearing congregations apart
Where	in Corinth
When	about AD 57,
Why	to show them how to rebuild a loving community

It Happened Then, Just as It Does Now

First-century Corinth (see Appendix A) was a busy city of some 250,000. Its population included native Greeks, a large number of Jews and other orientals, Roman settlers, government officials and businessmen. Priestess-prostitutes in Corinth's temple to **Aphrodite** helped create the climate of moral laxness for which Corinth was noted. Paul visited Corinth in AD 50, and stayed there for about eighteen months, establishing a large body of believers there, with members from every strata of society.

Some five years after the church was founded, messengers from Corinth told Paul about the dissension and disputes that were tearing the congregation apart. Commenting on these problems, the *Nelson Illustrated Bible Handbook* notes,

"The disturbing things which happened at Corinth still happen in modern congregations. There are still divisions, as believers exalt this or that human leader. There is still open immorality, for our society too is lax and wanton. Disputes between believers still lead to bitterness and law suits. Families break up. Pastors are caught in sin. And debates over doctrine divide our fellowship. Misunderstanding of basic truths still raises doubts and uncertainties. These facts make this letter of Paul to Corinth one of the most relevant of the New Testament epistles for us today."

Tracing Paul's Argument

The plan of Paul's first letter to the Corinthians is easy to follow, because the apostle simply addresses the problems one by one. Each new topic is introduced by a Greek phrase meaning "now concerning." Rather than give a short answer to problems in the church, Paul typically reviews basic truths the Corinthians need to understand, and then applies these truths to solve the problem. To trace Paul's argument in this book we'll follow his plan, and (1) look at each problem, (2) explain the truths needed to resolve it, and (3) apply it to solve the problem.

Select any one of the problems that interest you, and follow along the summary in your own Bible.

Divisions of the Church — My Leader Is Better Than Yours (1 Corinthians 1–4)

Greetings	1 Corinthians 1:1–10
THE PROBLEM The unity of the church is shattered by groups that quarrel over which leader they should be loyal to	1 Corinthians 1:10–17
INSTRUCTION IN BASIC CHRISTIAN TRUTH	1 Corinthians 1:18–3:23
• Human wisdom, which relies on human reasoning, and God's wisdom, which is exhibited in the cross, are different in nature	1 Corinthians 1:18–2:4

Divisions of the Church (cont'd)

• God's wisdom must be discerned by those who rely on the Spirit. The quarreling in Corinth shows that the believers there are worldly	1 Corinthians 2:5–3:4
• In truth, leaders are God's fellow workers, the Corinthians are God's building, and the foundation on which all must build is Jesus. So no more boasting about men	1 Corinthians 3:5–23
THE SOLUTION Human leaders are to be respected as servants entrusted with the secret things of God but not as founders of factions	1 Corinthians 4:1–21

ascetic
pertaining to rigorous self-denial

The Wicked Must Go — Impurity in the Church (1 Corinthians 5:1–6:20)

THE PROBLEM Sexual immorality goes on without confrontation by the church, and the Corinthians dare to be proud	1 Corinthians 5:1–2
INSTRUCTION IN BASIC CHRISTIAN TRUTH	1 Corinthians 5:3–6:20
• Christians must not associate with other believers who practice sexual immorality	1 Corinthians 5:3–13
• Similarly, disputes between believers should be resolved by judges appointed within the church	1 Corinthians 6:1–11
• Sexual immorality of any kind is especially corrupting and must be avoided	1 Corinthians 6:12–20
THE SOLUTION Expel the wicked man from among you	1 Corinthians 5:13

Stay Hitched — Confusion About Marriage (1 Corinthians 7:1–39)

THE PROBLEM Some had put an **ascetic** spin on Paul's comment that it is good for a man not to marry. A few of the married were refraining from sexual relations, others divorced, still others hesitated to wed	1 Corinthians 7:1
INSTRUCTION IN BASIC CHRISTIAN TRUTH	1 Corinthians 7:2–40
• One purpose of marriage is to meet the sexual needs of each partner; a person with a strong sex drive should marry	1 Corinthians 7:2–9
• The married should not divorce, but if a non-Christian spouse leaves a believer, the Christian need not remain unmarried	1 Corinthians 7:10–14

Stay Hitched (cont'd)

• Paul generally advises people to remain in whatever state they were in when saved, but each person has his or her own calling, and each must follow his or her own leading	1 Corinthians 7:15–40
THE SOLUTION	1 Corinthians 7:5, 10, 36
• The married should not give up sexual relations	1 Corinthians 7:5
• The married should not divorce	1 Corinthians 7:10
• There are good reasons to remain single, but any unmarried person may wed without sinning	1 Corinthians 7:36
• If an unmarried person desires to marry, he or she should wed another believer	1 Corinthians 7:39

Don't Offend Your Brother — Meat Sacrificed to Idols (1 Corinthians 8:1–11:1)

THE PROBLEM Most meat sold in the first century was from animals that had been sacrificed to pagan deities; some Corinthians shopped in markets associated with pagan temples, convinced that an idol is nothing at all; others were scandalized at this traffic with idolatry	1 Corinthians 8:1–7
INSTRUCTION IN BASIC CHRISTIAN TRUTH	1 Corinthians 8:7–10:22
• There is some truth in each party's argument, but this is an issue that should be approached on the basis of love, with consideration for the weaker brother who sees eating such meat as participating in idolatry	1 Corinthians 8:7–13
• Paul has himself set the example of giving up perfectly legitimate "rights" out of concern for others	1 Corinthians 9:1–27
• At the same time all must remain aware of the fact that immorality and idolatry are closely associated, and so contact with idolatry is to be avoided	1 Corinthians 10:1–22
THE SOLUTION Apply the principle that everything is permissible—but not everything is beneficial; so, within the church, seek first the good of others; when eating with an unbeliever don't ask, but if the unbeliever makes a point of telling you the meat has been dedicated to an idol, don't eat for the sake of your host's conscience; use your freedom to glorify God, not to cause others to stumble	1 Corinthians 10:23–11:1

Cover Your Head — Disorderly Public Worship (1 Corinthians 11:2–34)

THE PROBLEM	1 Corinthians 11:5, 17–21
• Women were praying and prophesying in public worship with their heads uncovered, and the well-to-do were treating the **Lord's Supper** as a social event and making distinctions between wealthier and poorer classes	1 Corinthians 11:5
INSTRUCTION IN BASIC CHRISTIAN TRUTH • The Creator made a distinction between male and female, and this is to be preserved in the Christian community; Christ himself established the pattern to be followed when we celebrate the Lord's Supper	1 Corinthians 11:3–16; 23–32
THE SOLUTION Women are to wear the head coverings that mark them as female and that signify the authority Christian women now have to pray and prophesy in church; the Lord's Supper is to be celebrated as the simple ceremony Christ instituted, with full awareness of its significance	1 Corinthians 11:10, 23–26, 10:23

Lord's Supper
Matthews 26:17–30

gift of tongues
1 Corinthians 12:10

Lord's Supper
Communion

gift of tongues
speaking to God in spiritual rather than human language

spiritual gift
a supernatural ability to minister to others in the body of Christ: all believers, united to Jesus and each other

Pentecost — Confusion About Spirituality (1 Corinthians 12:1–14:39)

THE PROBLEM In first-century paganism, ecstatic utterances and even epileptic seizures were thought to indicate closeness to a god; the young Christians in Corinth assumed that those who had the **gift of tongues** were especially spiritual and closer to God	1 Corinthians 12:1–3; 14:2–3
INSTRUCTION IN BASIC CHRISTIAN TRUTH	
• The Holy Spirit gives each believer a **spiritual gift**	1 Corinthians 12:1–14:25
• The gifts differ, but every gift is a sign of the Holy Spirit's presence in the believer's life	1 Corinthians 12:1–11
• Christians are like parts of a human body; the Spirit's gifts fit each person for his or her role in the body of Christ, and every person has an important part to play	1 Corinthians 12:12–31
• But the true test of spirituality is not one's gift but one's love	1 Corinthians 13:1–13
• Don't overemphasize tongues; unlike tongues, the intelligible words spoken by a prophet instruct and build others up, so this gift is more important	1 Corinthians 14:1–25

interpreting
translating

Pentecost (cont'd)

THE SOLUTION When you meet together let everyone take turns contributing to the service in an orderly way. And if someone with the gift of **interpreting** tongues is present, those who speak in tongues can take part too	1 Corinthians 14:25–33
• Regarding the disruptive women there—they should listen and learn quietly	1 Corinthians 14:34–40

Don't Worry About Tomorrow — Uncertainty About Resurrection (1 Corinthians 15:1–58)

THE PROBLEM Some are saying there is no resurrection	1 Corinthians 15:12
INSTRUCTION IN BASIC CHRISTIAN TRUTH	1 Corinthians 15:1–57
• It is a historical fact, witnessed by many, that Jesus rose from the dead	1 Corinthians 15:1–11
• If there is no resurrection, Christ wasn't , raised and the gospel is utter nonsense	1 Corinthians 15:12–19
• But Christ indeed has been raised from the dead, and in the end will destroy death itself; the resurrection body awaiting us will be glorious, powerful, and spiritual, and when we are clothed with immortality we will experience the victory Christ has won	1 Corinthians 15:20–28
THE SOLUTION Give yourselves fully to the work of the Lord, because you know that your labor in the Lord is not in vain	1 Corinthians 15:58
Closing remarks	1 Corinthians 6:1–29

2 Corinthians

. . . secrets of ministry

Who	The apostle Paul
What	carefully explained the Christian gospel
Where	to Christians in Rome
When	about AD 57
Why	so that they would understand the relationship between grace and righteousness

Sorry to Be So Blunt

Paul's second letter to the Corinthians was written within a year of the first. Paul had heard encouraging reports that many responded to his rather blunt epistle by facing their sins and working to resolve problems. But a hostile minority remained determined to reject Paul's guidance. In this warm and revealing letter, Paul opens his heart to share his love for the Corinthians and his vision of Christian ministry—and to warn those who still rejected his authority as an apostle of Jesus Christ.

Tracing Paul's Argument

This most personal of Paul's letters takes up three distinct topics. He begins with an explanation of his conduct and ministry (2 Corinthians 1–7). Paul then encourages the Corinthians to give generously to a collection being taken up for the saints and for Jerusalem (2 Corinthians 8–9). Finally Paul confronts and warns those who challenge his authority as an apostle (2 Corinthians 10–13).

Let's imagine that the apostle Paul made notes about what he wanted the Corinthians to understand about him and his ministry before writing this letter. His notes might have looked something like this.

Paul's "Notes"—Me and My Ministry (2 Corinthians 1:1–7:16)

PERSONAL MATTERS	2 Corinthians 1:1–2:11
• I hurt for your benefit	2 Corinthians 1:1–11
• I really did plan to visit you but decided a visit then would have hurt rather than helped you	2 Corinthians 1:12–2:4
• Oh yes. Tell them to forgive the man they disciplined. He's repented	2 Corinthians 2:5–11
MY MINISTRY	2 Corinthians 2:12–6:2
• Your transformation is proof that God called me, and	2 Corinthians 2:12–3:6
• That Jesus is real because we are being transformed, though we are not perfect	2 Corinthians 3:7–16
• Present failures don't cause us to lose heart; what is seen is temporary, but what is unseen is eternal	2 Corinthians 4:1–18
• How neat it will be when we are with the Lord in eternity!	2 Corinthians 5:1–10
• For now though, I rely on the love God has planted in your hearts to bring your lives into harmony with his will	2 Corinthians 5:11–6:2

Paul's "Notes"—Me and My Ministry (cont'd)

GETTING PERSONAL AGAIN	2 Corinthians 6:3–7:16
• It hasn't been easy, this ministry of mine, but I've been open with you	2 Corinthians 6:3–11
• Warn them about getting tied up with unbelievers!	2 Corinthians 6:12–7:1
• I take such pride in you, especially in the way most of you responded to my earlier letter. I am glad I can have complete confidence in you	2 Corinthians 7:2–15

Paul's "Notes"— As to Your Giving (2 Corinthians 8:1–9:15)

Be like the Macedonians: give yourselves first, then your money	2 Corinthians 8:1–7
God doesn't command giving, he invites us to follow Jesus' example	2 Corinthians 8:8–12
Really, giving is simply sharing so everyone will have enough	2 Corinthians 8:13–15
Mention that Titus is coming to help, so they'll be ready with the collection	2 Corinthians 8:16–9:5
Whoever sows sparingly will also reap sparingly	2 Corinthians 9:6–9
Give freely, because God will provide freely	2 Corinthians 9:10–12
Those who receive will praise God, and pray for you	2 Corinthians 9:13–15

Paul's "Notes"—About Apostles and Authority (2 Corinthians 10:1–13:11)

The true apostle's arsenal is filled with powerful spiritual weapons	2 Corinthians 10:1–6
You've been fooled by pseudo-apostles because you evaluate by the wrong criteria	2 Corinthians 10:7–18
I wouldn't even let you support me	2 Corinthians 11:1–14
Let them compare some of my meaningless "credentials"	2 Corinthians 11:15–33
What really counts isn't even visions, but weaknesses which make it plain that anything accomplished is done by Christ's power	2 Corinthians 12:1–10

Paul's "Notes"—About Apostles and Authority (cont'd)

I really care about you, and I'm worried that when I come, some of you will not have repented and changed	2 Corinthians 12:11–21
Jesus is not weak in in dealing with you. Christ did give me authority to build you up. Respond, or Jesus will deal with you	2 Corinthians 13:1–10
Final greetings	2 Corinthians 13:11–14

Paul's weaknesses
2 Corinthians 12:7–10

thorn in the flesh
2 Corinthians 12:7–10

orator
speaker

A Little Sample

The false super-apostles (2 Corinthians 11:5) who criticized Paul bragged about their strengths, and ridiculed Paul's weaknesses. Paul was hardly a compelling **orator**, nor was he an imposing figure physically. While Paul was given stunning revelations, he does not boast about them. In these verses Paul has a surprising response to his critics, and to his revelations.

2 Corinthians 12:7 ***Lest I should be exalted above measure by the abundance of the revelations, a thorn in the flesh was given to me, a messenger of Satan to buffet me.*** *(NKJV)*

Most believe the thorn in the flesh was a disfiguring and debilitating eye disease that made Paul even more vulnerable to ridicule by his opponents.

2 Corinthians 12:8 ***Concerning this thing I pleaded with the Lord three times that it might depart from me.*** *(NKJV)*

Paul's response was appropriate. Like others with an illness or disability, Paul prayed. We're told by some that healing is guaranteed to believers who have enough faith. Certainly Paul was a man of faith, and prayed with utter confidence. But as the next verse tells us, God's answer was "No."

2 Corinthians 12:9 ***And He said to me, "My grace is sufficient for you, for My strength is made perfect in weakness."*** *(NKJV)*

In Paul's case, God permitted the illness for more than one reason. First, the disability was to keep Paul from becoming conceited. Second, it was to make Paul a less-cluttered channel through which God's power might flow.

what others say

Dwight L. Moody

When God delivered Israel out of Egypt he didn't send an army. God sent a man who had been in the desert for 40 years, and had an impediment in his speech. It is weakness that God wants. Nothing is small when God handles it.[1]

2 Corinthians 12:9 ***Therefore most gladly I will rather boast in my infirmities, that the power of Christ may rest upon me. (NKJV)***

Paul understood God's message. His disability was a blessing, for it constantly reminded him to rely on God rather than on his own gifts and abilities.

what others say

Martin Luther

Those whom God adorns with great gifts he plunges into the most severe trials in order that they may learn that they're nothing . . . and that he is all.[2]

1 Thessalonians

. . . encouragement for holy living

Who	Paul wrote this letter
What	to encourage further commitment
Where	from believers in Thessalonica
When	about AD 51 or AD 52
Why	toward holy living

You're Doing Good

The city of Thessalonica (see Appendix A) was the capital of the Roman province of Macedonia. Rome maintained a great naval base there, and it was also a prosperous commercial center. Paul and his team spent only a brief time there, due to opposition aroused by Jews who were angry about the Gentiles' response to Paul's message. While Paul spent less than three months in Thessalonica, a flourishing church was planted there. This first letter to the church was written after Timothy visited the city and brought back a positive report to Paul.

This letter is probably the first of Paul's epistles. It is notable that the apostle mentions the return of Jesus in each of its five chapters.

Tracing Paul's Argument—Three Chief Aims

Paul had three chief aims in writing this epistle: (1) to express thanks to God for the healthy spiritual condition of the church (1 Thessalonians 1:2–10), (2) to reaffirm his affection for the congregation (1 Thessalonians 2:1–3:13), and (3) to encourage them to continue in their commitment to godly living (1 Thessalonians 4:1–5:23).

Paul's First Aim—to Express Thanks (1 Thessalonians 1:2–10)

GREETINGS	1 Thessalonians 1:1
WE THANK GOD, FOR YOU	1 Thessalonians 1:2–10
• You responded to the gospel	1 Thessalonians 1:2–7
• You are spreading the gospel	1 Thessalonians 1:8–10

Paul's Second Aim—to Reaffirm His Affection (1 Thessalonians 2:1–3:13)

REMEMBER	1 Thessalonians 2:1–3:12
• Remember how open we were with you	1 Thessalonians 2:1–6
• Remember how much we loved you	1 Thessalonians 2:7–9
• Remember how we parented each of you	1 Thessalonians 2:10–13
• Remember how you've responded despite the suffering it has cost you	1 Thessalonians 2:14–16
• I still long to see you	1 Thessalonians 2:17–20
• I had to send Timothy instead	1 Thessalonians 3:1–5
• I am overjoyed at his report	1 Thessalonians 3:6–13

Paul's Third Aim—to Encourage Them to Continue (1 Thessalonians 4:1–5:27)

I URGE YOU TO KEEP ON GROWING	1 Thessalonians 4:1–5:24
• Exercise self-control and avoid immorality	1 Thessalonians 4:1–8
• Keep on loving one another	1 Thessalonians 4:9–10
• Live quiet, responsible lives	1 Thessalonians 4:11–12

fallen asleep
died; appropriate for Christians who die and will awake

dead in Christ
Christians who have died

caught up
taken up to heaven in the **Rapture**

Rapture
when the Church is removed from the earth

Paul's Third Aim—to Encourage Them to Continue (cont'd)

• Encourage one another with the promise of Jesus' coming	1 Thessalonians 4:13–18
• Keep focused on serving Jesus now	1 Thessalonians 5:1–11
• And do all those "little things" that are to mark Jesus' people	1 Thessalonians 5:12–27
• Grace to you!	1 Thessalonians 5:28

A Little Sample

A few Thessalonian Christians had died, and some were devastated. They were certain the dead had missed the blessings Paul had taught were linked with the return of Jesus. Paul penned this famous passage to clarify what the future holds for all believers:

> 1 THESSALONIANS 4:13–14 *I do not want you to be ignorant, brethren, concerning those who have* ***fallen asleep****, lest you sorrow as others who have no hope. For if we believe that Jesus died and rose again, even so God will bring with Him those who sleep in Jesus. (NKJV)*

Second Corinthians 5:8 says that the Christian who has died and is "absent from the body" is "present with the Lord" (NKJV). Biological death closes the door on this world, but opens the door to heaven for the Christian. We pass through the curtain fully conscious and aware. But God has even more in store for his own.

> 1 THESSALONIANS 4:15 *This we say to you by the word of the Lord, that we who are alive and remain until the coming of the Lord will by no means precede those who are asleep. (NKJV)*

Those living when Jesus returns have no special advantage over believers who have died!

> 1 THESSALONIANS 4:16 *For the Lord Himself will descend from heaven with a shout, with the voice of an archangel, and with the trumpet of God. And the* ***dead in Christ*** *will rise first. (NKJV)*

When Jesus does return, the first event will be the resurrection of Christians who have died.

> 1 THESSALONIANS 4:17–18 *Then we who are alive and remain shall be* ***caught up*** *together with them in the clouds to meet the Lord in the air. And thus we shall always be with the Lord. Therefore comfort one another with these words. (NKJV)*

Then, together, the living and those who have died, transformed and in resurrection bodies like his own, will be caught up to be with the Lord forever.

Great Tribulation
Daniel 9:23–27

man of sin
the Antichrist

> **what others say**
>
> **Robert L. Thomas**
>
> Only after that will living Christians be caught up for the meeting with Christ. The interval separating the two groups will be infinitesimally small by human reckoning. Yet the dead in Christ will go first. They will be the first to share in the glory of his visit. In this rapid sequence the living will undergo an immediate change from mortality to immortality (1 Corinthians 15:52–53), after which they will be insusceptible to death.[3]

2 Thessalonians

. . . more on the Second Coming

Who	The apostle Paul wrote this letter
What	sharing more about Jesus' return
Where	to the Thessalonians
When	within a few months of his first letter,
Why	to encourage those who were being persecuted and to correct misunderstandings.

We're Not There Yet

Paul's first letter hadn't cleared up all the Thessalonians' confusion about the future. In particular the Thessalonians were under the impression that the persecution they were experiencing was part of the great tribulation Paul had told them was linked to history's end. Paul explains that this can't be, and reminds them that he told them about a **man of sin** the prophet Daniel and Jesus himself said would appear first.

This individual whose appearance will mark the beginning of history's end, also called the Antichrist (Against or Counterfeit—Christ), is described by Paul as one "who opposes and exalts himself above all that is called God or that is worshiped, so that he sits as God in the temple of God, showing himself that he is God" (2 Thessalonians 2:4 NKJV).

Tracing Paul's Argument

Calvary
the site in Jerusalem where Jesus died

Paul's brief letter is intended to help the Thessalonians put their troubles in perspective as well as correct misunderstandings. Compared to the awful judgment God will visit on the lost, present persecutions are nothing.

Paul's Intent—to Give Perspective

Greetings	2 Thessalonians 1:2
ABOUT PRESENT PERSECUTIONS	2 Thessalonians 1:3–12
• I thank God for your perseverance	2 Thessalonians 1:3–4
• which is evidence that God's terrible	2 Thessalonians 1:5–10
• future judgment of sinners is just, so I keep on praying Jesus will be glorified in you	2 Thessalonians 1:11–12
CONCERNING CHRIST'S COMING FOR US	2 Thessalonians 2:1–17
• first, the Day of the Lord has not come	2 Thessalonians 2:1–4
• for the power of lawlessness is being	2 Thessalonians 2:5–7
• temporarily restrained by the Holy Spirit; when the lawless one does come, Satan will	2 Thessalonians 2:8–12
• produce false miracles, and the world will follow the lawless one; stand firm in the gospel and be encouraged	2 Thessalonians 2:13–17
FOR NOW	2 Thessalonians 3:1–15
• pray for us	2 Thessalonians 3:1–5
• and don't sit around waiting for Jesus; work and take care of yourselves	2 Thessalonians 3:6–15
• Good-bye	2 Thessalonians 3:16–18

what others say

C. S. Lewis

In the long run the answer to all those who object to the doctrine of hell, is itself a question: "What are you asking God to do?" To wipe out all their past sins and, at all costs, to give them a fresh start, smoothing away every difficulty and offering every miraculous help? But he has done so, on **Calvary**. To forgive them? They will not be forgiven. To leave them alone? Alas, I am afraid that is what he does.[4]

Chapter Wrap-Up

- When Paul heard of problems in the churches he founded, he often wrote letters of instruction and encouragement.
- Many of the problems addressed in Paul's first letter to the Corinthians are common in modern churches as well.
- Paul's second letter to the Corinthians explains the spiritual principles on which his ministry was based.
- Paul wrote 1 Thessalonians to encourage the committed but persecuted Christian community, and to help them understand their future.
- In 2 Thessalonians Paul corrected misunderstandings about Christ's return to earth, and urged holy living during the interim.

Study Questions

1. Name Paul's four problem-solving epistles.
2. What solution did Paul give to the problem of immorality in the church?
3. What was wrong about the Corinthians' emphasis on the gift of tongues?
4. What are two reasons why Christians should be generous givers?
5. What were two reasons why God did not answer Paul's prayers for healing?
6. Why aren't Christians to grieve the death of loved ones in the same way unbelievers grieve?
7. How will God repay those who persecute believers?

Ephesians • Philippians • Colossians

Let's Get Started

Acts ends with Paul in a Roman prison awaiting trial. For two years Paul lived there under guard in a rented house, and was free to receive visitors. Often the visitors were from churches Paul had founded. In this way Paul was able to keep in close touch with Christians throughout the empire, and even to send letters of instruction to churches. The New Testament books of Ephesians, Philippians, and Colossians are letters written to churches during this time. Thus they are called the "Prison Epistles."

Ephesians

. . . the true church

Who	The apostle Paul wrote this letter,
What	exploring the true nature of Christ's Church
Where	with the Christians in Ephesus
When	about AD 62,
Why	to contrast Christianity with the religion of that great temple city

Illustration #16
Temple of Diana at Ephesus—Thousands of people came to the temple of Diana at Ephesus each year, and the city's prosperity depended on these visitors. The temple also served as a bank, in which individuals and rulers deposited vast sums.

pagan
someone who observes **polytheistic** religion

polytheistic
many gods

the big picture

Ephesians

The basic message of Ephesians is that Christ's Church is a living organism, not an institution. Father, Son, and Holy Spirit were each intimately involved in forming the New Testament community of faith, which can be understood as a living temple, as the body of Christ, and as the family of God the Father.

The Church Is You and Me

When the apostle Paul and his missionary team first reached Ephesus (see Appendix A), it was the leading city in Asia Minor made rich by the pilgrims who flocked to the city to visit the magnificent temple of Diana, or Artemis (see Illustration #16). Despite the success of Ephesus's religious institution, the population of the city was spiritually hungry, and deeply involved in dark occult practices. Paul's presentation of the gospel was so effective that it literally threatened the livelihood of citizens who depended on the sales of religious medals and on feeding and housing visitors.

Some years later, Paul wrote to the Ephesians to emphasize a vital difference between Christian faith and **pagan** "religion." Christianity is no institutional faith that finds expression in magnificent buildings or silver trinkets. Christianity is a relational faith. The "Church" is not a building but people who know God, who express his love in the way they live with one another, and who display his character in the holiness of their daily lives.

Two Main Sections of Ephesians

Greetings	Ephesians 1:1–2
UNDERSTANDING THE CHURCH	Ephesians 1:3–3:21
• As God's creation	Ephesians 1:4–23
• As one people	Ephesians 2:1–22
• As the family of God	Ephesians 3:1–21
LIVING AS THE CHURCH	Ephesians 4:1–6:20
• In ministry	Ephesians 4:1–16
• In purity	Ephesians 4:17–5:20
• In every relationship	Ephesians 5:21–6:9
• Enabled by God	Ephesians 6:10–20
• Farewell	Ephesians 6:21–24

What's Special in Ephesians?

1. What God has done for believers in Christ (Ephesians 1:3–14). Paul writes that God has blessed believers with every spiritual blessing in Christ. He then goes on to show how each person of the Trinity has been actively involved in providing the blessings Christians now enjoy.

events
Acts 3:23; Ephesians 1:11–12

God the Father	Christ the Son	The Holy Spirit
chose us to be holy and blameless	provided **redemption** through his blood	marked by his presence in us
predestined us to be adopted	provided forgiveness of our sins	guarantees our inheritance
made his will known to us		

redemption
the payment of a price to free sinners

predestined
chosen before hand

works
good deeds

trespasses
sinful acts

grace
God's favor shown to those who have done nothing to merit it

The idea of predestination troubles many. The word itself simply means "to ordain beforehand." Yet nowhere in the Bible does any writer suggest that individuals have been predestined to hell. Here as in other passages "predestination" emphasizes the certainty that God's purposes will accomplished, as in the events associated with the crucifixion of Christ.

2. Paul's prayers for the Ephesians (Ephesians 1:15–22; 3:14–20). Paul's prayers are a major feature of the Prison Epistles. In his first prayer for the Ephesians, Paul asks God to help him know him better, and to realize that his incomparably great power is at work in and for them. In his second prayer for the Ephesians, Paul asks God to so root the Ephesians in love for one another as members of the Father's family, that they may experience Christ's love, which surpasses knowledge.

3. The true relationship between faith and works (Ephesians 2:1–10). The raw material with which God constructed his Church is human beings who are spiritually dead in [their] **trespasses** and sins. By nature every human impulse is to satisfy the cravings of the sinful nature. To form Christ's Church, God made such persons alive in Christ. The new life God provides is entirely a gift of divine **grace**, not something anyone can earn by doing good. Yet once a person has trusted Christ and received the gift of life, he or she discovers a desire to do good out of gratitude to God.

new self
Ephesians 4:22–5:2

submit
submission is not giving in, but being responsive

what others say

Lewis Smedes

Realistic common sense tells you that you are too weak, too harassed, too human to change for the better; grace gives you the power to send you on your way a better person.[1]

Only after a person has experienced God's grace and been made alive through faith in Christ can he or she do anything to please God.

4. The Christian's new self (Ephesians 4:20–5:7). In Ephesians 2:10 Paul calls Christians God's workmanship, created in Christ Jesus. Now Paul applies this truth. God's creation is a new self that was created "according to God, in true righteousness and holiness" (Ephesians 4:24 NKJV). It follows that we are to get rid of such things as bitterness and anger and malice, which are associated with the old self, and to be kind, compassionate, and forgiving. Paul sums up the Christian's calling by saying, "Therefore be imitators of God as dear children. And walk in love, as Christ also has loved us and given Himself for us" (Ephesians 5:1–2 NKJV).

5. What it really means to be "head of the house" (Ephesians 5:21–32). The stereotype portrays the Christian husband as a dictator who demands that his wife **submit** by giving up her rights in order to serve him. But no one could read Paul's description of the man as head of the house and come up with such a notion. As head of the house, the Christian husband is to model himself on Jesus Christ, the head of the Church. As Christ loved the Church and gave himself for it, a husband is to love his wife, intent on caring for her and helping her achieve her full potential as a person. This kind of love makes it easy for a wife to respect her husband, and to be responsive to him.

what others say

Larry Christianson

Those who stubbornly hold that their own happiness and convenience are the highest goals of family life will never understand God's plan for marriage and the family.[2]

Philippians

. . . testimony to joy

Who	The apostle Paul wrote this letter
What	to share the joy he experienced
Where	with the Christians in Philippi,
When	about AD 62
Why	in the hopes of relieving their distress over his imprisonment in Rome.

Joy in the Midst of Trials

the big picture

Philippians

Philippi was a Roman colony city, settled by discharged army veterans. It had no Jewish community, but it did have a strong gentile Christian church to which Paul had strong, loving ties. One of the major features of this book is a powerful poetic passage which describes the humility of Jesus, who surrendered the prerogatives of deity to become a human being and die for us. Christ's subsequent exaltation is a reminder to believers everywhere that the way up is down, and that it is the path of selfless giving which leads to personal fulfillment.

Paul's imprisonment in Rome caused deep concern in many of the churches he had founded. The Christians in Philippi (see Appendix A) felt especially close to Paul, and had often sent him funds to help with his mission. In this very personal epistle, Paul shares his own feelings about being incarcerated. Rather than seeing his imprisonment as a setback for the gospel, Paul believes it will motivate believers throughout the empire to be even more bold in sharing the good news of Jesus Christ.

One striking feature of Philippians is the frequency with which Paul expresses his own sense of joy and rejoicing. How striking that in prison, where few would believe it is possible to be happy, the apostle finds so many sources of joy.

Here's help for following Paul's thoughts in this personal and newsy letter.

Paul's Thoughts in Philippians

Very personal greetings	Philippians 1:1–11
NEWS AND INSTRUCTIONS	Philippians 1:12–2:30
NEWS ABOUT PAUL	Philippians 1:12–26
INSTRUCTIONS FOR THE CHURCH	Philippians 1:27–2:18
• On stability	Philippians 1:27–30
• On humility	Philippians 2:1–11
• On obedience	Philippians 2:12–18
NEWS ABOUT FRIENDS	Philippians 2:19–30
WARNING AGAINST FALSE TEACHING	Philippians 3:1–21
• Against Judaizers	Philippians 3:1–11
• Against perfectionists	Philippians 3:12–17
• Against imitation	Philippians 3:18–21
EXHORTATIONS	Philippians 4:1–9
GRATITUDE	Philippians 4:10–20

What's Special in Philippians?

1. **The many sources of Paul's joy.** In Philippians Paul identifies a number of sources for his joy; sources which can provide joy for us as well. Reading one or two of the following verses will provide an introduction to the different sources of Christian joy.

Paul's Joys

Joy	Scripture
Partnering with others to share the gospel	Philippians 1:4
Stimulating others to share the gospel	Philippians 1:18
The prayers of others for him	Philippians 1:19
The unity and love of the Philippians	Philippians 2:2
The privilege of suffering for others	Philippians 2:17
The Lord himself	Philippians 3:1; 4:4
Fellow believers he loves	Philippians 4:1
The love others show him	Philippians 4:10

2. **Paul's inner conflict over dying** (Philippians 1:23). If the Roman court were to rule against Paul, he would be executed. In facing this reality Paul's inner conflict was not motivated by a fear of death. He writes, "I am hard-pressed between the two, having a desire to depart and be with Christ, which is far better.

Nevertheless to remain in the flesh is more needful for you" (Philippians 1:23–24 NKJV). Unselfishly, Paul expresses his willingness to continue living in this world, but only because he might be of further help to the churches he has planted.

How few realize what Paul realized—heaven is the soul's true home.

3. **Working out salvation is different from working for salvation** (Philippians 2:12–13). Paul encourages the Philippians to work out their salvation and reminds them that "it is God who works in you both to will and to do for His good pleasure" (Philippians 2:13 NKJV). The salvation Christians enjoy can be worked out only in those who already possess it!

what others say

Pope John Paul III

Every Christian—as he explores the historical record of Scripture and tradition and comes to a deep, abiding faith—experiences that Christ is the risen one and that he is therefore the eternally living one. It is a deep, life-changing experience. No true Christian can keep it hidden as a personal matter. For such an encounter with the Living God cries out to be shared—like the light that shines, like the yeast that leavens the whole mass of dough.[3]

4. **A vivid description of the confident Christian** (Philippians 3:2–11). Paul warns the Philippians against false Jewish teachers who brag about their credentials. Paul quotes his own qualifications, which are more impressive than theirs, and then consigns his credentials to the rubbish heap! What counts is knowing Christ. Paul's confidence is based on the fact that Christ's resurrection power can be experienced here and now by the believer whose earnest desire is to know Jesus better.

The confident Christian does not see himself or herself as perfected, but eagerly presses on to "lay hold of that for which Christ Jesus has also laid hold of me" (Philippians 3:12 NKJV). Our confidence is not in ourselves or in our achievements, but in his power to constantly lift us beyond ourselves.

5. **Freedom from anxiety is ours to claim** (Philippians 4:6–7). Paul's obvious sense of joy seems strangely out of place. Most of us in a similar situation would be worried and anxious. But Paul shares his secret with us: in everything, and with thanksgiving, he presents his requests to God. In return God floods his heart with a peace that transcends all understanding. Paul has turned his problems over to the Lord, and they no longer trouble him!

6. **The secret of contentment in all circumstances** (Philippians 4:12–13). The trouble with difficult circumstances is that they seem to rob us of our freedom of choice. The slave can't go where he wishes; the cripple can't run and jump. Paul, however, is content in any and every situation. He simply doesn't let circumstances bother him.

How can this be? Paul says, "I can do all things through Christ who strengthens me" (Philippians 4:13 NKJV). Circumstances have no power over Paul. God gives the strength needed to do whatever needs to be done in the situation. Confident in God's presence and power, you and I, like Paul, can be content.

A Little Sample

Philippians 2 is one of the most profound passages in the Bible. Paul urges the Philippians to maintain unity of heart and purpose by doing nothing out of selfish ambition or vain conceit, "but in lowliness of mind let each esteem others better than himself" (Philippians 2:3 NKJV). This will be possible only if the Christians in Philippi adopt the attitude displayed by Jesus Christ when he entered our world and went to the cross.

As Paul traces the course Jesus followed in setting aside the prerogatives of deity, he reminds us that Christ's path led to even greater glory.

> **PHILIPPIANS 2:6–11** ***Who, being in the form of God, did not consider it robbery to be equal with God, but made Himself of no reputation, taking the form of a bondservant, and coming in the likeness of men. And being found in appearance as a man, He humbled Himself and became obedient to the point of death, even the death of the cross. Therefore God also has highly exalted Him and given Him the name which is above every name, that at the name of Jesus every knee should bow, of those***

in heaven, and of those on earth, and of those under the earth, and that every tongue should confess that Jesus Christ is Lord, to the glory of God the Father. (NKJV)

Rather than suffer loss when we surrender our own interests to meet the needs of others we, like Christ, can only gain.

heresies
false teachings

Colossians

. . . God in daily life

Who	The apostle Paul
What	wrote this letter
Where	from prison to the Christians in Colosse (see Appendix A)
When	about 62 BC
Why	to clear up their confusion, which was the result of false teachers who divorced spirituality from daily life

God Is by My Side, All the Time

the big picture

Colossians

Curtis Vaughn, writing in the *Expositor's Bible Commentary,* sketches the leading features of the heresy Paul combats in Colossians: "(1) It professed to be a 'philosophy,' but Paul, refusing to recognize it as genuine, called it a 'hollow and deceptive philosophy' (Colossians 2:8). (2) It placed too much emphasis on ritual circumcision, dietary laws, and the observance of holy days (Colossians 2:11, 14, 16, 17). (3) Affirming the mediation of various supernatural powers in the Creation of the world and the whole process of salvation, the false teaching insisted that these mysterious powers be placated and worshiped (Colossians 2:15, 18, 19). As a result of this, Christ was relegated to a relatively minor place in the Colossian system. (4) Some of the errorists were ascetic (Colossians 2:20–23), teaching that the body is evil and must be treated as an enemy. (5) The advocates of this system claimed to be Christian teachers (Colossians 2:3–10)."

One of the early **heresies** that confused early Christians is demonstrated here in Colossians. Some people argued that all matter was evil. Only the "spiritual" and immaterial can be "good." If so, it follows that God could have nothing to do with the material universe. It must have been created by lesser beings far removed from God. What's more, if Jesus were God he could not have taken on a real human body. Conversely, if Jesus had a real human body, he could not be God. According to this heresy, it also follows that what Christians do in their daily lives has nothing to do with spirituality, for daily life is conducted in the material world.

Paul's letter to the Colossians confronts this notion and presents Jesus Christ as God come in the flesh.

To counter this false teaching, Paul presents a powerful portrait of Jesus Christ and his work on our behalf. He also offers an appealing description of the life by which Christians can honor him.

Paul's Portrait of Jesus and the Christian Life

Greetings	Colossians 1:1–2
THANKSGIVING AND PRAYER	Colossians 1:3–14
THE REAL JESUS	Colossians 1:15–2:7
• Christ is supreme	Colossians 1:15–23
• Paul ministers Christ	Colossians 1:24–2:7
WARNING AGAINST ERRORS	Colossians 2:8–23
• Against deceptive philosophy	Colossians 2:8–15
• Against legalism	Colossians 2:16–17
• Against angel worship	Colossians 2:18–19
• Against asceticism	Colossians 2:20–23
LIVING THE CHRISTIAN LIFE	Colossians 3:1–4:6
• Its heavenly source	Colossians 3:1–4
• Abandon sins	Colossians 3:5–11
• Cultivate virtues	Colossians 3:12–17
• Strengthen the family	Colossians 3:18–4:1
• Pray and witness	Colossians 4:2–6
CONCLUSION	Colossians 4:7–18
• Commendations	Colossians 4:7–9
• Greetings	Colossians 4:10–15
• Instructions	Colossians 4:16–17
• Benediction	Colossians 4:18

What's Special in the Book of Colossians?

1. **Paul's prayer points the way to spiritual growth** (Colossians 1:9–11). Paul's prayer outlines a step-by-step plan for anyone who wants to grow spiritually and deepen his or her personal relationship with God.

Paul's Prayer

Step	Description	Action to Take
1	Fill up with the knowledge of God's will	Study Scripture where his will is revealed
2	Exercise spiritual wisdom and insight	Seek to apply what you learn to daily life
3	Live a life worthy of the Lord	Act on what you learn, desiring to please him
4	Bear fruit in every good work	Bear fruit and God will produce fruit and good works
5	Grow in the knowledge of God	Grow and you will experience God's very presence

reconciled
brought into harmony

what others say

Edmund P. Clowney

Wisdom starts in heaven but works at street level, where we bump shoulders with others. It isn't satisfied with information retrieval: You can't access wisdom by the megabyte. Wisdom is concerned with how we relate to people, to the world, and to God.[4]

2. **The real Jesus is both fully God and truly man** (Colossians 1:15–23). The Bible makes absolutely clear who Jesus is. This brief passage (Colossians 1:15–23) is one of the clearest in Scripture.

Jesus—Fully God and Truly Man

Biblical Description	Characteristic
The image of the invisible God	Seeing Jesus is seeing God
The firstborn over all creation	The heir to all that exists
By him all things were created	He is the Creator God
All things were created by and for him	He is the beneficiary of Creation
In him all things hold together	His power holds the universe together even now
He is the head of the Church	He guides, directs his people
He is the firstborn from the dead	He is our living Lord
All God's fullness dwells in him	He is fully, completely God

3. **What Jesus did in our world makes all the difference** (Colossians 1:22). Paul challenges the notion that the material universe is irrelevant. He writes, "Now [God] has **reconciled** in the body of His flesh through death, to present you holy, and

blameless, and above reproach in His sight" (Colossians 1:21–22 NKJV). God the Son took on a flesh-and-blood human body, and in that body Christ died on the cross. In that act of self-sacrifice, Jesus paid for all our sins, bringing us back into conformity with God by making us holy in his sight. No one, realizing what Jesus has done, can ever claim that what human beings do in this world of space and time is irrelevant to God.

4. **Will the real Christian please stand up?** (Colossians 2:20–23; 3:12–17). Some people have a peculiar idea about what real Christians are like. Two passages in Colossians contrast the fake and the real Christian lifestyle. Compare them side by side:

Fake and Real Christians

Fake Christians	Real Christians
Make up rules	Are kind and compassionate
Emphasize don'ts	Forgive and love
Look pious	Enjoy worship
Punish themselves	Honor God in all they do

True Christianity isn't a matter of do's and don'ts, nor of appearances. True Christianity is about Jesus, and the authentic Christian seeks always to please him. It isn't lists that mark the authentic Christian, it's the love that overflows to others when a person loves and follows Jesus.

Chapter Wrap-Up

- While imprisoned in Rome the apostle Paul wrote letters of instruction to several churches he had founded.
- In Paul's letter to the Ephesians he contrasts Christianity with "religion," and Christ's living church with mere buildings.
- To create the Church God gave spiritual life to persons who were dead to God because of their sins.
- Paul urged the Philippians to work out or express the salvation that God had given them in Christ.
- Philippians chapter 2 shows how Christ surrendered the prerogatives of deity to become a human being and die on the cross.
- Paul's letter to the Colossians emphasizes the fact that Jesus Christ is God, who took on a real human body.
- Colossians reminds us that the way we live our daily lives is important to God, and that what we do daily can glorify him.

Study Questions

1. What is the theme of Ephesians?
2. According to Ephesians 2, what is the relationship between faith and works?
3. What are responsibilities of the husband as "head of the house"?
4. What key words recur again and again in Philippians?
5. What can a Christian do to gain freedom from anxiety?
6. What heresy is Paul combatting in Colossians?
7. What passage in Colossians makes it absolutely clear that Jesus is God?
8. What are two characteristics of "fake" Christians? What are two characteristics of "real" Christians?

1 and 2 Timothy • Titus • Philemon

Let's Get Started

Most of the New Testament letters of Paul were written to churches, but four were written to individuals.

Timothy and Titus were both young leaders who traveled from church to church. Their ministry was to correct false teaching and set local congregations on the path of godly living. The letters Paul wrote to them are filled with practical advice. The two letters to Timothy and the one letter to Titus are called the "Pastoral Epistles." The short letter to Philemon has another purpose entirely. In it Paul encourages a well-to-do Christian to welcome back a runaway slave who had become a Christian through Paul's witness.

1 Timothy

. . . the healthy local church

Who	The apostle Paul
What	wrote this letter of advice to Timothy, who was on a mission for Paul in Ephesus
Where	Ephesus
When	about AD 64
Why	to correct problems in the church and to restore spiritual health

Looking for a Church?

the big picture

1 Timothy

In this letter Paul describes the strong and healthy church that he expects Timothy to help establish in Ephesus. In addition Paul gives Timothy guidelines to follow.

TIMOTHY: Timothy had been a member of Paul's missionary team. He was a young man whose father was Greek and whose mother was Jewish. Paul had sent him on several missions (1 Corinthians 4:17; 16:10; Acts 19:22; 2 Corinthians 1:1, 19), and he had not always been successful. Paul guides this younger man who will be one of the Church's leaders when Paul dies.

Despite the fact that he had been taught the Scriptures by his mother and grandmother from childhood (2 Timothy 1:5–6) and had been trained by Paul himself, Timothy remained shy and unassertive. Also, he was young to be a leader in a culture that respected age and maturity. Despite this, Paul treated Timothy as a son and recognized his potential as a leader of the next generation of Christians. At the time Paul wrote, Timothy was in Ephesus, sent there to resolve problems that had emerged in the church and to establish stronger local leadership. It was a challenging mission, and Paul outlines many of the steps Timothy would need to take. Paul's instructions to Timothy paint a picture of the ideal church that may prove valuable to present-day Christians who are looking for a local congregation to join.

Variety of Topics in Paul's First Letter to Timothy

Greetings	1 Timothy 1:1–2
CORRECT FALSE TEACHING WITH SOUND DOCTRINE	1 Timothy 1:3–20
• See what the truth has done for me	1 Timothy 1:12–17
• Fight the good fight	1 Timothy 1:18–20
KEEP THE FOCUS ON THE LORD DURING WORSHIP	1 Timothy 2:1–15
REMEMBER THAT LEADERS ARE TO MODEL GODLINESS	1 Timothy 3:1–16
IDENTIFY FALSE TEACHING AND FALSE TEACHERS while serving as an example of godliness	1 Timothy 4:1–16
TREAT EVERYONE WITH RESPECT	1 Timothy 5:1–6:10
• Don't forget the "widows' corps"	1 Timothy 5:3–17
• Show respect to church elders	1 Timothy 5:18–25
• Remind slaves to respect their masters against a love of money	1 Timothy 6:1–2and warn 1 Timothy 6:3–10
AS FOR YOU, TIMOTHY, PURSUE RIGHTEOUSNESS	1 Timothy 6:11–21
• Oh yes, warn the wealthy, and	1 Timothy 6:17–19
• guard what has been entrusted to you	1 Timothy 6:20–21

what others say

J. Vernon McGee

In 1 Timothy we deal with the nitty-gritty of the local church, with the emphasis that it is the character and caliber of her leaders that will determine whether the church is really a church of the Lord Jesus Christ.[1]

mediator
a go-between who brings parties together

What's Special in 1 Timothy?

1. **The vital importance of sound doctrine** (1 Timothy 1:3–11). Paul gives an important reason why Timothy is to confront those who teach false doctrine. God's truth will produce love, which comes "from a pure heart, from a good conscience, and from sincere faith" (1 Timothy 1:5 NKJV). False doctrine promotes controversy and ungodliness.

In the next paragraphs (1 Timothy 1:12–17) Paul points out that he himself was once the worst of sinners, a persecutor and an insolent man. But the gospel message of the love and grace of God transformed Paul completely.

what others say

William Barclay

The Christian's dynamic comes from the fact that he knows sin is not only breaking God's Law but also breaking his heart. It is not the Law of God but the love of God which constrains us.[2]

2. **One God and one mediator between God and man** (1 Timothy 2:1–5). The Bible never apologizes for presenting faith in Christ as the only way that a person can establish a personal relationship with God. The common notion that all religions lead to the same God is, quite simply, false. Jesus Christ died to pay the price of sin for all human beings, and trust in him is the only avenue that leads to God.

JOHN 14:6 *I am the way, the truth, and the life. No one comes to the Father except through Me.* (NKJV)

3. Qualifications for church leaders (1 Timothy 3:1–16). It is striking that the list of qualifications for church leaders, whether elders, deacons, or deaconesses, emphasizes character rather than training or even spiritual gifts. The reason is that leaders are to be mature Christians who model the godly Christian character that the Holy Spirit seeks to produce in all believers. We see this clearly when we compare the words Paul used to describe the Christian way of life with those he used to describe the qualifications of a leader.

Christian Way of Life and Qualifications for Leadership

Christian Leaders Are to Be . . .	The Christian Lifestyle Involves . . .
Above reproach	Godliness
Temperate	Temperance
Self-controlled	Self-control
Respectable and upright	Trustworthiness
Hospitable	Love
Not alcoholics	Self-discipline
Not competitive but gentle	Gentleness
Not quarrelsome	Being considerate
Not quick tempered	Being peaceable
Not materialistic	Generosity
Respected by unbelievers	Integrity
Lovers of goodness	Dedication to goodness, faith, and endurance

4. Advice for every young believer (1 Timothy 4:12). Paul's advice to Timothy is ideal for any believer, whether young in years or young in the faith. "Let no one despise your youth, but be an example to the believers in word, in conduct, in love, in spirit, in faith, in purity" (1 Timothy 4:12 NKJV).

5. The widows' corps (1 Timothy 5:3–16). The New Testament Church, like the Jewish community, demonstrated a real concern for widows and the fatherless by providing support for them. With no occupations open to women in the first century, Paul advised younger widows to remarry. Those widows with adult children should be supported by their families (see 1 Timothy 5:16).

Having money can be a good thing—if the wealthy person is eager to be rich in good deeds, generous, and willing to share with others. But all too often the rich depend on their money rather than on God, and they become arrogant.

Paul's solution is for everyone to develop a passion for godliness, and to be content with whatever it takes to meet their basic needs. A good conscience and a good reputation are worth more than millions.

2 Timothy

. . . warning! warning! warning!

Who	The apostle Paul
What	wrote this letter to Timothy
Where	from prison in Rome
When	about AD 67,
Why	to warn him about the danger of false teachers who were infiltrating the Church.

They Speak with Lies

the big picture

2 Timothy

This book is a call to remain faithful to Christ and to sound teaching. It was vitally important because of the threat posed by false teachers. Highlights of Paul's letter are (1) his statement about the confidence we can have in Scripture, and (2) his description of the attitude that should be adopted by people sharing God's truth with others.

The book of Acts ended with Paul under house arrest in Rome. He was there for two years. Tradition reports that after being realeased, Paul went on a missionary journey to Spain. However, within five years Paul was arrested again and imprisoned in Rome. This time Paul did not survive but was executed under the Roman Emperor Nero.

Most believe that this was the last letter Paul wrote before his execution. While the Christian community had begun to experience governmental persecution, the apostle was more concerned about those who were corrupting the Church by false teaching. In this letter Paul urges Timothy to serve as a good soldier of Jesus Christ, and remain committed to the truth revealed by God.

Confidence and a Good Attitude

Greetings	2 Timothy 1:1–2
BE FAITHFUL	2 Timothy 1:3–2:13
• to the truth you learned as a child,	2 Timothy 1:3–7
• as I have been faithful,	2 Timothy 1:8–15
• as others have been faithful,	2 Timothy 1:16–18
• as also are . . .	2 Timothy 2:1–7
• soldiers,	2 Timothy 2:4
• athletes,	2 Timothy 2:5
• hard-working farmers,	2 Timothy 2:6
• and as Christ is faithful to us	2 Timothy 2:8–13
HOLD TIGHTLY TO GOD'S WORD	2 Timothy 2:14–26
• Handle it correctly	2 Timothy 2:8–19
• Prepare yourself to minister it	2 Timothy 2:20–23
PRESENT GOD'S WORD APPROPRIATELY	2 Timothy 2:24–26
BE PREPARED FOR DIFFICULT TIMES	2 Timothy 3:1–4:8
• with unresponsive people	2 Timothy 3:1–5
• led by false teachers	2 Timothy 3:6–9
LEAD A GODLY LIFE	2 Timothy 3:10–13
• guided by the Scriptures,	2 Timothy 3:14–17
• and keep on preaching,	2 Timothy 4:1–5
• for I am about to depart	2 Timothy 4:6–8
Final remarks	2 Timothy 4:9–18
Greetings	2 Timothy 4:19–22

What's Special in 2 Timothy?

1. **Parents have a vital role in their children's faith** (2 Timothy 1:5). The apostle Paul traces Timothy's faith back to his mother and grandmother, who passed the flame of faith on to young Timothy when he was a child. God's plan for communicating faith from generation to generation has always focused on the family.

> **what others say**
>
> **Roy B. Zuck**
>
> God placed the responsibility of developing godly character in our children squarely on the shoulders of parents. The Bible views fathers and mothers as teachers—those who instruct their own in the ways of God.[3]

2. The spiritual source of opposition to God's truth (2 Timothy 2:24–26). Paul describes the approach Timothy should take in addressing opposition. He warns against quarreling and prescribes an attitude of kindness which leads to gentle instruction. Why not rely on forceful argument and debate? Paul makes it clear that the real problem is spiritual, not intellectual. God alone can lead those who oppose the gospel to a knowledge of the truth, for they have been taken captive by the devil to do his will.

penitent
feeling sorrow for sin

form
outward appearance

what others say

William Barclay

It is God who awakens the repentance; it is the Christian leader who opens the door to the **penitent** heart.[4]

3. Beware of churches having a form of godliness without its power (2 Timothy 3:1–5). Paul looks ahead to terrible times and describes people who are lovers of money, boastful, proud, abusive, disobedient to their parents, ungrateful, unholy, without love, unforgiving, slanderous, without self-control, brutal, conceited, etc. Yet he notes that they will have a form of godliness. They'll go to church, sing the hymns, and congratulate the preacher on his sermon. But true godliness is exhibited in lives that Jesus Christ has transformed. Paul's admonition is good advice for the church where people go through the motions without exhibiting God's work in their hearts: have nothing to do with them.

4. The importance of knowing and living Scripture (2 Timothy 3:15–17). Paul focuses our attention on the holy Scriptures, which are able to make you wise for salvation through faith in Christ Jesus. What is it that makes Scripture so special?

What Makes Scripture Special?

The Bible is God-breathed	As a breeze fills the sails of a ship, the Spirit filled the writers of Scripture and carried them along, so what they wrote was what God intended to say
The Bible is useful for teaching	The Bible communicates God's truth
The Bible is useful for rebuking	The Bible corrects false ideas about God
The Bible is useful for correcting	The Bible directs us away from sin

What Makes Scripture Special? (cont'd)

The Bible is useful for training in righteousness	The Bible's teachings, when followed, enable us to be men and women of God. . . . It is sufficient to thoroughly equip believers for good works

If we expect God's Word to get into our lives, we must commit ourselves to get into God's Word—regularly!

Titus

. . . living as God's people

Who	The apostle Paul
What	wrote this letter
Where	to Titus, who was in Crete
When	about AD 65 or AD 66
Why	to correct problems in the church there and to motivate commitment to good

Be Eager to Do Good

the big picure

Titus

Paul's advice to Titus is similar to that which Paul set out in his first letter to Timothy. Both were to see to the establishment of a strong local leadership for the church. Both were to concentrate on teaching sound doctrine, with a view toward producing godly persons whose lives would glorify God. Particularly significant is Paul's emphasis on the importance of good works, to be done by those who have experienced the grace of God.

TITUS: Like Timothy, Titus was a young leader who carried the burden of instructing the churches once the apostles were gone. Titus successfully completed several missions for Paul, and the apostle had great confidence in his abilities.

The inhabitants of the Mediterranean island of Crete (see Appendix A) had a questionable reputation. Paul quotes the poet Epimenides in Titus 1:12, who had written centuries earlier that "cretans are always liars, evil beasts, lazy gluttons." Titus's mission to Crete was to motivate the Christians who had received the gospel to be transformed by God's grace into a people who are eager to devote themselves to doing what is good (Titus 3:8). When Paul wrote to Titus, he probably had less than two years to live. As Titus had been successful in other missions that Paul had assigned him, it seems likely that he was able to complete this mission too, and to lead members of this unruly church into a disciplined Christian life.

Paul's Advice to Titus

Greetings	Titus 1:1–4
WHAT TO DO ON CRETE	Titus 1:5–16
Appoint elders	Titus 1:5–9
Rebuke the rebellious	Titus 1:10–16
WHAT TO TEACH ON CRETE	Titus 2:1–15
Positive Christian character and	Titus 2:1–10
Rejection of ungodliness	Titus 2:11–15
WHAT TO EMPHASIZE ON CRETE	Titus 3:1–11
True humility toward all men,	Titus 3:1–2
Devotion to doing good, and	Titus 3:3–8
Avoiding divisive persons	Titus 3:9–11
Final remarks	Titus 3:12–15

What's Special in Paul's Letter to Titus?

1. **Appointing elders in every town** (Titus 1:5–9). It was and is vital to the health of a local congregation to be led by a team of godly leaders. Paul charged Titus with appointing these leaders, which are called elders, overseers, or bishops interchangeably throughout the New Testament.

The word translated "appoint" here and in other passages that have to do with leaders means to give official recognition to. Members of the local congregation were expected to recognize mature Christians whose lives exhibited the Christian character Paul describes here and in 1 Timothy, and who had a firm grasp of the truth. The apostle or his representatives then met with these local congregations, and, after examining the persons recommended, confirmed them as elders.

2. **Teaching that is in accord with sound doctrine** (Titus 2:1–15). We most often think of teaching as communicating information. But in Titus 2 Paul portrays it as encouraging a lifestyle that fits

Incarnation
the union of divinity and humanity in Jesus of Nazareth

justified
pronounced "not guilty" of sins that Jesus' death paid for

with the truth contained in God's Word. Words for this kind of teaching include "admonish" (Titus 2:4), "exhort" (Titus 2:6), and "showing yourself to be a pattern" (Titus 2:7).

What kind of life is fitting for those who are committed to what the Bible says? Paul emphasizes temperance, self-control, reverence, integrity, and uprightness, while warning against slander, addiction to much wine, and anything that would give others anything bad to say about believers. When Christians show that they can be fully trusted, they will make the teaching about God our Savior attractive.

3. **Emphasizing the transforming moral power of grace** (Titus 2:11–14). These verses are among the most powerful in the New Testament.

TITUS 2:11–14 ***For the grace of God that brings salvation has appeared to all men, teaching us that, denying ungodliness and worldly lusts, we should live soberly, righteously, and godly in the present age, looking for the blessed hope and glorious appearing of our great God and Savior Jesus Christ, who gave Himself for us, that He might redeem us from every lawless deed and purify for Himself His own special people, zealous for good works. (NKJV)***

what others say

William Barclay

There are few passages in the New Testament which so vividly set out the moral power of the **Incarnation** as this does. Its whole stress is on the miracle of moral change which Jesus Christ can work. Christ not only liberated us from the penalty of past sin; he can enable us to live the perfect life within this world of space and time; and he can so cleanse us that we become fit in the life to come to be the special possession of God.[5]

4. **Stressing rebirth and renewal by the Holy Spirit** (Titus 3:3–8). Paul reminds Titus that God has poured out his Spirit on those who have been **justified** by faith in Christ. Paul urges Titus to stress this truth because the Spirit's presence is the basis for all Christian living, and those who recognize his presence are to be careful to devote themselves to doing what is good. Simply put, faith in Jesus changes human beings—and that change is to be expressed in our daily lives.

Philemon

. . . pleading for a runaway slave

Who	The apostle Paul
What	wrote this letter to Philemon
Where	in Rome
When	during his first imprisonment
Why	to plead the case of Onesimus, a runaway slave who had been converted and wanted to return to his Christian master

Forgive and Press On

the big picure

Philemon

This one-chapter letter is the briefest of the New Testament Epistles. After a typical greeting and prayer, Paul pleads for his new son in the faith, Onesimus. Paul's letter of request has these features.

PHILEMON: Philemon was a wealthy Christian who had been converted under Paul's ministry. Like other wealthy men in the Roman Empire, Philemon owned slaves.

ONESIMUS: Onesimus had been a slave of Philemon. Apparently, he stole from his master and ran away to Rome, where he met Paul and became a Christian. Tradition reports that Onesimus became the bishop of Ephesus in the second century.

Onesimus stole money from his master Philemon, one of Paul's converts, and ran away to Rome where he met Paul and became a Christian. Paul sent him back to his master with a letter. In this letter Paul reminds Philemon of their close friendship, and urges him to welcome Onesimus back, not just as a slave but as a Christian brother. Paul offers to pay Philemon back for any loss due to Onesimus's past actions and delicately reminds Philemon that he owes his salvation to Paul's ministry.

Paul Pleads for Onesimus

slaves
Philemon;
1 Timothy 6:1–2;
Ephesians 6:5–9;
Colossians 3:22–4:1

Greetings	Philemon 1–3
Prayer	Philemon 4–7
PAUL PRESENTS A REQUEST, not a command,	Philemon 8
• for a new Christian	Philemon 9–10
• who formerly was worthless	Philemon 11
PAUL IS RETURNING ONESIMUS	Philemon 12–14
• as a slave but also as a brother in Christ	Philemon 15–16
PAUL APPEALS TO PHILEMON to welcome Onesimus as he would welcome Paul himself	Philemon 17–21
PAUL HOPES TO VISIT SOON	Philemon 22
• Final greetings	Philemon 23–25

Brothers in Christ

In the first-century Roman Empire, more than 20 percent of the population were slaves, viewed as property by their owners. The institution was so deeply woven into the social fabric that it would have been impossible to eliminate without creating an economic disaster.

The New Testament launches no crusade against the evil of slavery. But Christianity introduced a new dynamic reflected in this letter and other epistles. Slaves and masters alike became believers, and each was urged to show love and concern for the other. In a household where both were believers, they were to view each other as brothers in Christ. Where the gospel became entrenched, it was impossible to maintain the view that slaves were merely property, as Paul's letter to Philemon illustrates.

Chapter Wrap-Up

- Paul wrote four personal letters to individuals rather than to churches.
- Paul's first letter to Timothy urged the younger man to be an example of the truths he taught.
- One of the most important tasks in strengthening a church was to see to it that the congregation had godly leaders.

- Paul's second letter to Timothy is probably the last of his epistles, written just before his execution.
- Paul warns Timothy against false teachers, and stresses the importance of teaching and living God's Word.
- Paul's letter to Titus emphasizes the importance of performing good works.
- Paul reminds Titus that God's grace brings personal rebirth and renewal. Good works are the product of saving grace.
- Paul's letter to Philemon illustrates how Christian faith bridged the gap between slave and slave owner in the Roman world.

Study Questions

1. Which three of Paul's four personal letters are called pastoral letters?
2. What are two essential characteristics of persons qualified to become church overseers or elders?
3. What ministry did the early Church have for widows?
4. How would you correct the quote, "Money is a root of all evil"?
5. What guarantees the usefulness of Scripture in equipping Christians for good works?
6. What is involved in Christian teaching besides communicating biblical truths?
7. The one who has been justified by faith will express that reality by devoting oneself to what?
8. What was the change in the relationship between Philemon and Onesimus that Paul relied on to move Philemon to welcome back his runaway slave?

Hebrews

Let's Get Started

Most of the New Testament Epistles were written to predominantly gentile churches. But the letter called Hebrews was written specifically to converted Jews. They often felt a deep affection for the way of life they had known from birth, and sometimes wondered if they had been right in committing themselves to Christ. The writer of this powerful letter understands their feelings, and sets out to show them how faith in Christ promises a full experience of spiritual realities that Old Testament faith merely foreshadowed.

Hebrews

. . . the superiority of Christ

Who	An unnamed author
What	compares Old and New Testament revelations
Where	to Hebrew Christians everywhere
When	before AD 70
Why	to demonstrate the superiority of Christ and Christianity as a fulfillment of Old Testament promises

A New Covenant for All

the big picure

Hebrews

Hebrews compares Old and New Testament revelations point by point. The Old Testament is divine revelation, which offered great benefits to Israel as God's special people. But the New Testament is a superior revelation, and its benefits are not only superior; they are available to all who believe in Jesus. The following outline reflects the major themes developed in Hebrews.

In the beginning Christianity was a Jewish movement, centered in Jerusalem. The first Christians were Jews who, apart from their belief that Jesus was the Messiah, lived and worshiped like other Jews. But

New Covenant
Jeremiah 31:31–34

New Covenant
the promise offered by Jesus, the perfect High Priest

Old Covenant
Mosaic Law

within a few decades the church became predominantly gentile, and Jews who believed in Christ were cut off from the synagogue and the temple. This seemed a tragedy to many Jewish Christians, who had a deep affection for the ways and worship of Judaism, and who were now isolated from friends and relatives who continued in the old ways. These and other pressures led some Jewish Christians to waver, wondering whether they should return to their roots.

The unknown writer of the book of Hebrews determined to resolve their doubts. He saw clearly that Jesus was the fulfillment of all that the Old Testament promised, and that the **New Covenant** Christ instituted on the cross is vastly superior to the **Old Covenant** Moses introduced at Mount Sinai. Enthusiastically the writer of Hebrews set out to show the superiority of Jesus, and the wonderful benefits of a personal relationship with the living Savior.

Major Themes Developed in Hebrews

JESUS, THE LIVING WORD	Hebrews 1:1–4:13
• As ultimate revelation	Hebrews 1:1–14
• Warning against drifting	Hebrews 2:1–4
• As source of salvation	Hebrews 2:5–18
• As superior to Moses	Hebrews 3:1–6
• The urgency of response	Hebrews 3:7–4:13
JESUS, OUR HIGH PRIEST	Hebrews 4:14–8:13
• Jesus' priesthood	Hebrews 4:14–5:10
• Go on to maturity	Hebrews 5:11–6:20
• Superiority of Jesus' priesthood	Hebrews 7:1–28
• Implications of Jesus' priesthood	Hebrews 8:1–13
JESUS, THE PERFECT SACRIFICE	Hebrews 9:1–10:39
• His sacrifice cleanses	Hebrews 9:1–28
• His sacrifice removes sin	Hebrews 10:1–18
• Warning against turning from God	Hebrews 10:19–39
JESUS' CONTINUING MINISTRY	Hebrews 11:1–12:29
• Accessed by faith	Hebrews 11:1–40
• Experienced as discipline	Hebrews 12:1–13
• Missing God's grace	Hebrews 12:14–29
EXHORTATIONS	Hebrews 13:1–21
• Farewell	Hebrews 13:22–25

He's God's Son

the big picure

Living Word

In the past, God's revelation was transmitted in various ways, but now he has spoken through his Son. The Son, Jesus, is fully God and thus even greater than angels.

It would be disastrous to drift away from truth that is revealed by him. For the intended destiny of human beings depends on our link with Jesus, who became human to die for our sins, to free us from Satan's power, and to lift us with him far above the angels!

As for Moses, it is right to respect him, for he was a faithful servant in God's house. But Christ is the owner, architect, and builder of the house. He is worthy of far greater honor. It follows then that if anyone hears God's voice today, he must not be like the Israelites who followed Moses out of Egypt but disobeyed when God told them to enter Canaan.

What's Special in Hebrews 1–4?

1. **The identification of Jesus as God** (1:1–3). The writer begins by affirming Jesus' identity as God's Son, and by making clear just what this title means. As the radiance of God's glory, Jesus expresses God's very presence. As the exact representation of God's being, Jesus is identical with God, so that when we see Jesus we see exactly what God is like.

It is important to be completely clear about the identity of Jesus when examining Christianity. The fact that Jesus Christ is God incarnate is the central and foundational truth on which the New Testament rests.

2. **Jesus' superiority to angels** (Hebrews 1:5–14). The writer quotes seven Old Testament passages that establish the superiority of Jesus to angels. Jewish tradition held that angels served as mediators when God gave the Law to Moses. The active involvement of angels made the Law even more binding. But the new revelation was given personally by God's Son, who is superior to angels.

3. **Warning against drifting** (Hebrews 2:1–4). The writer presents the image of a ship drifting away from its moorings to warn of the

unbelief
Numbers 13:26–14:35

atonement
satisfying God's demand that sin be paid for

danger involved in drifting back into Judaism. His readers were familiar with the danger of disobeying God's Law. How much more dangerous to ignore a salvation announced by the Lord himself!

4. **Jesus as the source of man's salvation** (Hebrews 2:5–18). Jesus shared our humanity to save us in the only way possible—by making **atonement** for our sins. These verses compare the respective positions of Jesus and of human beings in relationship to angels before and after Jesus came.

Jesus not only reveals God, but through his suffering he brings "many sons to glory" (Hebrews 2:10 NKJV).

5. **Jesus is greater than Moses** (Hebrews 3:1–6). No one was more revered than Moses in Judaism. Demonstrating that Christ is greater than Moses was a powerful argument for the superiority of Christianity.

what others say

Leon Morris

Moses was no more than a member—even though a very distinguished member—of the household. He was essentially one with all the others. Christ has an innate superiority. He is the Son and as such is "over" the household.[1]

6. **Warning against unbelief** (Hebrews 3:7–4:13). The writer returns to an incident recorded in Numbers. Through Moses, God told the Israelites to enter Canaan, but the people refused. As a result, the whole generation was doomed to wander in the wilderness for four decades until all its adult members had died. All because when God spoke to the people they hardened their hearts, refused to trust him, and so disobeyed.

Today, God has spoken by his own Son. What a terrible loss contemporary Jewish Christians would experience if they hardened their hearts, and refused to listen to and trust him.

7. **The promise of a "Sabbath rest"** (Hebrews 4:1–13). The writer draws an analogy between the Israelites' rest when in Moses' day they finally conquered Canaan and the rest that is available to them as Christians. In both cases the victory has been won. When

a person fully trusts Jesus, he or she discovers that Christ has and in fact is the answer for all the needs of the heart.

intermediaries
go-betweens or mediators

perfected
not made him better, but equipped him

He's Our High Priest

the big picure

High Priest

The priests of the Old Testament era were **intermediaries** between God and man, offering the sacrifices that enabled worshipers to approach Israel's Holy God. But the high priest alone had the privilege of making the annual sacrifice that atoned for all the people's sins. Jesus is presented as the ideal High Priest, who can sympathize with our weaknesses, and who was called by God to a priesthood far superior to that of Aaron and his descendants. After pausing to warn his readers again, the writer continues to explore the superiority of Jesus' priesthood. He explains why a change in the priesthood was essential. He further explains the benefits inherent in the fact that Jesus is not under an Old Law Covenant; he is under a New Covenant of transforming grace.

What's Special in Hebrews 4:14–8:43?

MELCHIZEDEK: He was both king of Jerusalem and a priest in the time of Abraham. Psalm 110:4 announced that God's Son would be a priest like Melchizedek. After Abraham's victory over some marauding kings (Genesis 14), Melchizedek blessed Abraham, and Abraham gave a tenth of what he had to this priest and king. To the writer of Hebrews, this indicated that the priesthood of Melchizedek was superior to that of Aaron, a descendant of Abraham.

1. **Seeing Jesus as a caring High Priest** (Hebrews 4:14–5:10). Jesus lived among us as a human being and so experienced the weaknesses that flesh and blood are heir to. Thus we can appeal to Jesus with complete confidence that he will hear us sympathetically. While Jesus was ordained to his priesthood by God, it was his obedient life as a human being that **perfected** him for his high priestly role.
2. **Warning—go on to maturity!** (Hebrews 5:11–6:12). The Hebrew Christians' failures to commit fully to Jesus had stunted their spiritual growth. Faith's foundation had been laid, and they were to build their lives on that foundation. A paraphrase of an

often misunderstood passage (Hebrews 6:4–6) helps us grasp the writer's point. The writer challenges his readers, who want to go back to the old era, by asking them a hypothetical question:

What would you want to do? View your failure as a falling away of God, so access is now lost? How then would you ever be restored—you who have been enlightened, tasted the heavenly gift, shared in the Holy Spirit, and known the flow of resurrection power? Do you want to crucify Jesus all over again, and through a new sacrifice be brought back to repentance? How impossible! What disgrace, this hint that Jesus' work for you was not enough!

The implicit warning is clear. Anyone who abandons hope in Christ abandons all hope! Jesus has been crucified for us, and this ultimate expression of God's love will never be repeated. Apart from Jesus their lives will be barren; with him their lives will be fruitful indeed.

3. **God's promises are an anchor for the soul** (Hebrews 6:13–20). The writer reminds his readers that God has done everything possible to make the unchanging nature of his purpose very clear. Only now do we have God's promises and his oath, we have the resurrected Jesus in heaven itself, representing us as our High Priest. His presence there is an anchor for the soul, firm and secure. (Hebrews 6:19–20)

what others say

F. F. Bruce

Our hope, based on his promises, is our spiritual anchor. And our hope is fixed there because Jesus is there, seated, as we have already been told, at the right hand of Majesty on high (Hebrews 1:3). Abraham rested his hope in the promise and oath of God; but we have more than that to rest our hope upon: we have the fulfillment of his promise in the exaltation of Christ. No wonder our hope is secure and stable.[2]

4. **The superiority of Jesus' priesthood** (Hebrews 7:1–28). Returning to the theme of Christ's priesthood, the writer contrasts Jesus as High Priest with the priests of the Old Testament.

Jesus' Superiority Is Shown in . . .

- Melchizedek's blessing of Abraham (Hebrews 7:1–10).
- Scripture's prediction of another priesthood (Hebrews 7:11–14).
- the fact that Christ's priesthood does not rest on lineage but on the power of an indestructible life (Hebrews 7:15–17).
- the inability of the old system to perfect, in contrast to the Christian's privilege of direct access to God (Hebrews 7:18–19).
- the fact that God himself ordained his priesthood to Jesus (Hebrews 7:20–22).
- the fact that the ever-living Jesus has a permanent priesthood which cannot be ended by death, and thus is able to save completely those who come to God through him (Hebrews 7:23–25).
- the fact that Christ offered only one sacrifice for sins, and then sat down, his saving work complete (Hebrews 7:26–28).

5. **Implications of Jesus' priesthood** (Hebrews 8:1–13). Earlier the writer of Hebrews noted that where there is a change of the priesthood there must also be a change of the Law (Hebrews 7:12). His point was that each element of Old Testament religion—law, sacrifices, priesthood, worship, etc.—was linked to form a balanced whole.

The Old Testament itself contains the promise that God would one day replace the Old Mosaic Covenant with a New Covenant. With the death and resurrection of Christ, that Old Covenant became obsolete, and God began to work in a new way in the hearts of his own.

The writer of Hebrews quotes Jeremiah's words to make the difference clear:

sacrifices
Leviticus 1–5;
Psalm 51

Hebrews 8:10–12 ***I will put My laws in their mind and write them on their hearts; and I will be their God, and they shall be My people. None of them shall teach his neighbor, and none his brother, saying, "Know the Lord," for all shall know Me, from the least of them to the greatest of them. For I will be merciful to their unrighteousness, and their sins and their lawless deeds I will remember no more.*** *(NKJV)*

With Christ as our High Priest, the New Covenant is now operative. The Law that God wrote in stone is now being written on the living hearts of believers, each of whom has a personal relationship with the Living God, and each of whom has been forgiven all his or her sins.

what others say

Kay Arthur

Man can be right with God! Righteousness is more than goodness; it is right standing with God. Righteous means to be straight. It is to do what God says is right, to live according to his standards. But righteousness in man requires a new heart.

And man can have a new heart! I "will put my Law within them, and on their heart I will write it . . . for I will forgive their iniquity, and their sin I will remember no more" (Jeremiah 32:40).[3]

He's the Perfect Sacrifice

the big picure

Perfect Sacrifice

The Old Testament had its earthly sanctuary where priests offered sacrifices. While these sacrifices provided a superficial cleansing, they were not able to purify human beings within. The fact that they had to be repeated endlessly showed how ineffective they really were. But Jesus offered himself, not in an earthly temple but in heaven itself. By his one sacrifice Jesus has cleansed forever those who believe in him.

While the repeated sacrifices of the Old Covenant were annual reminders of the fact that human beings are sinners, the once-and-for-all sacrifice of Jesus is evidence that our sins truly have been forgiven. Because of Jesus there is no longer any sacrifice for sin.

Surely then, Hebrew Christians have all the more reason to persevere in their new faith.

What's Special in Hebrews 9:1–10:39?

prefigured
foreshadowed

1. **Significance of the earthly sanctuary** (Hebrews 9:1–10). The writer points out that every aspect of Old Testament religion had symbolic significance. For instance, the fact that the high priest could only enter the inner room of the tabernacle or temple, the Holy of Holies, once a year, and then only with a sacrifice, showed that people had no direct access to God under the old system. The sacrifices offered there were unable to clear the conscience of the worshiper.

> **what others say**
>
> **Leon Morris**
>
> The reference to conscience is significant. The ordinances of the Old Covenant had been external. They had not been able to come to grips with the real problem, that of a troubled conscience.[4]

2. **The power of the blood of Christ** (Hebrews 9:11–14). Unlike Old Testament animal sacrifices, Christ's blood can cleanse our consciences from dead works, so that we may serve the living God (Hebrews 9:14). Christians are no longer held in the deadly grip of past sins; forgiveness sets the believer free to serve God.
3. **The Old Testament sacrificial system prefigured Christ's death** (Hebrews 9:15–28). The Old Covenant required that blood be shed if sins were to be forgiven and persons purified. But the blood of sacrificial animals was only for purifying material things, which themselves were merely copies of heavenly realities. All the Old Testament sacrifices pointed toward the one ultimate sacrifice Jesus would make on Calvary, shedding his blood to take away our sins.
4. **The finality of Christ's sacrifice** (Hebrews 10:1–18). The writer keeps the focus on the fact that Jesus, unlike the priests of the Old Testament, needed to offer only the one sacrifice, for we have been made holy through the sacrifice of the body of Jesus Christ once for all (Hebrews 10:10). The fact that Jesus offered only one sacrifice is proof that we have been forgiven: where these have been forgiven, there is no longer any sacrifice for sin (Hebrews 10:18). There is no longer any need for sacrifice—Christ's sacrifice is final.

faith
a trust in God that moves a person to respond to his Word

Old Testaments Saints
true believers in God who lived before the death of Christ

5. **A warning against turning away from God** (Hebrews 10:19–39). The writer showed what a wonderful salvation God provided in Christ. The appropriate response to this is to accept him and spur one another on toward love and good deeds (Hebrews 10:24). To deliberately turn one's back on Jesus would be treating Christ's blood as an unholy thing and would be an insult to the Spirit of grace.

the big picure

Faith

By this point in the epistle, the readers understand why life under the New Covenant is superior to life under the Old; at every point the salvation Jesus provides is superior! The writer then goes on to show that New Covenant blessings are accessed by faith, and that God will continue to discipline his children that they might share his holiness. After warning his readers against refusing to respond to the Lord, the writer closes his letter with a series of exhortations.

What's Special in Hebrews 10–13?

1. **The importance of faith** (Hebrews 11:1–40). The writer of Hebrews has clearly laid out the ways in which the gospel message is better than the Old Testament revelation. It was **faith**—the conviction that God exists and that he rewards those who seek him—that enabled **Old Testament Saints** to accomplish the things for which we honor them.

What can't we accomplish if we meet our challenges with their kind of faith?

2. **Jesus as the "author and finisher of our faith"** (Hebrews 12:1–3). Jesus is not only the object of our faith, he is the supreme example of one who lived by faith, and thus is our inspiration.

3. **A new perspective on hardships** (Hebrews 12:4–13). The writer encourages his readers—including us—to maintain a healthy perspective on our hardships. These are experiences provided by God himself as discipline. Rather than signaling our abandonment by God, they signal his great love for us. For every father who loves his children disciplines them to strengthen their character. And God disciplines us that we may share in his holiness. No lordship we experience is pleasant, but God will use it to produce a harvest

of righteousness and peace for those who have been trained by it. (Hebrews 12:11)

what others say

Leon Morris

It is important that suffering be accepted in the right spirit; otherwise it does not produce a right result.[5]

4. Warning—against missing God's grace (Hebrews 12:14–28). The writer contrasts Mount Sinai, representing the Old Covenant of Law, with Mount Zion, representing the gospel of grace.

The sight at Mount Sinai was terrifying, for it spoke of judgment. The view at Mount Zion is one of blessing. If anyone refuses God's offer of grace to turn back to the Law, he will not escape the wrath of God.

5. Concluding exhortations (Hebrews 13:1–21). The book of Hebrews closes with a variety of brief encouragements to godly living, and with one of the most beautiful benedictions to be found in Scripture:

HEBREWS 13:20–21 ***Now may the God of peace who brought up our Lord Jesus from the dead, that great Shepherd of the sheep, through the blood of the everlasting covenant, make you complete in every good work to do His will, working in you what is well pleasing in His sight, through Jesus Christ, to whom be glory forever and ever. Amen.*** *(NKJV)*

Chapter Wrap-Up

- Jesus the Son of God brought humankind God's final and superior revelation.
- As God's Son, Jesus is superior to angels and to Moses, so the revelation he brought deserves our fullest attention.
- Jesus has been ordained by God as our High Priest: because he lives forever he can save to the uttermost all who come to God by him.
- Jesus offered his own blood to God as a sacrifice for sins.

- Jesus' one sacrifice cleanses believers and guarantees their forgiveness.
- Jesus' death initiated the promised New Covenant, not only promising forgiveness but also the inner transformation of believers.
- As with Old Testament Saints, it is faith that claims God's promises and enables believers to accomplish great things.

Study Questions

1. To whom is Hebrews addressed?
2. Why did the author write this book?
3. What makes the fact that the New Testament revelation was delivered by Jesus so significant?
4. In what ways is Jesus a superior High Priest to the Old Testament's high priesthood?
5. What does the New Covenant do for believers that the Old Covenant could not do?
6. What is the significance of the fact that Jesus offered only one sacrifice for sins?
7. What does Hebrews 11 explore the significance of?
8. How are hardships evidence of the love of God?

James • 1 and 2 Peter • 1, 2, and 3 John • Jude

Let's Get Started

In the past few chapters, we have learned about the epistles of Paul. However, others wrote letters to some of the first-century churches, and these are usually called the "general epistles." They include writings of Peter and John, who were apostles, and Jesus' half brothers James and Jude, who were leaders in the church. They also include the book of Hebrews.

creed
accepted systems of religious or other beliefs

Each writer had a special reason for writing, and each letter makes a definite contribution to our understanding of Christian faith and life.

James

. . . faith at work

Who	James
What	wrote this letter
Where	in Jerusalem, to Jewish Christians in the Middle East
When	around AD 48
Why	to encourage practical Christian living as an expression of true faith in Christ

the big picure

James

This letter urges readers to pay attention to how faith is expressed in daily life. Writing within fifteen years or so of Christ's resurrection, James is rightly concerned that no one confuse **creeds** with vital Christianity. This brief letter makes even more mention of faith than Paul's letter to Galatians.

JAMES: James was a half brother of Jesus, and became a leader of the church in Jerusalem. Tradition portrays him as a man of prayer, whose nickname was the Just.

You Gotta Have Faith

every situation
Mark 10:27

James is probably the earliest of the New Testament Epistles, written by a pastor who is deeply concerned that Christian faith find practical expression in daily life. In the early days of the Church, when James wrote, the debate of justification by faith alone, which Paul addresses, had not yet emerged. But James does distinguish between mere intellectual assent and a faith that involves both trust in and commitment to Jesus as Lord. James's concern is that the lives of those who claim Jesus as Savior honor him.

Expressing Faith in Daily LIfe

Greetings	James 1:1
PRACTICING FAITH'S LIFESTYLE	James 1:2–2:13
• In our personal life	James 1:2–18
• In our interpersonal relationships	James 1:19–2:13
PRINCIPLES UNDERLYING FAITH'S LIFESTYLE	James 2:14–26
PROBLEMS FOR FAITH'S LIFESTYLE	James 3:1–4:17
• Taming the tongue	James 3:1–12
• Subduing the self	James 3:13–4:10
• Judging	James 4:11, 12
• False pride	James 4:13–17
THE PROSPECTS AND PROMISES OF FAITH	James 5:1–19
• Future redress	James 5:1–6
• Patience rewarded	James 5:7–20

What's Special in the Book of James?

The book of James is filled with special insights for Christians who want to honor the Lord by the way they live. Here are a few highlights:

1. **Understanding temptation** (James 1:13–15). Let's not blame God for our reactions to situations in which we feel tempted. James says that God never tempts anyone. The pull we feel toward sin comes from within us, not from the situation. In fact, God only gives good gifts.

key point

James's point is that <u>every situation</u> in which God places us is intended to bless us, not to trip us up. Harm will result only when we give into the inner pull toward sin. When we respond in a godly way, blessing will result, and this is what God intended all along.

2. Faith that counts (James 2:14–26). James does not argue that faith and deeds are necessary for salvation. Instead, he insists that a faith which does not produce right actions is a false, dead faith.

James does not teach that Abraham was pronounced righteous on the basis of his actions. James teaches that Scripture's announcement that Abraham was righteous is vindicated on the basis of Abraham's subsequent obedience. He did right because God had actually worked within him to make him righteous! James is speaking of two kinds of faith, only one of which is saving faith. He teaches that any claim of having saving faith will be vindicated by the actions that flow from that faith, and which in that sense complete it.

what others say

Leon Morris

The kind of faith [James] objects to is the kind of faith the devils have (James 2:19). They believe in God, but that does nothing more than produce a shudder. A faith that does not transform the believer so that his life is given over to doing good works is not faith as James understands it. That is dead faith.[1]

3. Two problems with prayer (James 4:1–3). James's practical approach to life is illustrated in two statements about prayer. He notes that some people go about getting what they want the wrong way. James writes, "You do not have because you do not ask" (James 4:2 NKJV). The Christian life is to be one of dependence on the Lord. But then James adds, "You ask and do not receive, because you ask amiss, that you may spend it on your pleasures" (James 4:3 NKJV). We're not to approach prayer as a magic lamp. The person who prays in Jesus' name should seek from God what Jesus sought—the Father's will, and the privilege of serving others.

what others say

C. S. Lewis

When the event you prayed for occurs your prayer has always contributed to it. When the opposite event occurs your prayer has never been ignored; it has been considered and refused, for your ultimate good and the good of the whole universe.[2]

1 Peter

. . . following Jesus' example

believers
Galatians 2:7

dangers
1 Peter 1:6

Who	The apostle Peter
What	wrote this letter
Where	from Rome, to Christians everywhere
When	about AD 64 or AD 65
Why	urging Christians to follow Jesus' example and live holy lives

And You Think You Have It Bad

the big picure

1 Peter

This letter of Peter provides Christians with the needed perspective on persecution, and reminds them that believers are called to both holiness and suffering. Peter wants his readers to see that suffering can be a gift of God, replete with benefits.

PETER: The apostle Peter had been Jesus' leading disciple from the beginning. After Jesus' resurrection, Peter preached the first gospel sermons and developed a special ministry to Jewish believers. He and Paul were both executed in Rome under the emperor Nero.

Thirty years after the resurrection of Jesus, Christianity had been carried throughout the Roman Empire. By this time it was seen as distinct from Judaism, and as such was viewed by the Roman government as a foreign, illicit religion. The emperor Claudius had been intent on restoring traditional Roman religion, and now a half-mad Nero ruled. Nero would torture and kill thousands of believers in the city of Rome, and the decades ahead would hold great suffering for those who identified themselves with Jesus and his people.

Peter was well aware of the dangers that lay ahead and his letter, directed to all Christians scattered throughout the empire, was a call to holiness as well as an attempt to help his readers better understand the purpose of suffering in the believer's life.

Called to Holiness and Suffering

Greetings	1 Peter 1:1–2
A CALL TO HOLINESS	1 Peter 1:3–2:12
• Our living hope	1 Peter 1:3–12
• Our holy calling	1 Peter 1:13–2:12
A CALL TO SUBMISSION	1 Peter 2:13–3:7
A CALL TO SUFFERING	1 Peter 3:8–4:10
• Exhortations	1 Peter 5:1–11
• Final greetings	1 Peter 5:12–13

What's Special in Peter's First Epistle?

1. **Joy in the midst of trials** (1 Peter 1:3–9). Peter writes of a joy that the believer experiences even while suffering in all kinds of trials. He likens our trials to the hot furnaces in which goldsmiths melt precious metal to rid it of impurities. "That the genuineness of your faith . . . may be found to praise, honor, and glory at the revelation of Jesus Christ" (1 Peter 1:7 NKJV). The fact that the salvation God provides is real enables us to feel joy despite the pain, and this is proof that God truly has saved us!

2. **Three characteristics of the Christian experience** (1 Peter 1:13–25). The image people have of Christians is that of sour and mean spoilsports. Peter reminds us that God has a very different idea of what Jesus' followers are to be like. This passage gives us three attractive characteristics:

    - Christians are hope-filled and holy (1 Peter 1:13–16).
    - Christians have a deep respect for God (1 Peter 1:17–21).
    - Christians lead lives of love for one another (1 Peter 1:22–25).

All this grows out of the fact that believers have been born again. They have been given a vital new life, which is God's own and which breaks through our hardness to find loving expression in our lives.

3. **The significance of Jesus' example** (1 Peter 3:8–18). What about situations where Christians suffer unfairly? What about those times when we do what is good, but bad things happen? Peter acknowledges that such things happen. He tells us that when they do, we should not be afraid, but remember that Christ is still Lord and

remain positive. When people are amazed that we can remain positive despite being treated unfairly, we are to witness to the basis of our hope (1 Peter 3:15). What enables us to remain positive? Peter points to Jesus, the prime example of one who suffered unfairly (1 Peter 3:18).

1 Peter 3:18 ***For Christ also suffered once for sins, the just for the unjust, that He might bring us to God.*** *(NKJV)*

What appears to be history's greatest injustice was used by God to bring salvation to humankind!

Peter's point? If God could use such unfair treatment to bring about this wonderful good, he can use the unfair things that happen to us for good too!

4. **Suffering as a Christian** (1 Peter 4:12–19). Peter reminds his readers that Christians should not be surprised at suffering. In a sense, suffering enables us to draw closer to Christ, who suffered before us. Peter's final word on the topic is good advice indeed.

1 Peter 4:19 ***Therefore let those who suffer according to the will of God commit their souls to Him in doing good, as to a faithful Creator.*** *(NKJV).*

2 Peter

. . . following Jesus' example

Who	The apostle Peter wrote this letter
What	both warning and encouraging Christians
Where	while in Rome
When	just before his death in 67 BC or 68 BC
Why	in view of emerging dangers from false teachers

Evil from Within

the big picure

2 Peter

In this short letter Peter addresses two issues that most concerned him. He urges believers to concentrate on living productive lives, and he describes false teachers and their end.

Near the end of his life Peter became deeply concerned about the future of Christ's Church. In his first epistle, he wrote about dangers from outsiders who would persecute Christians. In his second epistle, Peter writes about dangers from the inside. Insiders who are pseudo-Christians were corrupting the faith by introducing false teaching. No foe from without could defeat Christ's Church, but the emerging dangers from within constituted a real threat. To overcome this menace, Christians would have to remain committed to the truth and to holy living.

heresy
false teaching

This second epistle of Peter's is especially helpful in understanding **heresy**, and in showing how to deal with false teaching.

Peter Addresses Two Issues

Greetings	2 Peter 1:1–3
CONFIRMING OUR CALLING	2 Peter 1:1–21
• By productive lives	2 Peter 1:1–11
• By God's sure Word	2 Peter 1:12–21
FALSE TEACHERS	2 Peter 2:1–22
THE END OF THE WORLD	2 Peter 3:1–18

What's Special in 2 Peter?

1. **God's part and our part in Christian experience** (2 Peter 1:3–9). God has done all that's needed to equip us for life and godliness, by giving us promises that permit us to share in the divine nature itself. But we cannot be passive in our pursuit of godliness. Rather we are to focus on developing godly character.

The qualities that Peter lists are both important and practical:

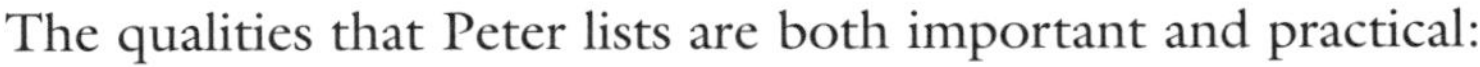

Quality	Expression in Daily Life
Faith	Faithful commitment to revealed truth
Goodness (virtue)	Faithful comment to moral excellence
Knowledge	Practical application of revealed truth
Self-control	Personal discipline and restraint
Perseverance	Steadfastness in the face of opposition
Godliness	Reverence for God expressed in conduct
Brotherly kindness	Affection for fellow believers
Love	Commitment to act for others' benefit

2. **Descriptions of false teachers and false teaching** (2 Peter 2:1–22). Peter emphasizes the fact that God will deal with false teachers. In the meantime, this is one of three Bible passages that specify the signs by which false teachers can be recognized.

Sign of a False Teacher

Sign	Jeremiah	2 Peter	Jude
DOCTRINAL			
• Introduce heresies, denying the Lord who bought them	23:13	2:11	
PERSONALITY			
• Bold, arrogant	23:10	2:10	16
• Despise authority		2:10	3
• Follow desires of sin nature	23:14	2:10	4, 19
• Love money		2:15	12
MINISTRY			
• Appeal to "lustful desires"	23:14	2:17	16
• Promise "freedom" to be depraved	23:16–17		

3. **The coming end of the world motivates the godly** (2 Peter 3:1–14). Peter describes two attitudes that people adopt in response to Christ's promise to come again.

The unbeliever scoffs, assuming that everything goes on as it has since the beginning of creation. They ignore Scripture's testimony to the Genesis Flood, which is evidence that God can and does step into history to judge sin.

The believer chooses to live a holy and godly life, in preparation for life in the new heaven and new earth that God will one day create.

what others say

William Law

If you attempt to talk with a dying man about sports or business, he is no longer interested. He now sees other things as more important. People who are dying recognize what we often forget, that we are standing on the brink of another world.[3]

1, 2, and 3 John

. . . on leading lives of love and obedience

Who	The apostle John
What	wrote these letters
Where	while living in Ephesus,
When	near the end of the first century
Why	to encourage love for others and obedience to God as vital Christian qualities

Light, Love, and Faith

the big picure

John's Letters

Each of John's three letters is warmly relational, encouraging intimate fellowship with the Lord and with other Christians. In John's first letter, he introduces various themes and keeps returning to them, which makes his letter difficult to outline, but no less valuable. Perhaps the best way to approach this letter is to focus on three themes: John wants Christians to live in the light, to live lovingly, and to live by faith.

JOHN: The apostle John was especially close to Jesus during Christ's life on earth. John outlived the other apostles of Jesus, and spent most of his life ministering in Asia Minor. These letters, and the book of Revelation, were written near the end of the first century when John was in his nineties.

With the crowning of the emperor Domitian in AD 81, persecution of Christians became state policy. Even though John himself was later exiled, the apostle's letters ignore the external threat. John is most concerned with the inner life of God's people, and so focuses on the need to live in intimate fellowship with God and fellow believers.

Themes in 1, 2, and 3 John

Invitation	1 John 1:1–4
LIVING IN THE LIGHT	1 John 1:5–2:29
• Being honest with ourselves	1 John 1:5–2:2
• Being loving toward others	1 John 2:3–11
• Being separate from the world	1 John 2:12–17

Themes in 1, 2, and 3 John (cont'd)

light
in the books of John, in touch with reality

confess
to acknowledge, admit

• Being alert for antichrists	1 John 2:18–29
LIVING IN LOVE	1 John 3:1–4:19
• As God's children	1 John 3:1–10
• As concerned for others	1 John 3:11–20
• In fellowship with God	1 John 3:21–24
• In allegiance to God	1 John 4:1–6
• As moved by God's love	1 John 4:7–21
LIVING BY FAITH	1 John 5:1–21
• Assured of eternal life	1 John 5:1–12
• Assured that God hears us	1 John 5:13–15
• Freed from sin's control	1 John 5:16–21
HOLDING FAST TO TRUTH	2 John
COMMENDATION FOR LOVING	3 John

What's Special in 1 John?

1. **Walking in the light means being honest about sin** (1 John 1:8–10). John calls on Christians to be honest with themselves and with God. In saying God is light with no darkness at all, he reminds us that God sees everything as it really is. The only way to get along with God is to be real, without deceiving ourselves or others.

This is particularly important when we sin, as all human beings do. John says If we claim to be without sin, we deceive ourselves and the truth is not in us (1 John 1:8). What are we to do? We are to **confess** our sins—to acknowledge them to God and to ourselves. John reminds us that he is faithful and just and will forgive us our sins and purify us from all unrighteousness! (1 John 1:8–9)

what others say

John Wesley

He says not, the blood of Christ will cleanse (at the hour of death or in the day of judgment) but it cleanses at the present time.[4]

2. **The warning against loving the world** (1 John 2:15–17). What passions make human society corrupt? John identifies three:

- the lust of the flesh (desires generated by the sin nature)

- the lust of the eyes (the desire for material things)
- the pride of life (pride in possessions)

The person who is worldly is in the grip of the same desires that motivate the lost—desires which are totally out of harmony with God's nature and of which he is not the source. Why is it foolish as well as wrong to adopt the values of human society? John says, "The world is passing away, and the lust of it; but he who does the will of God abides forever" (1 John 2:17 NKJV).

go to

antichrists
1 John 4:1–3;
2 Peter 2;
Revelation 3

love one another
1 John 4:7
John 13:34–35

> **what others say**
>
> **François Fénelon**
>
> You must violently resist the tides of the world. Violently give up all that holds you back from God. Violently turn your will over to God to do his will alone.[5]

antichrists
all who oppose God and Jesus

brothers
any fellow believer

3. The warning against antichrists (1 John 2:18–23). John warns his readers against false teachers and others who would lead them astray. He calls such persons antichrists. How do we guard against antichrists? By being sensitive to the Holy Spirit within, who provides a built-in spiritual instinct that enables us to distinguish truth from falsehood by a simple objective test. Anyone who denies the deity of Jesus, who refuses to acknowledge that Jesus Christ has come in the flesh, is a false teacher.

4. The call to love one another (1 John 4:11–24). John frequently reminds his readers of the importance of loving one another. God himself is love, so a failure to love fellow Christians is a sign that the believer is out of touch with God. Here is a sampling of what John says about loving our **brothers**.

John's Call to Love Fellow Christians

Verse	What John Says
1 John 2:10	"He who loves his brother abides in the light." (NKJV)
1 John 3:11	"Whoever does not practice righteousness is not of God, nor is he who does not love his brother." (NKJV)
1 John 3:14	"We know that we have passed from death to life, because we love the brethren." (NKJV)
1 John 3:17	"Whoever has this world's goods, and sees his brother in need, and shuts up his heart from him, how does the love of God abide in him?" (NKJV)

John's Call to Love Fellow Christians (cont'd)

Verse	What John Says
1 John 3:23	"This is His commandment: that we should believe on the name of His Son Jesus Christ and love one another, as He gave us commandment." (NKJV)
1 John 4:7	"Let us love one another, for love is of God." (NKJV)
1 John 4:8	"He who does not love does not know God, for God is love." (NKJV)
1 John 4:11	"Beloved, if God so loved us, we also ought to love one another." (NKJV)
1 John 4:12	"If we love one another, God abides in us, and His love has been perfected in us." (NKJV)
1 John 4:20	"If someone says, 'I love God,' and hates his brother, he is a liar." (NKJV)
1 John 4:21	"And this commandment we have from Him: that he who loves God must love his brother also." (NKJV)

Jude

. . . contending for the faith

Who	Jude, a half brother of Jesus, wrote this brief epistle
What	about false teachers who were infiltrating the Church
Where	to Christians everywhere
When	in the AD 80s
Why	to challenge believers to contend for the faith

Sounds Just Like the Church Today

the big picure

Jude

The writer had hoped to write about the glories of salvation, but found himself led instead to urge his readers to contend for the faith that had once for all been entrusted to God's saints. The bulk of Jude's letter is spent drawing analogies between false teachers threatening the Church and Old Testament enemies of God, emphasizing the fact that such persons are under the judgment of God.

Jude's Encouragement to Contend for the Faith

Greetings	Jude 1:1–2
Descriptions of false teachers	Jude 1:3–16
Encouragement and conclusion	Jude 1:17–25

JUDE: Early Church fathers identify the author of this letter as the half brother of Jesus and brother of James, named in Matthew 13:55 and Mark 6:3.

Like Paul, John, and Peter, Jude recognized the danger false teachers posed to the Church. Both non-Christian, Jewish, and pagan teachers were active in the first century, busy reinterpreting Christian teachings to fit their philosophical presuppositions. Jude's letter, filled with allusions to the Old Testament, seems addressed primarily to Jewish Christians. Jude sums up the danger from false teachers by saying they are "ungodly men, who turn the grace of our God into lewdness and deny the only Lord God and our Lord Jesus Christ" (Jude 4 NKJV).

But Jude closes with a word of advice for true believers on how to defeat those who would divide them.

What's Special in Jude?

Jude's closing advice to his readers is on target for Christians today.

> **JUDE 20–21** ***But you, beloved, building yourselves up on your most holy faith, praying in the Holy Spirit, keep yourselves in the love of God, looking for the mercy of our Lord Jesus Christ unto eternal life.*** *(NKJV)*

Chapter Wrap-Up

- The general epistles in the New Testament include James, 1 and 2 Peter, 1, 2, and 3 John, Jude, and also Hebrews.
- The epistle of James was the first of the New Testament books to be written.
- James gives practical advice on how faith in Jesus should work itself out in daily life.
- In his first letter Peter encourages believers about how to experience persecution, and helps them put suffering in Christian perspective.

- In Peter's second letter he warns against false teachers, and reminds Christians to live godly lives in view of the coming end of this world.
- The apostle John wrote three letters that have found a place in our New Testament.
- In his first letter John emphasizes the importance of loving one another and obeying God.
- Jude, a half brother of Jesus, adds an urgent warning against false teachers who reinterpret truths delivered by the apostles.

Study Questions

1. What are the seven general epistles discussed in this chapter?
2. What is the theme of the book of James?
3. What is the difference between a true faith in Christ and a dead or merely intellectual faith?
4. Why did Peter write about all sorts of trials that Christians were about to experience?
5. How does the example of Christ's suffering on the cross encourage Christians who suffer unjustly?
6. What are at least three characteristics of the false teachers against whom Peter warns in his second letter?
7. Why does John warn Christians against deceiving themselves after they sin?
8. What is one objective test that helps identify false teachers who infiltrate the Church?
9. Why does John believe loving our Christian brothers is so important?

Revelation

Let's Get Started

The last book of the New Testament, **Revelation**, is a book of prophecy. While events in the first chapters of this mysterious book take place in the past, most of Revelation is about history's end and the eternity that lies beyond. The book of Revelation reminds us that God will one day act to judge sin, to purge evil from his universe, and to welcome those who have trusted Jesus as Savior to the new heavens and the new earth that he will create.

revelation
disclosure of what was previously unknown

lost
those who have not trusted Christ

saved
those who have trusted Christ as Savior and have had their sins forgiven

predictive prophecy
a description of future events

Revelation

. . . of things to come

Who	The apostle John
What	wrote this record of God-given visons
Where	while exiled on the island of Patmos
When	about AD 90
Why	to describe what God intends to accomplish at history's end

Wow!

the big picure

Revelation

This book can be divided into three main parts. John is given a vision of the risen Christ, and is told to write letters to seven churches in Asia Minor. John is then caught up into heaven, and from this vantage point he observes terrible punishments that God hurls against the wicked on earth. The final section of Revelation pictures what will happen after Jesus physically returns to earth, and describes what eternity holds for both the **lost** and the **saved**.

Much of the Old Testament is **predictive prophecy**, which describes events to take place at or near history's end. Jesus also spoke about the future, as did writers of the New Testament Epistles. But these scattered references did little to fit future events together.

Then, near the end of the first century, the apostle John was given a vision while he was on the Mediterranean Island of Patmos. He saw the resurrected Jesus in his glory, and in a vision observed history's culminating events. John's description of what he saw helps us to fit earlier prophecies together, and reassures us as well. God truly is in control, and history is moving toward his intended end. When that end comes, God will triumph, and those who have trusted in him will be welcomed to an eternity of blessing and joy.

John's Visions in the Book of Revelation

The setting	Revelation 1:1–3
CHRIST AND THE CHURCHES	Revelation 1:4–3:21
RAPTURE TO THE SECOND COMING	Revelation 4:1–19:21
• Events in heaven	Revelation 4:1–5:14
• Seven seal judgments	Revelation 6:1–7:17
• Seven trumpet judgments	Revelation 8:1–11:19
• Satanic intervention	Revelation 12:1–15:8
• Seven bowl judgments	Revelation 16:1–21
• Destruction of man's religious and economic system	Revelation 17:1–18:24
• The second coming of Jesus	Revelation 19:1–2
MILLENNIUM AND BEYOND	Revelation 20:1–22:21
• Millennium and rebellion	Revelation 20:1–10
• Final judgment	Revelation 20:11–15
• Heaven ahead	Revelation 21:1–2:6
• Coming soon	Revelation 22:7–21

Seven Examples

the big picure

Seven Churches

While on Patmos John was stunned by the sudden appearance of the risen Jesus. Christ dictated letters to seven churches in Asia Minor. Many believe the seven churches are representative either of the spiritual condition of churches from every era, or of the spiritual condition of Christians at different periods in history.

What's Special in Revelation 1–3

1. The appearance of the risen Jesus (Revelation 1:12–16). The vision uses symbolic images drawn from the Old Testament to emphasize the deity of Jesus. John had been close to Jesus while he was on earth. Yet when John saw Jesus in his glory, the apostle "fell at His feet as dead" (Revelation 1:17 NKJV). The Jesus of history is the eternal God.

symbolic images
Daniel 7:9

2. Past, present, and future (Revelation 1:19).

> REVELATION 1:19 ***Write the things which you have seen, and the things which are, and the things which will take place after this. (NKJV)***

This verse gives us the key for understanding the book of Revelation. What you have seen (past tense) is the vision of Jesus in chapter 1. What is now (present tense) refers to the seven churches to whom Jesus will dictate letters (Revelation 2, 3). And what will take place later (future tense) reveals what will happen after the **Church Age** is over (Revelation 4–22).

Church Age
from the first century until Jesus takes Christians to heaven (the Rapture)

3. The letters to the seven churches (Revelation 2:1–3:22). The seven churches to which the letters are addressed existed in Asia Minor at the time John wrote down what Christ dictated. But the descriptions of the churches, with Christ's warnings and promises, surely apply to congregations today.

what others say

Alan F. Johnson

Even though the words of Christ refer initially to the first-century churches located in particular places, by the Spirit's continual relevance they transcend that time limitation and speak to all the churches in every generation.[1]

Trouble on the Way

the big picure

Tribulation

John is taken to heaven, symbolizing the rapture of the Church, where he witnesses preparations for terrible judgments about to strike the people left on earth. John struggles to describe what he sees as powerful angels pour out judgment after judgment on a rebellious earth.

False Prophet
the second beast of Revelation, it seeks devotees for the Antichrist

apocalyptic
refers to writings from God that use symbolic language to tell of a divine intervention soon to come

During this time of judgment, called the Great Tribulation or the Day of the Lord in the Old Testament, Satan marshals his forces to do battle with God. Satan energizes two individuals, the Beast (the Antichrist) and the **False Prophet**, who unite mankind against God's Old Testament people, Israel. Continuous acts of divine judgment destroy the unified religious and political system that the Antichrist establishes, and the struggle is ended by Christ himself, who returns from heaven with an army of angels.

What's Special in Revelation 4–19?

1. **It's often difficult to know just what John is describing.** Some dismiss the language of Revelation as **apocalyptic**, implying that the visions of John have no relation to reality. But in fact John describes actual events that will surely take place here on earth, just as portrayed. The difficulty with the language of Revelation is that John was forced to use the vocabulary available to him in the first century.

Imagine that a Pilgrim who came to America on the *Mayflower* in the 1600s was suddenly given a vision of twenty-first-century America. The Pilgrim witnesses a landing on the moon shown on TV, watches as planes take off and land at a major airport, and observes traffic hurtling along Los Angeles highways. Imagine how that individual, with only a seventeenth-century vocabulary, might try to describe what he saw to friends on the *Mayflower*, and you will have some insight into why it is so difficult to understand John's description of real events in Revelation.

2. **The terrible judgments of history's end do not bring repentance** (Revelation 6:15–17). The nature of the judgments makes it unmistakably clear that God himself is their source. Even knowing the great day of God's wrath has arrived, the people of earth refuse to repent. They continue in their sins, while trying to call on the mountains to hide them from "the face of Him who sits on the throne and from the wrath of the Lamb!" (Revelation 6:16 NKJV).

Don't wait to trust Christ until it's too late. Judgment is coming soon.

what others say

J. H. Melton

The Lord Jesus Christ will either be your Savior or your judge. Your sins will either be judged in Jesus Christ or they will be judged by Jesus Christ. Now he offers his mercy to save you. If you reject his mercy he will judge you in absolute justice and wrath.[2]

sealed
a mark, sign, or symbol serving as visible evidence of something

cult
a religion or sect considered to be false, unorthodox, or extremist

3. **The 144,000 people sealed from the tribes of Israel** (Revelation 7:1–8). The **cult** of Jehovah's Witnesses was launched with the conviction that the 144,000 represented all who would be saved, and that this group would be made up of their members only. But the text clearly states that these 144,000 people are Jews, who come from the twelve tribes of Israel. Who are they really, and what is their role during this period of terrible tribulation on earth? The simple answer is that they are Jews who will convert to Christ during this time, and will witness to him throughout the world.

what others say

Daymond R. Duck

Once God has sealed his 144,000, the whole world will hear his message. Multitudes will believe and be saved. The Antichrist and his False Prophet will be furious and try to stop the revival by forcing new believers to turn away from the faith. They will deny people food and medicine. Executions will be frequent and numerous.[3]

4. **Praise for God and Christ in heaven.** While terrible judgments cause terror for the peoples of earth, John portrays a very different reaction in heaven. There, angels and the saved join in praise of God. Both the judgments and the praise are appropriate, for at last God is acting to establish what is right. In the words of the elders and angels in heaven . . .

Revelation 11:18

The nations were angry, and Your wrath has come,
And the time of the dead, that they should be judged,
And that You should reward Your servants the prophets and the saints,
And those who fear Your name, small and great,
And should destroy those who destroy the earth. (NKJV)

Millennium
thousand-year reign of Christ on earth

Lake of Fire
the final abode of Satan and his follow

what others say

Ed Hindson

The real tragedy in all this talk of global unity is the absence of any emphasis on the spiritual roots of democracy and freedom. The Gospel has been blunted in Western Europe for so long that there is little God-conscientiousness left in the European people. Without Christ, the Prince of Peace, there can be no hope for manmade orders of peace and prosperity. There will be no **Millennium** without the Messiah![4]

6. **The age ends with the return of Christ in triumph** (Revelation 19:1–21). The final scene on earth is that of the Antichrist and his forces gathered to do battle with Christ, who returns to earth at the head of the armies of heaven. The Antichrist and False Prophet are immediately thrown alive into the **Lake of Fire**, and their armies are destroyed.

what others say

Alan F. Johnson

John is showing us the ultimate and swift downfall of these evil powers by the King of kings and Lord of lords. They have met their master in this final and utterly real confrontation.[5]

Peace at Last

the big picure

The Millennium

At last Jesus rules on earth, fulfilling the predictions of the Old Testament prophets. The reign will last for a thousand years (a millennium), during which Satan will be bound. At the end of these thousand years Satan is released and again deceives human beings into rebelling against God. This time God responds by putting an end to the universe. Lost human beings are called before God's throne for final judgment, and all those who have not trusted Christ as Savior are consigned to the Lake of Fire. God then creates a new and perfect universe, to be populated by the saved forever and ever.

What's Special in Revelation 20–22?

1. **The Millennium** (Revelation 20:1–6). This is the only passage in the Bible that speaks specifically of a thousand-year period. Some

have dismissed the idea of a millennial reign of Christ for this reason. However, the Old Testament prophets pictured just such a role of the Messiah, and Christ's reign on this earth is mentioned dozens of times.

Christ's reign on this earth
Revelation 20:6

what others say

Hal Lindsey

The heart of the Old Testament prophetic message is the coming of the Messiah to set up an earthly kingdom over which he would rule from the throne of David. The only important detail which Revelation adds concerning this promised Messianic kingdom is its duration—one thousand years.[6]

2. **Satan's doom** (Revelation 20:7–10). Satan began his existence as a bright and powerful angel, who then rebelled against God and tricked Adam and Eve into joining his side. But from the very beginning Satan's doom has been fixed.

REVELATION 20:10 ***The devil, who deceived them, was cast into the lake of fire and brimstone where the beast [Antichrist] and the false prophet are. And they will be tormented day and night forever and ever. (NKJV)***

3. **God's final judgment of the lost** (Revelation 20:11–14). John speaks of two books to be referred to at the final judgment. One book, the Book of Life, is a record of the deeds of every human being. The other book is called the Lamb's (or Christ's) Book of Life, where the names of those who have trusted Christ and whose sins have been paid for are written. Anyone judged on the basis of what he or she has done is condemned to the Lake of Fire. At that time all will know that hell is not a fiction, but is utterly and eternally real.

what others say

David Hocking

Those who are cast into hell are not annihilated as some religious groups teach. They experience torment forever and ever; it is an everlasting fire into which they are cast. Satan deserves it, and the justice of God demands it.[7]

4. God's new heaven and new earth (Revelation 21:1–22:6). We cannot know how wonderful eternity will be for those who have trusted God until we are welcomed into the new heaven and earth God will create. But these last chapters of the Bible tell us that it will be wonderful indeed.

What Will Heaven Be Like?

- God himself will be with us.
- God will wipe away every tear.
- There will be no more death, mourning, crying, or pain.
- The glory of the Lord will provide its light.
- Nothing impure will ever enter it.
- No longer will there be any curse.
- The throne of God will be in the city, and we will serve him.
- We will reign forever and ever.

5. Jesus is coming soon (Revelation 22:12–21). Revelation closes with a wonderful promise. Jesus says he is coming. He is coming soon. How eagerly all who are Christians can look forward to that wonderful day!

Chapter Wrap-Up

- The bulk of Revelation is "predictive prophecy."
- The prophecy in Revelation reveals what will happen at history's end.
- God will bring devastating supernatural judgments on those who continue to rebel against him.
- Satan will give supernatural powers to an Antichrist who will build a one-world political and economic empire.
- God will destroy the Antichrist and his forces when Jesus returns personally to set up a thousand-year reign on earth.

- Satan will lead a final rebellion at the end of Christ's reign, and will then be consigned to the Lake of Fire.
- This present universe will be dissolved, and all the dead will be revived to face God's judgment.
- Those who have failed to trust in God during their lives will be judged by their actions, and consigned to the Lake of Fire forever.
- Those who have trusted in God will be welcomed into a new heaven and earth which God will create, and will be with him eternally in glory.

Study Questions

1. What is the subject of Revelation?
2. What is special about Jesus when John sees him?
3. How does Revelation 1:19 help us understand the book of Revelation?
4. What is the significance of the seven churches to which Jesus sends letters?
5. Will the terrible judgments predicted for history's end cause sinners to repent?
6. Who is the Antichrist and what does he do?
7. What is the Millennium?
8. What is the fate of those who fail to trust Christ in the final judgment?
9. What is the destiny of those who have trusted Christ and whose names have been written in the Lamb's Book of Life?

Appendix A - Paul's Missionary Journeys

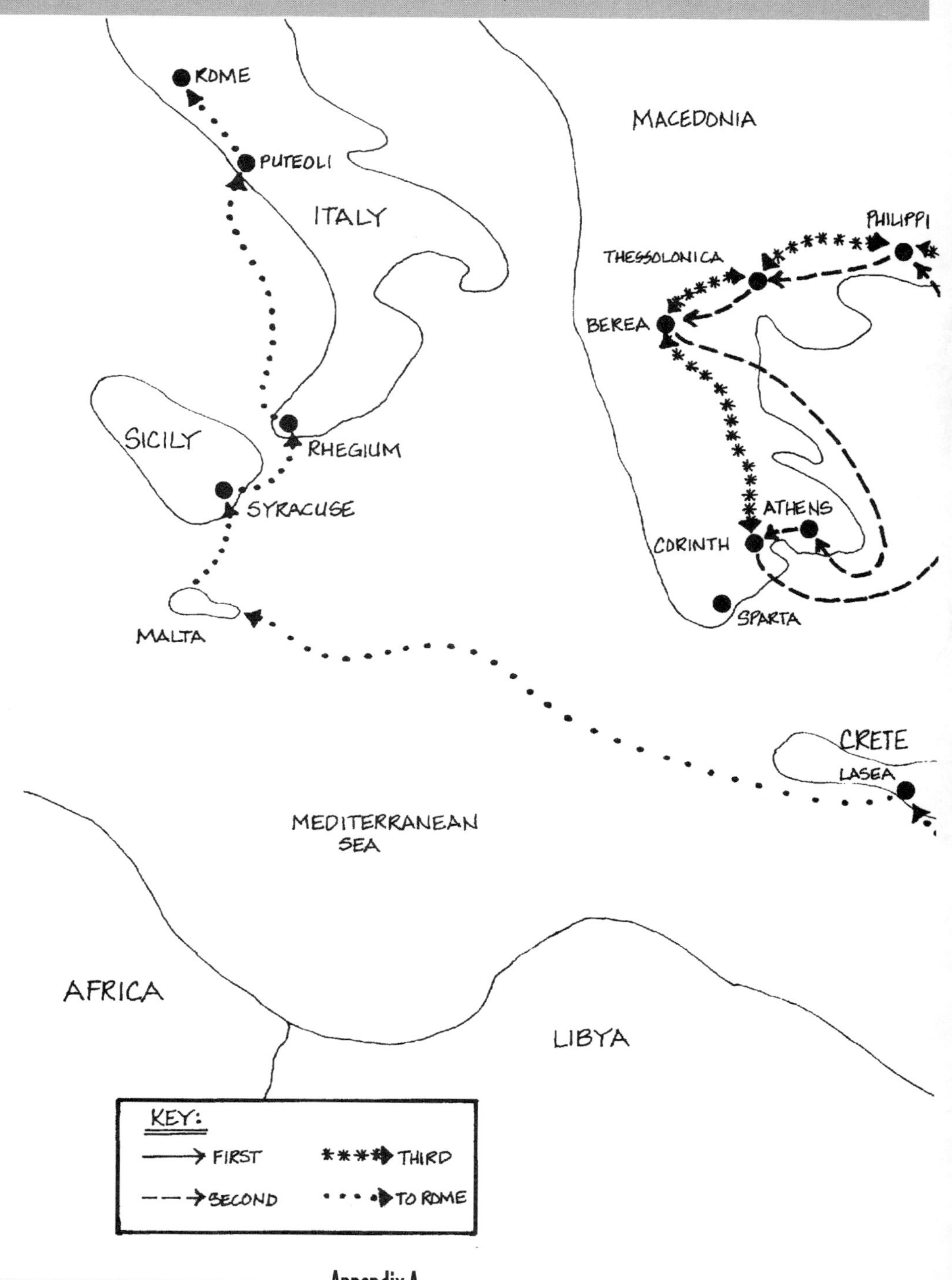

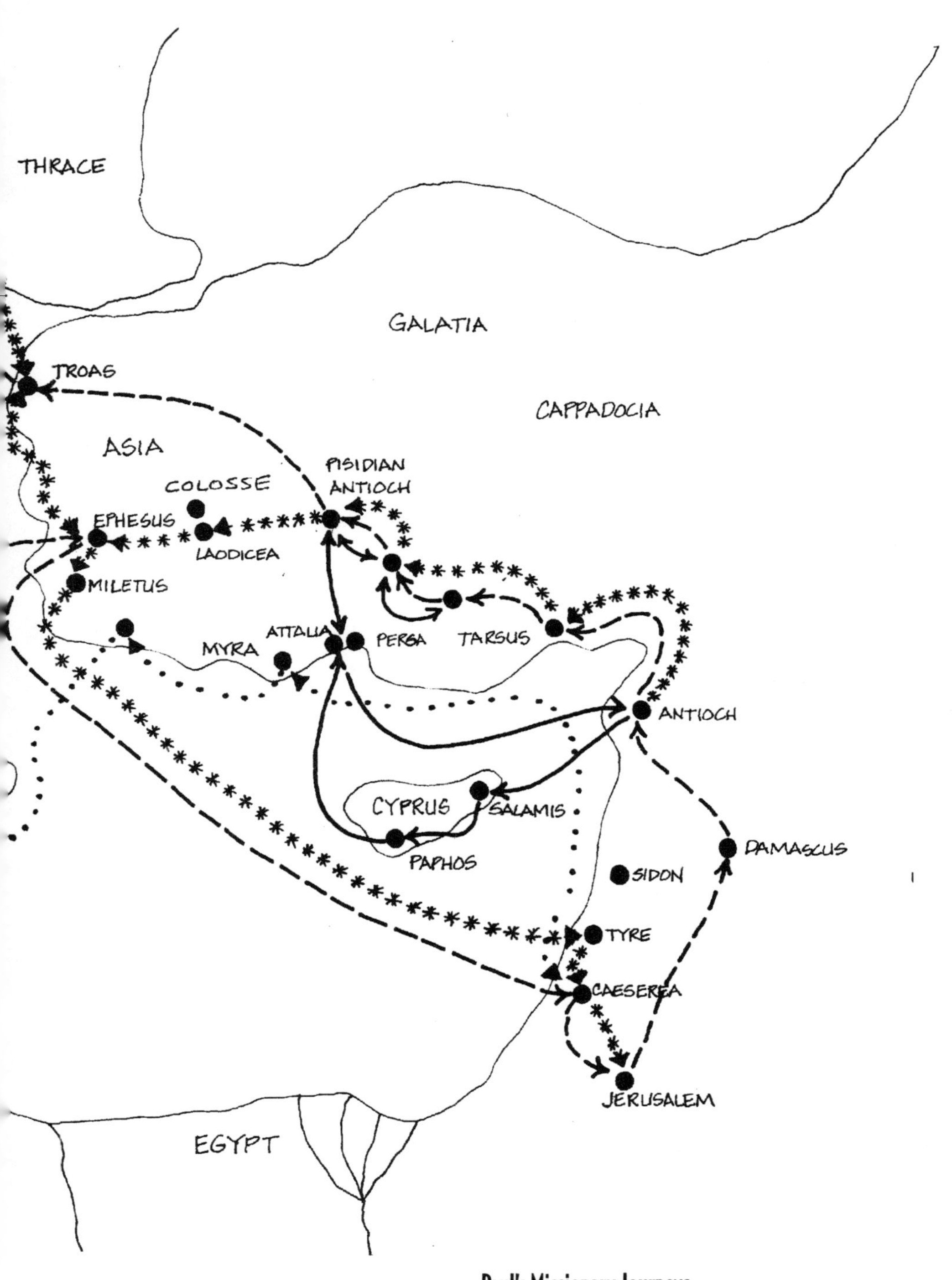
THRACE
GALATIA
TROAS
CAPPADOCIA
ASIA
PISIDIAN
ANTIOCH
COLOSSE
EPHESUS
LAODICEA
MILETUS
ATTALIA
MYRA
PERGA
TARSUS
ANTIOCH
CYPRUS
SALAMIS
PAPHOS
DAMASCUS
SIDON
TYRE
CAESEREA
JERUSALEM
EGYPT

Appendix B - The Answers

CHAPTER 1 Genesis 1— 11

1. If God did not create, then the universe "just happened"; life has no meaning or purpose, and death is the end.
2. Human beings are special because we were created in the image and likeness of God. (Genesis 1:26–27)
3. The evils in society and our own tendency to sin are consequences of the Fall. (Genesis 4)
4. The Fall was the choice of Adam and Eve to disobey God. The Fall corrupted human nature and gave all human beings a sinful nature. (Ephesians 2:1–4)
5. The Flood tells us that God is a moral judge who will punish sin. (Genesis 6:5–7)

CHAPTER 2 Genesis 12 — 50

1. Abraham was chosen by God to receive special promises, and Abraham responded to God with faith. (Genesis 15:6)
2. A covenant is a commitment, contract, oath, or treaty. The biblical covenants are commitments made by God. (Hebrews 6:13–20)
3. The Abrahamic covenant is important because it spells out what God has committed himself to do through Abraham and his descendants. (Genesis 1–3)
4. The Abrahamic covenant passed to Isaac, Jacob, and to the Jewish people who descended from them. (Genesis 21–50)
5. Faith is important because God will declare those who hold true faith to be righteous. (Romans 4:18–25)

CHAPTER 3 Exodus

1. Moses is important because God used him to deliver the Israelites from slavery in Egypt, to give Israel his law, and to write the first five books of the Old Testament. (Exodus 3–5)
2. A miracle is an event caused directly by God to accomplish a purpose of his own.
3. God struck Egypt with a series of devastating plagues which forced Pharaoh to release his Hebrew slaves. (Exodus 7:3)
4. A "promise covenant" states what God will most certainly do no matter what human beings do. A "contract covenant" states what God will do depending on what human beings choose to do. (Compare Genesis 12:1–3 with Exodus 19:5.)
5. The Ten Commandments reveal the moral character of God and define the behavior he expects from human beings. (Exodus 20:1–17)

CHAPTER 4 Leviticus • Numbers • Deuteronomy
Answers to which of the five rules below do you think are examples of ritual law:

1. Do not eat shrimp.—ritual law
2. Sacrifice after giving birth.—ritual law
3. Do not commit adultery.—moral law
4. Help your enemy if his cattle get loose.—moral law
5. Wash clothing after touching dead body.—ritual law

Answers to "Fear, Love, or Drive Out" table:

Deuteronomy 6:1–3—Fear
Deuteronomy 6:20–24—Love
Deuteronomy 7:1–6—Drive Out
Deuteronomy 7:7–10—Love
Deuteronomy 10:12–22—Love
Deuteronomy 11:16–17—Fear

Answers to Study Questions:

1. The theme of the book of Leviticus is holiness.
2. Important terms linked with the teaching of Leviticus on sacrifice include: guilt, forgiveness, blood, sacrifice, and atonement. These are important because they lay the foundation for understanding the meaning of Jesus' death on the cross. (Leviticus 1–5, 16)
3. Ritual laws defined actions that made an Israelite ritually unclean. Moral laws defined acts that were sin. (Compare Leviticus 11 with Leviticus 18.)
4. Violation of a ritual law made an Israelite unclean. Normally ritual uncleanness would be removed by washing with water after a specified period of time, or the offering of a sacrifice. (Leviticus 11:26–28; 12:1–8)
5. The Israelites refused to obey God when he commanded them to enter Canaan. (Numbers 14)
6. Love motivated the giving of the Law, as God revealed to Israel the way to experience his blessings. Love for God is the only motive that will produce true obedience to the Law God gave. (Deuteronomy 11)
7. A prophet is a person who delivers a message directly from God. True prophets could be recognized, for they had to be Israelites, who spoke in the name of the Lord, whose messages were in harmony with God's Word, and whose predictions came true. (Deuteronomy 18:14–22)

CHAPTER 5 Joshua • Judges • Ruth
Answer to Jephthah's Daughter puzzle:

The Old Testament displays an absolute revulsion toward human sacrifice (Leviticus 18:21; 20:2–5; Deuteronomy 12:31; 18:10.). While some argue that Jephthah must have fulfilled his vow by killing and burning his daughter, this is not required by the text or Hebrew practices. Old Testament Law introduces a principle in Exodus 38:8 and illustrates it in 1 Samuel 1:28 and Luke 2:36–37. This principle is that a person or thing dedicated to God might fulfill the vow with a lifetime of service and the surrender of one's life.

Indicators that this is what happened in the case of

Jephthah's daughter are (1) Jephthah had previously displayed knowledge of Old Testament history and Law, as in his letter to the Ammonites (Judges 11:15–17); (2) every sacrifice to the Lord required that a priest officiate, and no Hebrew priest would offer a human sacrifice; (3) the reaction of Jephthah's daughter, who went out with her friends to lament not over her immediate death but because I will never marry (Judges 11:37). All this leads us to the conclusion that Jephthah did fulfill his vow, by dedicating his daughter's life to the service of the Lord.

Answers to Study Questions:

1. These books cover a period from about 1390 BC to 1150 BC.
2. The major message of Joshua is that obedience brings victory, and disobedience brings defeat. (Joshua 6–8)
3. The major message of Judges is commitment to worshiping and obeying God is essential to maintain a just society. (Judges 3:6–15)
4. The Judges of Israel were military, political, and religious leaders. They offered the Israelites someone to turn to for moral and spiritual leadership. (Judges 6:1–8)
5. The persons emphasized in the book of Judges are Deborah, Gideon, Jephthah, and Samson.
6. The major message of the book of Ruth is that godly people can live meaningful lives even in a corrupt society. (Ruth 3)

CHAPTER 6 1 Samuel • 2 Samuel • 1 Chronicles

1. The three key figures in the transition to monarchy are Samuel, Saul, and David.
2. When Samuel was born, Israel was a loose confederation of poverty-stricken tribes oppressed by foreign enemies. (1 Samuel 2:12–4:27)
3. When David died, Israel was a wealthy, powerful nation whose territory had been expanded tenfold. (1 Chronicles 18)
4. Both Saul and David had weaknesses, but David loved God and was willing to take responsibility for and openly confess his sins. Saul was unwilling to repent, however, and God rejected his kingship. (Compare 1 Samuel 15 with 2 Samuel 12.)
5. David unified the Hebrew kingdom, organized it armies, defeated foreign enemies, established Jerusalem as the political and religious center of the nation, and organized Temple worship. (1 Chronicles)
6. The Davidic covenant established the fact that it would be a descendant of David who would fulfill the promises God had made to Abraham. (2 Samuel 7)
7. A study of David's life teaches the importance of loving God, the vulnerability of the greatest saints to sin, and the willingness of God to forgive those who confess their sins to him. (Psalm 51)

CHAPTER 7 1 Kings 1–11 • 2 Chronicles 1–9 • Job • Psalms • Proverbs • Ecclesiastes • Song of Solomon (Song of Songs)

1. The two kings who ruled Israel during the golden age were David and Solomon. (1 Chronicles – 2 Chronicles 10)
2. The golden age was marked by prosperity, military strength, and literary accomplishment. (1 Kings 4:20–34)
3. Books of Bible poetry associated with the golden age are Proverbs, Psalms, Ecclesiastes, and the Song of Solomon.
4. Hebrew poetry relied on symmetry of thought rather than on rhyme and rhythm. (Psalm 1)
5. The theme of these books is:
   Job—faith's response to suffering. (Job 1, 2)
   Psalms—personal relationship with God, worship. (Psalm 9)
   Proverbs—guidance in making wise and right choices. (Proverbs 1:1–6)
   Ecclesiastes—the futility of seeking any meaning in life apart from a relationship with God. (Ecclesiastes 1:1–11)
   Song of Solomon—the delights of married love. (Song of Solomon 4)

CHAPTER 8 1 Kings 12–22 • 2 Kings • Jonah • Amos • Hosea

1. Jeroboam established a counterfeit religious system. (1 Kings 12:25–33)
2. All the kings of Israel were evil and maintained the counterfeit religious system instituted by Jeroboam I. (2 Kings)
3. Elijah and Elisha are the two speaking prophets in the Bible's second age of miracles. (1 Kings 18–2 Kings 8)
4. Jonah, whose mission to Nineveh showed God's willingness to withhold punishment of those who would repent. Amos, whose preaching condemned Israel's false religion and social injustice. (Jonah 4; Amos 4)
5. The Day of the Lord is any period in which God acts directly to accomplish his purposes. (Amos 5:18–27)
6. The sins of Israel that called for judgment included institutionalized injustice and immorality. The newspaper headlines highlight similar sins in our own society. (Amos 2)

CHAPTER 9 1 and 2 Kings • 2 Chronicles • Obadiah • Joel • Micah • Isaiah

1. Second Kings and 2 Chronicles record the history of Judah after the division of Solomon's kingdom.
2. Godly kings stimulated religious revivals, which permitted God to act for his people. (2 Chronicles 19:20)
3. Pagans turn to occult practices to seek supernatural guidance. God provided his people with prophets through whom the Lord himself gave guidance. (Deuteronomy 18:9–22)
4. The true prophet must be an Israelite who speaks in the name of the Lord, whose message is in harmony with Scripture, and whose predictions come true. (Deuteronomy 18:19–22)
5. Joel, plague of locusts (Joel 1); Obadiah, judgment on Edom (Obadiah 1); Micah, the Savior to be born in Bethlehem (Micah 5:2); Isaiah, God's sovereign rule (Isaiah 44).

CHAPTER 10 2 Kings 15–25 • 2 Chronicles 29–36 • Nahum • Zephaniah • Habakkuk • Jeremiah • Ezekiel

1. Revival under Hezekiah saved Judah from destruction by Assyria. (2 Chronicles 29–32)
2. The prophets of Judah pointed to idolatry and the worship of pagan deities. (Isaiah 1)
3. Nahum, Zephaniah, Habakkuk, and Jeremiah all preached in the surviving kingdom of Judah.
4. Ezekiel preached to the exiles in Babylon before the fall of Jerusalem. (Ezekiel 1:1)

CHAPTER 11 Lamentations • Daniel • Esther • Ezra • Nehemiah • Haggai • Zechariah • Malachi

1. Lamentations expresses the despair of those Jews taken captive to Babylon.
2. The book of Daniel contains a specific prediction about the date of the entrance of the Messiah into Jerusalem. (Daniel 9:20–27)
3. The books of Ezra and Nehemiah tell of the return to Judah.

4. The book of Esther teaches that God is in control of every aspect of our lives.
5. Isaiah predicted that Cyrus would be the ruler who permitted the Jews to return to Jerusalem. (Isaiah 45:11–13)
6. Zechariah and Haggai encouraged the people to finish building God's temple.
7. The last book of the Old Testament, Malachi, was written around 400 BC.

CHAPTER 12 Jesus, the Promised Savior

1. Jesus Christ is the central figure in the New Testament.
2. Psalms 2:7; 45:5–6; Isaiah 7:14; 9:6–7; Micah 5:2; and Malachi 3:1 all indicate that the Messiah will be God himself.
3. John 5:17–18; 8:58–59; Matthew 16:16–17; and Matthew 26:63–64 all report Jesus' claim to be God.
4. Philippians 2 says that being in very nature God Jesus was made in human likeness.
5. The Resurrection proved that Jesus was truly God. (Romans 1:1–4)

CHAPTER 13 Jesus' Birth and Preparation

1. Matthew wrote the Gospel directed to the Jews. (Matthew 1:22)
2. Mark wrote the Gospel directed to the Romans.
3. The Gospel of John is not in chronological order.
4. The two genealogies of Jesus are different because one genealogy is Mary's and the other is from Jesus' stepfather, Joseph. (Matthew 1:1–17; Luke 4:21–38)
5. The appearances of angels marked Jesus' birth as unusual. (Matthew 1:15, 24; Luke 1:11, 26–38)
6. The message of John the Baptist was "Repent, because the Messiah is about to appear." (Matthew 3:2)
7. God spoke from heaven and the Holy Spirit descended as a dove. (Matthew 3:16–17)
8. To deliver us from our sins Jesus needed to be without sin. (Hebrews 4:14–16)

CHAPTER 14 Jesus' Early Ministry

1. The disciples were twelve men, specially chosen by Jesus, who followed Christ from the beginning of his ministry. (Mark 3:13–19)
2. The Pharisees and Sadducees were religious parties in Jesus' day.
3. Jesus performed miracles of healing, control of nature, control of demons, and power over death itself. (Mark 4, 5)
4. The Beatitudes define what God values in human beings. (Matthew 5:1–10)
5. Jesus explained the Law and exposed its true meaning. (Matthew 5:17–47)
6. God's character as Father helps define the relationship he seeks with human beings. (Matthew 6)
7. The Pharisees started the rumor that Jesus' miracles were performed by Satan's rather than God's power. (Matthew 12:22–32)

CHAPTER 15 Jesus Faces Opposition

1. The Pharisees brought the false charges against Jesus. (John 8)
2. The fact that Jesus had not "studied" allowed the Pharisees to falsely charge that he was not qualified to teach. (Matthew 13:53–58)
3. God hears the prayers of the godly, not of wicked men. (John 9:13–21)
4. Jesus began to use parables after the crowds had refused to acknowledge him as the Messiah. (Matthew 13)
5. The subject of Jesus's parables was the kingdom of God. (Matthew 13)
6. The mark of a true disciple is the belief that Jesus is God the Son. (Matthew 16:13–20)
7. The key to greatness for a disciple of Jesus is willingness to serve others. (Matthew 20:20–28)
8. Jesus' "new commandment" was to love one another as he had loved them. (John 13:33–34)

CHAPTER 16 Jesus' Death and Resurrection

1. His triumphal entry into Jerusalem began Jesus' last week on earth. (Matthew 21)
2. He drove out the merchants. (Mark 11:12–19)
3. The Jews resented paying taxes to Rome and viewed it as a betrayal of their faith. Regardless of how Christ answered the Pharisees, he would be "guilty," of either commanding revolt against Caesar, or betraying the Jews. (Luke 20:29–36)
4. Jesus called the Pharisees hypocrites. (Matthew 23)
5. By raising Jesus from the dead after his crucifixion, God answered Jesus' prayer. (Matthew 26:36–46)
6. In the Jewish courts, he was charged with blasphemy. Pilate charged him with being a king and rival of Caesar. (John 19)
7. The body was taken down from the cross and sealed in a tomb. (John 27:32–66)
8. By viewing it as a sacrifice for sins, made on our behalf. (Hebrews 10)
9. Jesus is alive to save and to guard us. (Hebrews 7:11–28)

CHAPTER 17 Acts

1. Acts is a historical narrative. (Acts 1:1–2)
2. The ascension of Christ begins Acts. (Acts 1)
3. The coming of the Holy Spirit provides the disciple with power to witness to Christ. (Acts 1:8; 2:1–12)
4. Jesus is a historical person who was crucified, is risen again, and saves those who trust in him. (Acts 2:14–41)
5. Peter and Paul are the dominant figures in Acts.
6. Cornelius was the first gentile convert. (Acts 10)
7. Three of Paul's missionary journeys are reported in Acts. (Acts 13–19)
8. It determined that a person did not have to adopt Jewish practices to be a Christian. (Acts 15)
9. At the end of the book of Acts, Paul is imprisoned in Rome. (Acts 28)

CHAPTER 18 Romans • Galatians

1. The epistles are letters of correspondence.
2. Tracing the argument of an epistle means to follow the writer's train of thought.
3. The theme of Paul's letter to the Romans is righteousness. (Romans 1:16–17)
4. Romans teaches us no human being is righteous, God requires us to be righteous, and God will declare those who trust in Jesus to be righteous. (Romans 3)
5. Our sinful nature. Ever since the Fall, humans have been inheritors of original sin. This means that humans are inherently flawed and in need of redemption. (Romans 5:12–20)
6. People have their own sense of right and wrong, and all have acted against their own standards. (Romans 2:12–16)
7. God's Law is meant to convince us that we are sinners and cannot help ourselves. (Romans 3:19–20)
8. The theme of Paul's letter to the Galatians is the inadequacy of the Law vs. the power of the Holy Spirit and grace.
9. The two contrary principles of a Christian's life are Law and grace. (Romans 7)
10. Relating to God through the Law involves dependence

on our own on self-effort. Relating to God through the Spirit involves relying on God to do in us what we cannot do alone. (Romans 8)

CHAPTER 19 1 and 2 Corinthians • 1 and 2 Thessalonians

1. First and 2 Corinthians; 1 and 2 Thessalonians
2. Paul's solution was to expel the Christian who refuses to stop sinning. (1 Corinthians 5)
3. They thought it indicated a special closeness to God. (1 Corinthians 12:1–11)
4. God loves cheerful givers, we can meet the needs of others, and God is able to provide for all our needs. (2 Corinthians 8–9)
5. God did not answer Paul's prayer for healing in order to keep him from becoming proud and to teach him to rely on God. (2 Corinthians 12)
6. We should not grieve the death of loved ones because we will see them again when Jesus comes. (1 Thessalonians 4:13–18)
7. God will punish those who persecute believers. (2 Thessalonians 1:5–10)

CHAPTER 20 Ephesians • Philippians • Colossians

1. The theme of Ephesians is the Church of Jesus Christ as a living entity. (Ephesians 4)
2. Faith produces works. (Ephesians 2:8–10)
3. A husband's responsibility is to love his wife as Christ loved the Church. (Ephesians 5:25)
4. Joy and rejoice are the key words in the book of Philippians.
5. To gain freedom from anxiety, Christians can present requests to God with thanksgiving. (Philippians 4:8–9)
6. In the book of Colossians, Paul battles a heresy which argues that everything material is evil and only the immaterial can be spiritual, or good.
7. Colossians 1:15–17 shows that Jesus is God.
8. Fake Christians live by lists of do's and don'ts; real Christians show love, compassion, and forgiveness toward others. (Colossians 2:6–23)

CHAPTER 21 1 and 2 Timothy • Titus • Philemon

1. The three "pastoral" letters are 1 and 2 Timothy and Titus.
2. See list on page 278.
3. The widows' ministry was teaching younger women. (2 Titus 2:3–5)
4. A love of money is a root of every evil. (1 Timothy 6:3–10)
5. The fact that God inspired the Scriptures ensures their usefulness. (2 Timothy 3:16–17)
6. Also involved in Christian teaching is teaching to live in harmony with the truths. (2 Timothy 2)
7. One justified by faith expresses that reality through good works. (James 2)
8. Philemon and Onesimus had become brothers in Christ. (Philemon 12–16)

CHAPTER 22 Hebrews

1. Hebrews is addressed to Jewish Christians.
2. Hebrews was intended to show that Christianity and Christ is better than Judaism.
3. The New Testament message was delivered by God the Son himself, rather than a messenger. (Hebrews 1:1–4)
4. Jesus brought a better revelation and offered a more effective (ultimate) sacrifice. (Hebrews 1)
5. It works an inner transformation by writing God's Law within our hearts. (Hebrews 8)
6. This shows that the sacrifice was efficacious and that we truly are forgiven. (Hebrews 10:1–18)
7. Hebrews 11 explores the significance of faith.
8. All loving fathers discipline (train) their children, and hardships are evidence of God's discipline in our lives. (Hebrews 12)

CHAPTER 23 James • 1 and 2 Peter • 1, 2, and 3 John • Jude

1. The six epistles discussed in this chapter are James, 1 and 2 Peter, 1, 2, and 3 John, and Jude.
2. The theme of the book of James is faith at work.
3. A true faith is transforming and will be expressed in the way we live. (James 2)
4. Christians need to understand how to relate to suffering. (1 Peter)
5. God turned the injustice into good, and can do the same for us. (1 Peter 3:13–18)
6. See the chart on page 308.
7. We need to confess our sins to remain in fellowship with God. (1 John 1:9)
8. Are they willing to confess that Jesus is God come in the flesh. (1 John 4:1–6)
9. Love is God's nature and he commands us to love our brothers. (1 John 4:16–21)

CHAPTER 24 Revelation

1. The subject of Revelation is the events to take place at history's end. (Revelation 2:19)
2. Jesus is seen in his essential nature, and he is so glorious that John is stunned. (Revelation 1:9–20)
3. Revelation 1:19 divides the content into "what was, what is now, and what is to come."
4. The churches are representative, and/or may symbolize periods in the Christian era.
5. Even in the face of the terrible judgments, the sinners will not repent. (Revelation 9)
6. The Antichrist will be a human being in league with Satan, who will claim the prerogatives of Christ and demand to be worshipped. (Revelation 13)
7. The Millennium will be the thousand-year period during which Jesus will rule on earth, fulfilling Old Testament prophecy. (Revelation 20:1–6)
8. Those who fail to trust Christ are thrown into the Lake of Fire. (Revelation 20:11–15)
9. Those who have trusted Christ will spend eternity with God in the new heavens and earth God will create. (Revelation 21, 22)

Endnotes

CHAPTER 1 Genesis 1— 11

1. Ronald F. Youngblood *The Book of Genesis*, p. 23.

CHAPTER 2 Genesis 12 — 50

1. Max Lucado, *The Applause of Heaven*, p. 32.
2. Robert C. Girard, *My Weakness: His Strength*, p. 77.
3. Mother Teresa, *A Gift from God*, p. 37.

CHAPTER 3 Exodus

1. William S. LaSor, *Old Testament Survey*, p. 136.
2. C. S. Lewis, *Miracles*, p. 60.
3. Norman L. Geisler, *Miracles and Modern Thought*, p. 123.
4. Robert Schuller, *The Be (Happy) Attitudes*, p. 176.

CHAPTER 4 Leviticus • Numbers • Deuteronomy

1. Joni Eareckson Tada, "Spiritually Active," in *The Women's Devotional Bible*, p. 123.
2. Lewis Goldberg, quoted in *The 365-Day Devotional Commentaryry*, p. 163.

CHAPTER 5 Joshua • Judges • Ruth

1. Howarad Hendricks, *Say It with Love*, p. 79.
2. Martin Luther, quoted in *The 365-Day Devotional Commentaryry*, p. 343.

CHAPTER 6 1 Samuel • 2 Samuel • 1 Chronicles

1. Blaise Pascal, quoted in *Christianity Today*, March 2, 1998, p. 62.
2. Saint Augustine, quoted in *The 365-Day Devotional Commentary*, p. 207.

CHAPTER 7 1 Kings 1–11 • 2 Chronicles 1–9 • Job • Psalms • Proverbs • Ecclesiastes • Song of Solomon (Song of Songs)

1. Albert H. Baylis, *From Creation to the Cross*, p. 243.
2. Bruce Wilkinson, *God's Masterwork*, p. 69.
3. Charles Swindoll, *God's Masterwork*, pp. 75–76.

CHAPTER 8 1 Kings 12–22 • 2 Kings • Jonah • Amos • Hosea

1. Billy Graham, *Peace with God*, p. 38.

CHAPTER 9 1 and 2 Kings • 2 Chronicles • Obadiah • Joel • Micah • Isaiah

1. King Solomon, Proverbs 14:34.
2. John Alexander, quoted in *Christianity Today*, February 9, 1998, p. 78.

CHAPTER 10 2 Kings 15–25 • 2 Chronicles 29–36 • Nahum • Zephaniah • Habakkuk • Jeremiah • Ezekiel

1. Norman L. Geisler, *Miracles and Modern Thought*, p. 260.
2. Kay Arthur, *Lord, Heal My Hurts*, p. 23.

CHAPTER 11 Lamentations • Daniel • Esther • Ezra • Nehemiah • Haggai • Zechariah • Malachi

1. Samuel Schultz, *The Old Testament Speaks*, p. 343.
2. William S. La Sor, *Old Testament Survey*, p. 632.
3. Martin Luther, quoted in *The 365-Day Devotional Commentary*, p. 1075.

CHAPTER 12 Jesus, the Promised Savior

1. James Smith, *The Promised Messiah*, p. 180.
2. John F. MacArthur Jr., *God with Us*, p. 46.
3. Edward J. Young, *The Book of Isaiah*, p. 338.
4. C. F. Kiel, *Commentary on the Old Testament*, vol. 10, p. 329.
5. Craig S. Keener, *The IVP Bible Background Commentary*, p. 287.
6. C. S. Lewis, *Christian Reflections*, p. 137.
7. F. F. Bruce, *The Epistle to the Hebrews*, p. 48.

CHAPTER 13 Jesus' Birth and Preparation

1. Graham Scroggie, *A Guide to the Gospels*, p. 505.
2. J. W. Shepherd, *The Christ of the Gospels*, p. 1.
3. Alfred Edersheim, *The Life and Times of Jesus the Messiah*, p. 221.
4. G. Campbell Morgan, *The Crises of Christ*, p. 183.

CHAPTER 14 Jesus' Early Ministry

1. Charles C. Ryrie, *The Miracles of Our Lord*, p. 11.
2. Ibid., p. 37.
3. J. Dwight Pentecost, *The Words and Works of Jesus Christ*, p. 159.
4. John Wesley, *The Works of John Wesley*, 5:278.

CHAPTER 15 Jesus Faces Opposition

1. F. F. Bruce, *The Gospel of John*, p. 169.
2. Ibid., p. 219.
3. John Wesley, quoted in *The 365-Day Devotional Commentary*, p. 671.
4. Thomas à Kempis, *The Imitation of Christ*, 6.1.
5. F. F. Bruce, *The Gospel of John*, p. 301.
6. J. Dwight Pentecost, *The Words and Works of Jesus Christ*, p. 346.

CHAPTER 16 Jesus' Death and Resurrection

1. Alfred Edersheim, *The Life and Times of Jesus the Messiah,* Volume 2, p. 385.
2. J. Dwight Pentecost, *The Words and Works of Jesus Christ,* pp. 391–392.
3. Ibid., p. 455.
4. John Stott, *Commentary on Romans,* p. 144.
5. Max Lucado, *No Wonder They Call Him the Savior,* p. 140.

CHAPTER 17 Acts

1. Craig S. Keener, *The IVP Bible Background Commentary,* p. 354.

CHAPTER 18 Romans • Galatians

1. Max Lucado, *In the Grip of Grace,* p. 92.
2. Wolfheart Pannenberg, "Homosexuality and Revelation," in *Christianity Today,* November 11, 1996, p. 37.
3. Everett F. Harrison, *The Expositor's Bible Commentary,* p. 31.
4. Max Lucado, *In the Grip of Grace,* p. 92.
5. John Wesley, *The Works of John Wesley,* 6:452.
6. James Montgomery Boice, "Galatians," in *The Expositor's Bible Commentary,* p. 409.
7. Ibid., p. 495.

CHAPTER 19 1 and 2 Corinthians • 1 and 2 Thessalonians

1. Dwight L. Moody, quoted in *The 365-Day Devotional Commentary,* p. 954.
2. Martin Luther, *The Best of All His Works,* p. 276.
3. Robert L. Thomas, "Thessalonians," *The Expositor's Bible Commentary,* p. 233.
4. C. S. Lewis, quoted in *The 365-Day Devotional Commentary,* p. 1025.

CHAPTER 20 Ephesians • Philippians • Colossians

1. Lewis Smedes, quoted in *Christianity Today,* November 13, 1995, p. 69.
2. Larry Christianson, *The Christian Family,* p. 270.
3. Pope John Paul II, quoted in *Christianity Today,* November 13, 1995, p. 69.
4. Edmund P. Clowney, quoted in *Christianity Today,* April 27, 1998, p. 78.

CHAPTER 21 1 and 2 Timothy • Titus • Philemon

1. J. Vernon McGee, *The Epistles of 1, 2 Timothy, Titus, & Philemon,* p. 14.
2. William Barclay, *Letters to Timothy, Titus, and Philemon,* p. 36.
3. Roy B. Zuck, *Precious in His Sight,* p. 114.
4. William Barclay, *Letters to Timothy, Titus, and Philemon,* p. 181.
5. Ibid., p. 256.

CHAPTER 22 Hebrews

1. Leon Morris, "Hebrews" in *The Expositor's Bible Commentary,* p. 32.
2. F. F. Bruce, *Epistle to the Hebrews,* p. 155.
3. Kay Arthur, Lord, *I Want to Know You,* p. 157.
4. Leon Morris, *New Testament Theology,* p. 306.
5. Ibid., p. 138.

CHAPTER 23 James • 1 and 2 Peter • 1, 2, and 3 John • Jude

1. Leon Morris, *New Testament Theology,* p. 313.
2. C. S. Lewis, *Miracles,* p. 181.
3. William Law, quoted in *Christianity Today,* June 19, 1995, p. 33.
4. John Wesley, *The Works of John Wesley,* 6:15.
5. François Fénelon, quoted in *Christianity Today,* November 13, 1995, p. 69.

CHAPTER 24 Revelation

1. Alan F. Johnson, "Revelation" in *The Expositor's Bible Commentary,* Volume 10, p. 432.
2. J. H. Melton, 52 *Lessons in Revelation,* p. 93.
3. Daymond R. Duck, *The Book of Revelation—The Bible Smart Guides™,* p. 109.
4. Ed Hindson, ed., *Final Signs,* p. 107.
5. Alan F. Johnson, "Revelation" in *The Expositor's Bible Commentary,* p. 576.
6. Hal Lindsey, *There's a New World Coming,* p. 252.
7. David Hocking, *The Coming World Leader,* p. 288.

The following excerpts are used by permission with all rights reserved:

Kay Arthur, *Lord, I Want to Know You; Lord, Heal My Hurts; Lord, Where Are You,* Multnomah Publishers, Sisters, OR.

F. F. Bruce, *The Epistle of Hebrews,* Wm. B. Eerdmans Publishing Co., Grand Rapids, MI.

Daymond Duck, *The Book of Revelation—The Bible Smart Guides™,* Thomas Nelson Publishers, Nashville, TN.

Max Lucado, *Applause of Heaven; In the Grip of Grace,* Word Publishing, Nashville, TN.

J. Dwight Pentecost, *The Words and Works of Jesus Christ,* Zondervan Publishing, Grand Rapids, MI.

Charles Swindoll, *Living Beyond the Daily Grind; God's Masterwork,* Word Publishing, Nashville, TN.

Warren Wiersbe, *Wiersbe's Expository Outlines; Wiersbe's Expository Commentary; Be Rich; Be Confident,* Chariot-Victor Publishing, Colorado Springs, CO.

Index

F

G

H

I

J

S

T